THE
SAINTS

THE
POCKET GUIDE
TO

THE
SAINTS

RICHARD P. McBRIEN

HarperSanFrancisco
A Division of HarperCollins*Publishers*

HarperCollins books may be purchased for educational,
business, or sales promotional use. For information please
write: Special Markets Department, HarperCollins Publishers,
10 East 53rd Street, New York, NY 10022.

HarperCollins Web site: http://www.harpercollins.com

HarperCollins®, 📖®, and HarperSanFrancisco™
are trademarks of HarperCollins Publishers.

FIRST EDITION

Book design by rlf design

Library of Congress Cataloging-in-Publication Data
    McBrien, Richard P.
        The pocket guide to the saints / Richard P. McBrien. —
    1st ed.
        p.   cm.
    Includes index.
    ISBN-13: 978-0-06-113774-7
    ISBN-10: 0-06-113774-X
        1. Christian saints—Biography   I. Title

    BX4655.3.M33   2006
    282.092'2—dc22
    [B]   2006043412

06 07 08 09 10   (WE)   10 9 8 7 6 5 4 3 2 1

CONTENTS

THE
POCKET GUIDE
TO

THE
SAINTS

INTRODUCTION

*T*his book contains the abridged profiles of canonized saints and other saintly figures, organized according to their respective feast days or days of death. For the complete profiles, readers should consult the full edition, published in hardcover by HarperSanFrancisco in 2001 and released in paperback in 2003.

Although the Catholic Church has always been the principal agency of saint making, this book is also attentive to the devotional traditions and practices of other Christian denominations, particularly the Greek and Russian Orthodox Churches, the churches of the Anglican Communion, including the Episcopal Church USA, and the churches of the Lutheran World Federation, especially the Evangelical Lutheran Church in America. There are also occasional references to holy persons not yet formally recognized as saints, including non-Christians.

There is no more basic question than the question of sanctity, because it touches the very meaning and depths of our lives on this earth. In what does a fully human life consist? What does it mean not only to be "good," but to be heroically so? And what role does a global and multicultural community like the Church have in inspiring others to live up to such standards of human behavior, and what responsibility does it have to live up to those standards itself?

In the eyes of the Church, saints are personifications of what the truly good life is all about, and that is why, for centuries, devoted members of the Church have looked to the saints as models for their own lives and as sources of inspiration and hope. Indeed, the veneration of saints has been an integral part of the Church's life ever since the death of its first martyr, Stephen [December 26]. Most Christians (and many non-Christians as well) are named after saints, as are some major and mid-sized cities in the United States: for example, St. Louis, St. Augustine, St. Paul, San Francisco, San Jose, San Juan, Santa Anna, Santa Barbara, San Bernardino, and San Antonio. The most famous golf course in the world is named after St. Andrew [November 30] as is one of the world's most beloved mythical characters, Santa Claus (St. Nicholas [December 6]).

Catholic parents once were carefully instructed to choose a saint's name for their newly born infants; otherwise, the priest would not baptize them. Boys and girls were expected to select a saint's name for Confirmation. Catholics of all ages routinely prayed to St. Anthony of Padua [June 13] to find lost articles or to St. Jude [October 28] in the face of seemingly hopeless situations. There were popular novenas to St. Anne [July 26], the Little Flower (St. Theresa of the Child Jesus [October 1]), the Miraculous Medal (a devotion promoted by St. Catherine Labouré [November 28]), and St. Jude. Children and adults alike wore medals imprinted with the images of St. Joseph [March 19], St. Benedict of Nursia [July 11], and St. Christopher [July 25]. The last was such a popular item in automobiles that it was a matter of widespread concern, even anxiety, for many Catholics (and some non-Catholics too) when Christopher was dropped from the liturgical calendar in 1969.

This book summarizes the lives and achievements of these and so many other saints who have been key participants not only in the history of the Church, but of humankind itself.

WHO IS A SAINT?

Saints are holy people. Because God alone is holy, to be a saint is to participate in, and to be an image of, the holiness of God. "Be holy, for I, the Lord, your God, am holy" (Lev. 19:2). To share in the holiness of God is to share in the very life of God, also known as grace. To be in the "state of grace" is to be permeated and transformed by the presence of God. Saints are persons in whom the grace of God, won for us by Christ, has fully triumphed over sin—which is not to say that the saints were without sin. Jesus alone was without sin (John 8:46; 14:30; 2 Cor. 5:21; 1 Pet. 2:22; Heb. 4:15), and only he could be called "the Holy One of God" (John 6:69).

The Second Vatican Council (1962–65) clearly shifted the emphasis from the saints as miracle workers and intercessors to the saints as models. "No devotion to the saints is more acceptable to God," the great Christian humanist Erasmus once wrote, "than the imitation of their virtues. . . . Do you want to honor St. Francis? Then give away your wealth to the poor, restrain your evil impulses, and see in everyone you meet the image of Christ."

In the Catholic tradition, there are at least four possible applications of the word "saints": (1) all those who have been sanctified, or made holy, by the grace of Christ, whether they be living or dead, Catholic or non-Catholic, Christian or non-Christian, people of explicit religious faith or none; (2) those who, having been sanctified by Christ on earth, have entered into the joy of eternal life in heaven; (3) biblical figures in the time before Christ who lived by the Spirit of God and who became luminous examples of holiness; and (4) those whom the Church, either through popular acclaim or formal canonization, has declared to be members of the Church triumphant (i.e., those already in the company of God, the angels, and the saints in heaven) and who are commemorated and invoked in the Church's public worship and in private prayer. The Church attests to that broadly inclusive tradition each year in its celebration of the feast of All Saints [November 1].

In the beginning, Jesus' disciples were considered "saints" and were addressed as such by St. Paul in his Letters to the various churches of the first century. The first saints in a more restricted sense of the word were the *martyrs,* who had died for the faith and whose reward was believed to have been immediate transition to eternal life with Christ. From the reign of Constantine in the early fourth century and with the end of the intermittent periods of persecution, the cult of saints (the so-called red martyrs) was extended to *confessors* (the so-called white martyrs, and not to be confused with priests who "hear" confessions), namely, those who suffered imprisonment, torture, expropriation of property, hard labor, or exile for the faith but who did not directly suffer the martyrdom of death; *ascetics,* especially those, such as monks, hermits, and holy women, who lived a life of celibacy or virginity; *wise teachers,* including theologians and spiritual writers; pastorally effective *church leaders,* including bishops, outstanding members of the diocesan and religious clergy, and the founders and foundresses of religious orders; and *those who cared for the sick and the poor.*

Saints are integral members of the Church and, as such, manifest its corporate holiness. They bear within themselves the hope and the assurance that the Church, which is called to be holy, will in fact achieve that end. That hope is succinctly expressed in the words of the First Eucharistic Prayer of the Catholic Mass: "For ourselves, too, we ask some share in the fellowship of your apostles and martyrs, with John the Baptist, Stephen, Matthias, Barnabas, Ignatius, Alexander, Marcellinus, Peter, Felicity, Perpetua, Agatha, Lucy, Agnes, Cecilia, Anastasia, and all the saints. Though we are sinners, we trust in your mercy and love. Do not consider what we truly deserve, but grant us your forgiveness."

THE PROCESS OF CANONIZATION

Saints do not come about like the Ten Commandments. No one ascends a high mountain, consults with God, and then returns with a list. Canonization is an essentially human process that Catholics believe is guided by the wisdom and inspiration of the Holy Spirit. During the first Christian millennium saints were popularly acclaimed at the local level, that is, where they lived much of their lives and where they died, often as martyrs. In most instances, it was the prerogative of the local bishop to grant approval for a new cult, usually centered on the tomb. In the second Christian millennium the process shifted from the local church to the papacy. Only those candidates who survived scrutiny by Roman offices (the Congregation of Rites, and later the Congregation for the Causes of Saints) and ultimately by the pope himself could be advanced to canonization in a step-by-step fashion: from "Servant of God" to "Venerable" to "Blessed" to "Saint." To be sure, this process was never completely immune from external and internal pressures, whether from temporal rulers, powerful families, religious orders, or influential bishops and cardinals. In other words, there has been a political as well as a spiritual dimension to the process.

Examples of overtly political canonizations abound throughout history. Celestine V was canonized because the king of France, Philip IV, pressured a French pope, Clement V (1305–14), to do so. The canonization was a form of posthumous retribution on the part of the king toward his bitter enemy Boniface VIII (1295–1303), who had coaxed Celestine into resigning the papacy and then placed him under house arrest, lest he become the focal point of a schism. On the other hand, Boniface had canonized Philip's IV's grandfather, Louis IX [August 25], as part of the negotiated settlement of a dispute between the pope and the king over the latter's power to tax the French clergy without papal approval. At the time of Rose of Lima's [August 23] canonization, Clement X (1670–76) was engaged in intense struggles with Louis XIV of France over the independence of the Church and was looking to Spain for support. (Rose's home country of Peru was a Spanish colony at the time.) Finally, Benedict XV (1914–22) canonized Joan of Arc [May 30] in 1920 as part of an effort to restore diplomatic relations between the Holy See and France following World War I.

But apart from such occasional politics, how does the Church ordinarily go about making its saints? On January 25, 1983, Pope John Paul II issued an apostolic constitution, *Divinus perfectionis Magister,* that significantly modified the traditional process leading to canonization. The new procedures place the entire responsibility for gathering the evidence in support of a cause in the hands of the local bishop in whose diocese the candidate died. He is expected, however, to consult with the other bishops of his region about the case, in keeping with the doctrine of episcopal collegiality.

The bishop appoints a postulator of the cause, who seeks out accurate information about the life of the candidate (known as the Servant of God) and develops the arguments in favor of moving the cause forward. This process includes the taking of testimony and the examination of historical records. The judgment of orthodoxy is now rendered at the local level rather than in Rome. The bishop must see to it that both publications and unpublished writings (letters and diaries) by the candidate are examined by theological censors. If there is nothing contrary to faith or morals in these, the bishop may proceed to the calling of witnesses by the postulator.

The bishop or his delegate must then carefully inspect the tomb of the Servant of God, the room in which he or she lived or died, and any other relevant places and be able to attest that there are no signs of a cult in the Servant of God's honor. In 1634 in order to curb abuses, Pope Urban VIII had decreed that the presence of an unauthorized cult would disqualify the candidate from papal canonization. When the investigations have been completed, two copies of the record, or transcript, of the proceedings are sent to the Congregation for the Causes of Saints in Rome, along with a copy of the books written by the candidate and the judgment by the theological censors. The bishop or his delegate also must attest in writing that the witnesses were trustworthy and all of the acts of the process were carried out according to law.

Once the cause has been accepted, the congregation appoints a relator, drawn from a College of Relators assigned to the congregation. The relator is responsible for selecting someone, known as a collaborator, to assist in writing the *positio* (or printed version of the case in support of canonization). The relator may select additional collaborators, including specialists in the history of a particular period or country in which the candidate lived. Witnesses are still appropriate, but the chief source of information is now a well-documented biography, written "according to the rules of criticism used in hagiography." The document must contain everything necessary for the consultors and prelates of the congregation to render a judgment about the fitness of the candidate for beatification and canonization, namely, that the candidate was a person of heroic virtue or was truly martyred for the faith. The document is submitted for discussion before the congregation only after it has been reviewed by theological consultors and the Promoter of the Faith (an office of the congregation charged with thoroughly investigating any objections to the cause). Their opinions and conclusions are submitted in writing to the cardinals and bishops of the congregation.

One relator is specially assigned to prepare a *positio* on the miracles attributed to the candidate, in consultation with a board of medical doctors and another of theologians. Only two miracles are now required: one for beatification and one for canonization. In the case of martyrs, only one miracle is required, and that for canonization. Once evidence of heroic virtue is established at the beatification stage, it need not be investigated further for canonization. The judgments of the cardinals and bishops of the congregation are reported to the pope, who alone has the right to declare that a public cult may be accorded to the Servant of God.

At the canonization ceremony itself, the pope proclaims: "We solemnly decide and define that [name] is a saint and inscribe him [or her] in the catalog of saints, stating that his [or her] memory shall be kept with pious devotion by the universal Church." And so it is done.

JANUARY

1   SOLEMNITY OF MARY,
     MOTHER OF GOD

The *Blessed Virgin Mary* is the greatest of the Church's saints, and "Mother of God" (Gk. *Theotokos;* Lat. *Deipara*) is the highest of her titles. It is the basis for every other title and dignity accorded to her. Although she was the Mother of God from the moment she conceived Jesus in her womb by the power of the Holy Spirit (Luke 1:26–38), her motherhood of God was not formally recognized by the Church until the first half of the fifth century, in response to a theological controversy.

Nestorius (d. ca. 451), the patriarch of Constantinople, argued that there are two whole and distinct natures in Christ, one human and one divine, each having its own "personal" manifestation. Nestorius and his supporters wanted to emphasize that the Son of God really took on our humanity. He became one of us in the flesh. It was Jesus, not the Second Person of the Trinity, who nursed at his mother's breast and who later suffered on the cross. According to Nestorius, Mary was the mother of the human person Jesus, and not of the Son of God.

A crisis erupted when, in his preaching, Nestorius publicly denied to Mary the title "Mother of God" (*Theotokos*), calling her instead the mother of Christ (*Christotokos*). A general council convened at Ephesus to address the issue. The council condemned Nestorius's views and affirmed that Mary was not only the mother of Christ in his human nature, but also of Christ as a divine Person. Therefore, Mary could indeed be proclaimed as the Mother of God.

After Ephesus, Marian feasts began to multiply and churches were dedicated to her in all major cities. By the middle of the seventh century, four separate Marian feasts were observed in Rome: the Annunciation [March 25], the Purification [February 2], the Assumption [August 15], and the Nativity of Mary [September 8]. The growth of Marian piety was accelerated in the nineteenth century with the promulgation of the dogma of the Immaculate Conception by Pope Pius IX in 1854. During the same century, a spate of Marian apparitions were reported: at La Salette and Lourdes (in France) and in many other places. Various devotional customs developed, including the living Rosary, May processions with the crowning of a Marian statue, and the wearing of the Miraculous Medal and the scapular. The Second Vatican Council (1962–65) brought about a major change in Marian devotion by grounding it more firmly in the Bible and the liturgy of the Church and in situating Mary herself in the context of the mystery of the Church, as the first among the redeemed, as the disciple par excellence.

Formerly the feast of the Circumcision of Jesus (still celebrated as such by the Greek and Russian Orthodox

Churches), January 1 has been devoted liturgically to
Mary, the Mother of God, since 1970, following the revision of the General Roman Calendar in 1969.

2   BASIL THE GREAT AND GREGORY
NAZIANZEN, BISHOPS AND DOCTORS
OF THE CHURCH

Basil, bishop of Caesarea, and Gregory, bishop of Constantinople, were two of the three famous Cappadocian
Fathers. Their writings and sermons effectively put an
end to Arianism, a fourth-century heresy that denied the
divinity of Christ, referring to him instead as the greatest
of creatures.

Basil, also known as "the Great" (ca. 330–79), was born
in Caesarea, the capital of the Roman province of Cappadocia. One of nine children, he came from a distinguished
and pious family. His father and mother, his sister, his two
brothers, and his grandmother are all venerated as saints.
Basil was educated first at home by his father and grandmother and then in Constantinople and Athens, where he
befriended Gregory of Nazianzus. In 359 he and Gregory
joined an ascetic community in Pontus, where Basil developed his monastic Rules, which were later to influence
all of Western monasticism; the longer Rule emphasizes
community life, liturgical prayer, and manual work.

With great reluctance on his part, Basil was ordained
a priest (presbyter) ca. 362 for the diocese of Caesarea. His
bishop later summoned him to the see city to lend support against the persecution waged against the Church
by the Arian emperor Valens (364–80) and specifically to

rebut the teachings of the Arians. Basil led relief efforts during a famine in 368, distributing his own inheritance to the poor. He was elected bishop in 370. Basil's episcopal ministry continued to emphasize aid to the poor, but it also drew him inevitably into direct controversy with the Arians and also with the Pneumatomachians, who denied the divinity of the Holy Spirit. His writings provided solid defenses of the teachings of the Council of Nicaea (325) and anticipated the teaching of the Council of Constantinople (381) on the divinity of the Holy Spirit. Basil died on January 1, 379, at the relatively young age of forty-nine.

Gregory Nazianzen, also known as Gregory of Nazianzus (ca. 329–90) and as Gregory the Theologian, was the son of the bishop of Nazianzus in Cappadocia. Like Basil, Gregory came from a family of saints: his father, mother, sister, and brother. He was broadly educated in Christian writings and in Greek philosophy in Caesarea, Alexandria, and Athens, where he began a deep but sometimes troubled friendship with Basil.

Soon after the death of the Arian emperor in 380, bishops of various neighboring dioceses appealed to Gregory to help restore the beleaguered Christian community at Constantinople. It had been under Arian rule for over thirty years, and orthodox Christians lacked even a church for worship. Gregory, now bent over with age, accepted under protest. Here, he preached famous sermons on the Trinity and, in the process, earned the surname "the Theologian." Named bishop of Constantinople, he played a prominent part in the Council of Constantinople (381), which confirmed his teaching on the divinity of the Holy Spirit.

Gregory Nazianzen died in 390. The feast of Basil and Gregory Nazianzen is on the General Roman Calendar and is also celebrated on this day by the Church of England.

3 GENEVIÈVE OF PARIS, VIRGIN

Geneviève, patron saint of Paris (ca. 422–ca. 500), was born to wealth in Nanterre, but moved, after the death of her parents, to Paris, where she continued her life of prayer and asceticism as a consecrated virgin. When Paris was besieged by the Franks under Childeric, she is said to have accompanied a group to obtain food and other provisions from neighboring towns and, in the process, to have won the respect of the Frankish leader, who spared the lives of many citizens in response to her pleas. She is also said to have encouraged the Parisians to fast and pray in order to avert an attack by Attila and his Huns. The invaders changed their route and the city was spared.

The most famous miracle attributed to her was in connection with the great epidemic that afflicted France in the early twelfth century. All efforts, both medicinal and spiritual, had failed to halt its progress—until 1129, when the casket containing Geneviève's bones was carried in solemn procession to the cathedral. (She is patron saint of those suffering from fever.) Her feast is not on the General Roman Calendar.

4   ELIZABETH ANN SETON, WIDOW AND FOUNDRESS

Baptized Elizabeth Bayley (1774–1821), *Elizabeth Ann Seton* was the first American-born saint. She was raised in a devout and well-to-do Episcopalian family. At age twenty Ann married a wealthy merchant, William Magee Seton. Together they had five children. She became involved in social work and established the Society for the Relief of Poor Widows with Children in 1797, earning the epithet the "Protestant Sister of Charity." After her husband's bankruptcy and death from tuberculosis, Elizabeth became a Catholic in 1805.

The rector of St. Mary's Seminary in Baltimore learned of her plight and invited her to establish a school for girls there. It opened in 1808. With four companions the following year, she founded a religious community, the Sisters of St. Joseph, and also a school for poor children near Emmitsburg, Maryland. She was elected superior and, with eighteen other sisters, took vows the following year. Thereafter, she was known as Mother Seton. Hers was the first American religious society, formally known as the Daughters of Charity of St. Joseph, devoted to the service of the poor and to teaching in parochial schools. Historians often credit her with laying the foundation for the Catholic parochial-school system in the United States.

Mother Seton died in Emmitsburg on January 4, 1821. She was canonized in 1975 by Pope Paul VI. Her feast is on the Proper Calendar for the Dioceses of the United States, but is not on the General Roman Calendar.

5 JOHN NEPOMUCENE NEUMANN, BISHOP

John Nepomucene Neumann (1811–60), the fourth bishop of Philadelphia, was born in Bohemia of a German father and Czech mother. Named after John Nepomucen, the patron saint of Bohemia, he came to the United States with the intention of doing missionary work after the Austrian government forced the local bishop to postpone ordinations. Neumann arrived in Manhattan in June 1836 and was ordained within three weeks. After joining the Redemptorists, he became a popular preacher among the immigrant communities of Pittsburgh and Baltimore.

In 1852 he was appointed the fourth bishop of Philadelphia and embarked on a vigorous program of building some one hundred churches and eighty schools in Delaware and the eastern half of Pennsylvania. He completed the unfinished cathedral and founded a new congregation of women, the Sisters of St. Francis of Philadelphia, to help staff the increasingly crowded schools. On January 5, 1860, Bishop Neumann died suddenly. Pope Paul VI canonized him on June 17, 1977. His feast is celebrated in the United States according to the Proper Calendar for the Dioceses of the United States, but is not on the General Roman Calendar.

6 PETER OF CANTERBURY, ABBOT

Peter of Canterbury (d. ca. 607) was a member of the original group of Benedictine monks sent to Briton by Pope Gregory the Great [September 3], under the leadership of Augustine of Canterbury [May 27], to evangelize the Anglo-Saxons. King Ethelbert [February 24] was eventually baptized and gave the monks a house in Canterbury that would become the monastery of Sts. Peter and Paul, later called St. Augustine's. Peter was appointed its first abbot. Peter later drowned in the English Channel while on a missionary journey to Gaul and was buried in Boulogne. His feast is not on the General Roman calendar.

7   RAYMOND OF PEÑAFORT, PRIEST

Raymond of Peñafort (ca. 1180–1275) was a distinguished Dominican and canonist. He was born of a family of high station in Catalonia, Spain, and received doctorates in canon and civil law at the University of Bologna and also taught there. Raymond joined the Dominicans in Barcelona, where he combined the tasks of preaching with those of study and meditation. Called to Rome in 1230 to be the pope's confessor, he produced the *Decretals of Gregory IX,* the basis for the Code of Canon Law, and later wrote an influential guide for confessors. In 1238 he was elected third master general of the Dominican order. In 1240, at age sixty-five, he voluntarily resigned his office and devoted the rest of his life to preaching and working for the conversion of the Jews and the Moors, the latter especially through dialogue, and was instrumental in establishing the Inquisition in Catalonia. He was canonized in 1601 and is the patron saint of canon lawyers. His feast is on the General Roman Calendar.

8 LAWRENCE GIUSTINIANI, BISHOP

Lawrence Giustiniani (1381–1455), the archbishop of Venice, was renowned for his extraordinary concern for the poor. Born of a noble Venetian family, he entered an Augustinian monastery early in his life, was ordained a priest in 1406, and eventually became general of the congregation of Canons Regular of St. Augustine from 1424 until 1431. He was appointed bishop of Castello, which included a portion of Venice, in 1433. When the region was reorganized, Castello was suppressed and Lawrence became archbishop of Venice. His episcopal ministry was marked by personal austerity and extraordinary generosity to the poor. He died on a bed of straw on January 8, 1455. He was canonized in 1690. His feast is not on the General Roman Calendar.

9 ADRIAN OF CANTERBURY, ABBOT

An African by birth, *Adrian of Canterbury* (d. ca. 710) was the abbot of the monastery of Sts. Peter and Paul (later St. Augustine's) in Canterbury. Under his leadership and that of the archbishop, Theodore, the monastery became a major center of learning, producing a number of future bishops and archbishops. Adrian taught at the school for some forty years. He died on January 9, probably in 710, and was buried in the monastery. His tomb became associated with various miracles, and his feast was added to English liturgical calendars. It does not, however, appear on the General Roman Calendar.

10   GREGORY OF NYSSA, BISHOP

Gregory of Nyssa (ca. 330–ca. 395) was the third of the three great Cappadocian Fathers (along with his older brother, Basil the Great [January 2], and Gregory Nazianzen [January 2]). He became bishop of Nyssa in 371, a remote outpost near Armenia where Arianism (the heresy that denied the divinity of Christ) was strong. But Gregory was more skilled as a thinker and writer than as an administrator. He played an important role, along with Gregory Nazianzen, in the Council of Constantinople (381), which defined the divinity of the Holy Spirit. The significance of his writings—in which he argued that the purpose of the Christian life is to imitate God in Christ and that the ideal milieu for such a process is the monastic community—was not fully appreciated until the second half of the twentieth century, thanks to the work of several leading scholars. Gregory's name does not appear on the General Roman Calendar, but his feast is celebrated in the East on this day and he is commemorated on the Benedictine and Cistercian calendars.

11   THEODOSIUS THE CENOBIARCH

Theodosius (423–529) was a leading pioneer of cenobitic, or communal, monasticism, rather than the life of solitude. Born in Cappadocia in Asia Minor, he made a pilgrimage early in life to Jerusalem, where he began to attract disciples. He built a large monastery at Cathismus near Bethlehem. He attached three infirmaries to the monastery: one for the sick, one for the aged, and one for the mentally disturbed. There were also four churches: one for Greeks, one for Armenians, one for Slavs, and one for those doing penance or recovering from mental illness. The Liturgy of the Word was celebrated within each language group, and then all came together for the liturgy of the Eucharist in Greek. The monastic complex became a model of its kind in the East. After Theodosius's death, many miracles were attributed to his intercession. His feast is celebrated by the Greek and Russian Orthodox Churches, but it is not on the General Roman Calendar.

12 BENEDICT BISCOP, BISHOP

The founder and first abbot of Wearmouth and later of Jarrow, both in England, *Benedict Biscop* (628–89) was born Biscop Baducing, of a noble Northumbrian family. He decided at age twenty-five to become a monk, taking the name Benedict, and eventually made six separate visits to Rome as well as to seventeen different monasteries, from which he produced a synthesis of Rules for later use in his own foundations. After serving only two years as abbot of Sts. Peter and Paul (later St. Augustine's) in Canterbury, he founded, with the help of King Egfrith, a new monastery in Wearmouth in 674, for which he later secured the special protection of the Holy See. Benedict's extensive library holdings made possible the work of the Venerable Bede [May 25], a monk of Jarrow, where he wrote the *Ecclesiastical History of the English People.* Benedict Biscop is the patron saint of English Benedictines. His feast is not on the General Roman Calendar, but is commemorated by the Church of England.

13   HILARY OF POITIERS, BISHOP AND DOCTOR OF THE CHURCH

Hilary of Poitiers (ca. 315–ca. 367) was a vigorous and out-spoken defender of orthodoxy against Arianism (which held that Jesus Christ was the greatest of creatures, but not the equal of God). Born at Poitiers (in the central southwest of modern-day France) of wealthy pagan parents, Hilary became a Christian in 350 after a long period of study. About three years later he was elected bishop of his hometown, probably while still a married layman. He was exiled to Phrygia (in Asia Minor) by the Arian emperor Constantius II. His return from exile was greeted with great enthusiasm in Gaul, which became the center of Nicene orthodoxy in the West, and Hilary its chief proponent. He was not yet sixty when he died. Hilary was named a Doctor of the Church by Pope Pius IX in 1851. His feast is on the General Roman Calendar and is also observed on this day by the Church of England and the Episcopal Church in the United States.

14   SAVA OF SERBIA, BISHOP

Sava (1174–1237), patron saint of the Serbs, was the youngest of three sons of Prince Stephen I, who secured the independence of the Serbian state from Byzantium. At age seventeen Sava became a monk on Mt. Athos in Greece. His father later abdicated and joined his son there, and together they founded a monastery for Serbian monks called Khilandari, which survives as one of the seventeen "ruling monasteries" of Mt. Athos. Sava became its abbot for a time, but returned home in 1206 to attempt to settle a dispute between his brothers over their inheritance. He was struck by the sad state of the Church in his homeland. Ordained archbishop of Zica in 1219, Sava established a number of bishoprics, built churches and monasteries, and generally reformed the religious life of the country. He died on January 14, 1237. His feast is not on the General Roman Calendar.

15 PAUL THE HERMIT;
MARTIN LUTHER KING JR.,
CIVIL RIGHTS LEADER

Paul the Hermit (ca. 233–ca. 345), also known as Paul of Thebes, is traditionally regarded as the first hermit in Christian history. He fled to the desert during a period of persecution (probably during the reign of the Roman emperor Decius [249–51]) and is reputed to have lived there to well over a one hundred. Life in solitude was a way of following Christ, but also a defiant "no" to the newly comfortable Church under Constantine. His feast was suppressed from the General Roman Calendar in 1969, but continues to be celebrated in the East on this day.

Lutherans commemorate the American civil rights leader *Martin Luther King Jr.* (1929–68) on this day as a "renewer of society" and "martyr." The United States Catholic bishops recommended to the Vatican that his name be included on a list of twentieth-century martyrs announced by Pope John Paul II in May 2000.

16 HONORATUS OF ARLES, BISHOP

Honoratus (d. ca. 429), born of an aristocratic pagan Gallo-Roman family, was the founder (ca. 405) of one of the most famous monasteries of the early Church, that of Lérins, off the southern coast of Gaul opposite modern-day Cannes. The island is now called Saint-Honorat in his honor. This monastery produced several of southern Gaul's leading bishops and writers, including Vincent of Lérins. Honoratus was named archbishop of Arles in 426, and died there about three years later. He is patron saint of bakers and cake makers. His feast is not on the General Roman Calendar.

17 ANTHONY OF EGYPT, ABBOT

Anthony (also Antony) *of Egypt* (251–356) is generally regarded as the founder of monasticism. Born in Upper Egypt of a prosperous landowning family, at about the age of twenty, following his parents' deaths, he sold all of his possessions and gave the money to the poor in keeping with the Gospel injunction in Matthew 19:21. He took up the life of a hermit, first near his home under the tutelage of an elderly hermit; then for twelve to fifteen years he lived in empty tombs in a cemetery at some distance from his village, and later still in an abandoned fort deep in the desert (286–306). He eventually attracted many disciples and established his first monastery, which was actually a collection of hermits' cells. Athanasius's *Life of Antony* made him a well-known figure, "the father of monks." Anthony's feast is on the General Roman Cal-

endar and is also celebrated on this day by the Greek and
Russian Orthodox Churches.

18 MARGARET OF HUNGARY, NUN

Margaret of Hungary (1242–70), daughter of King Bela IV,
was a Dominican nun who entered the convent at age
thirteen. When her father ordered her to withdraw from
the convent to marry the king of Bohemia, she adamantly
refused, threatening to cut off her nose and lips if forced
to leave. Her life in the convent was described as one of
self-crucifixion because of her preference for the most
menial and even degrading tasks, especially in the care
of the sick and dying. She died at age twenty-eight. She
was canonized by Pope Pius XII in 1943, at a time when
Hungary was under Nazi domination. The Dominicans
commemorate her on this day, but her feast is not on the
General Roman Calendar.

19 WULFSTAN, BISHOP

Born of Anglo-Saxon parents, *Wulfstan* (ca. 1008–95) entered the Benedictine priory at the Worcester cathedral
sometime following his ordination as a diocesan priest.
He became prior of this small community and did such an
excellent job that, when the local diocese became vacant,
he was appointed bishop of Worcester while retaining his
responsibilities at the priory. He visited parishes throughout the diocese, encouraged the building of churches on
his own lands and those of other nobles, promoted clerical celibacy, rebuilt the cathedral, and was exceedingly

generous to the poor. He also abolished the slave trade between Bristol and Ireland (then under Viking control). Wulfstan died at age eighty-seven. He was canonized by Pope Innocent III in 1203. Although he is not on the General Roman Calendar, his feast is celebrated on this day by the Church of England and the Episcopal Church in the United States.

20 FABIAN, POPE AND MARTYR;
SEBASTIAN, MARTYR

Fabian (d. 250) was one of the most respected and accomplished popes of the earliest Christian centuries. Elected as a layman, he reorganized the local clergy, dividing the growing Roman church into seven ecclesiastical districts with a deacon in charge of each, and supervised numerous building projects in the cemeteries, which were also places of worship for the Christian community. Almost all of Fabian's pontificate (236–50) was peaceful, until Decius rose to power in 249 and unleashed a new and vicious persecution against the Church. Fabian was the first to be arrested and put in prison, where he died after suffering brutal treatment.

  Sebastian (d. ca. 300) was martyred under Diocletian and buried on the Appian Way close to the site where a basilica was erected in his honor, possibly by the emperor Constantine. He is usually depicted being pierced with arrows (which, according to legend, did not kill him). For that reason, he is regarded as the patron saint of archers. Both Fabian and Sebastian are on the General Roman Calendar.

21 AGNES, VIRGIN AND MARTYR

Liturgical sources indicate that *Agnes* (d. ca. 305) was one of the most famous of the early Roman martyrs. There is strong evidence of an early cult. She was killed at a very young age (probably twelve or thirteen) during the persecution of Diocletian in the Stadium of Domitian, now the Piazza Navona. Because of the similarity of her name to the Latin word for lamb (*agnus*), the lamb has been her emblem since the sixth century. Her feast is on the General Roman Calendar. She is patron saint of young girls and the Children of Mary, a pious sodality dedicated to the Blessed Virgin Mary.

22 VINCENT OF SARAGOSSA, DEACON AND MARTYR

Vincent of Saragossa (d. 304), a patron saint of Portugal, was a deacon trained by the bishop of Saragossa. He was martyred under Dacian, governor of Spain, during the imperial reign of Maximian. The fact of his martyrdom is clear, but not the manner. Some accounts say that he was imprisoned and nearly starved to death, then racked and roasted on a gridiron when he refused to sacrifice to the gods or hand over the sacred books, then returned to prison and placed in stocks. He eventually died from this brutal treatment. In Burgundy and elsewhere he is regarded as patron of vine growers and wine makers because of the protection he offers against frosts, which often occur on or near his feast day. His feast is on the General Roman Calendar.

23 ILDEPHONSUS OF TOLEDO, BISHOP

Ildephonsus of Toledo (ca. 607–77) was a leading figure in the Spanish Church of the seventh century. Born of a noble Spanish family, he became a monk early in his life against the opposition of his parents, was ordained to the priesthood ca. 637, and was appointed abbot of Agalia ca. 650. As an abbot, he participated in the councils of Toledo in 653 and 657 and was appointed archbishop of Toledo in 657. Ildephonsus had great devotion to the Blessed Virgin Mary and wrote a tract on her perpetual virginity that exercised great influence on the development of Marian devotion in Spain. His feast is not on the General Roman Calendar.

24 FRANCIS DE SALES, BISHOP AND DOCTOR OF THE CHURCH

Francis de Sales (1567–1622) was one of the originators of lay spirituality and author of the classic work *Introduction to the Devout Life*. Several religious congregations have been founded under his patronage: the Missionaries of St. Francis de Sales, the Oblates of St. Francis de Sales, the Salesians of Don Bosco, and the Sisters of St. Joseph. Born in the duchy of Savoy, he eschewed a civil career and was ordained in 1593, soon distinguishing himself as a preacher and as a minister to the poor and the sick. After several years of difficult but eventually successful efforts to reconvert many of the Calvinists of Geneva to Catholicism, he became bishop of Geneva in 1602, where he excelled in administration, preaching, catechesis, clergy education, and spiritual direction.

The central message of his *Introduction to the Devout Life* (1608) was a novel one for the times, namely, that the way of spiritual perfection is not only for the elite few and it does not require great austerities or withdrawal from the everyday life of the world. Francis died on December 28, 1622, was canonized in 1665, and declared a Doctor of the Church in 1877. His feast day is on the General Roman Calendar and is also celebrated by the Church of England.

25 CONVERSION OF PAUL, APOSTLE

Paul (ca. 1/5–ca. 62/67) was the most prominent early Christian missionary, known as the "apostle to the Gentiles." Born in Tarsus in Asia Minor of a Hellenistic-Jewish family and given the name Saul, he received both a Greek and a Jewish education and probably possessed Roman citizenship. A self-described Pharisee (Phil. 3:5), he was zealous in his persecution of the early disciples of Jesus. However, he had a profound conversion experience, liturgically commemorated on this day, while on his way to Damascus around the year 35 (Gal. 1:15–16), an experience he interpreted as a call to preach the Risen Christ to the Gentiles. After remaining in the Damascus area for the next three years, he spent ten years (38–48) on his first great missionary journey, in Syria and Asia Minor.

Paul spent the next eight years (49–57) establishing Christian communities around the eastern Mediterranean.

During these journeys, he wrote letters that form part of the New Testament. In the year 57 he returned to Jerusalem, where he was arrested and imprisoned for two years. Exercising his rights as a Roman citizen, he appealed his case to Caesar and was sent to Rome, where he was held under house arrest for about two more years (59–60). Sometime between 62 and 67 he was executed in Rome by order of the local authorities. His feast is on the General Roman Calendar, and is also celebrated by the Church of England and the Episcopal Church in the United States.

26 TIMOTHY, BISHOP AND MARTYR, AND TITUS, BISHOP

Although the first-century disciples Timothy and Titus are the addressees in three of Paul's New Testament Letters, virtually nothing is known about them. *Timothy* (d. 97) came from Lystra in Asia Minor, the son of a Jewish-Christian mother and a Greek father (Acts 16:1). Paul first met him during his second missionary journey, and Timothy accompanied him on this and the third journey. Paul sent him to strengthen the Thessalonians (1 Thess. 1:1; 3:2, 6) and to help solve problems in Corinth (1 Cor. 4:17; 16:10) and Philippi (Phil. 2:19). In later Christian tradition Timothy was considered the first bishop of Ephesus (probably based on 1 Tim. 1:3). Paul's Letters to Timothy in the New Testament direct him to correct innovators and teachers of false doctrine and to appoint overseers (bishops) and deacons. His feast, along with that of Titus, is on the General Roman Calendar.

Titus was of Greek origin and perhaps a native of Antioch. In the year 48 he accompanied Paul and Barnabas from Antioch to Jerusalem to meet with the leaders of the Jerusalem church about whether gentile Christians had to be circumcised and observe the Mosaic law. Paul pointed to the example of Titus, a Greek, who was not forced to be circumcised upon his conversion to Christ (Gal. 2:3). Titus served as Paul's co-worker and secretary at Ephesus. Paul sent Titus to Corinth to serve as an intermediary in his bitter dispute with the Corinthian Christians. We know that Titus was successful because Paul was later comforted by the news Titus had brought from Corinth (2 Cor. 2:13; 7:6, 13–14). It is thought that Titus was the first bishop of Crete (Titus 1:5).

27 ANGELA MERICI, VIRGIN

Angela Merici (ca. 1470/74–1540) was the foundress of the Ursuline nuns. Born in Desenzano, in the Republic of Venice, she was orphaned at an early age and moved to Brescia, where she became a Franciscan tertiary and began to devote her life to the education of poor girls. She and several companions placed themselves under the patronage of Ursula, thought to have been a fourth-century British princess who fled to Cologne to preserve her virginity and was martyred there with some companions. The Company of St. Ursula took no vows and wore lay clothes, but its Rule prescribed virginity, poverty, and obedience. Angela Merici died on January 27, 1540, and was canonized in 1807. Her feast is on the General Roman Calendar.

28 THOMAS AQUINAS, PRIEST AND DOCTOR OF THE CHURCH

Thomas Aquinas (ca. 1225–74), a Dominican friar known as the "Angelic Doctor," is one of the greatest and most influential theologians in the entire history of the Church. Born in a castle near the small town of Aquino, Thomas was educated at the Benedictine monastery at Monte Cassino and at the University of Naples. He entered the Order of Preachers in 1244 over the strong opposition of his family. His brothers kidnapped him, held him in a castle for a year, and then tried to seduce him away from his vocation with a courtesan. Upon regaining his freedom, he went to Paris for further studies, and then to Cologne, where he studied under Albertus Magnus [November 15] from 1248 until 1252, during which period he was ordained a priest.

From 1259 to 1268, Thomas was in Naples and then at Orvieto, Viterbo, and Rome, teaching his fellow Dominicans. It was in Rome that he began writing his most famous work, the *Summa Theologiae* (Lat., "Synthesis of Theology"), which he continued to write for the next five years in Paris and Naples. On December 6, 1273, he suddenly stopped all of his writing. Whether this was due to a recognition of the limitations of his work or a medical condition from which he died a few months later, on March 7, 1274, cannot be known.

Thomas's entire ministry as a teacher and preacher was a matter of giving to others what he had himself contemplated, which was for him the highest of all activities when done out of charity. It was this same openness and generosity of mind and heart that inspired him to use extensively the works of any authors—whether Christian, Jewish, or pagan—who might lead him to the truth.

Thomas was canonized in 1323 and declared a Doctor of the Church in 1567. Pope Leo XIII, in his encyclical *Aeterni Patris* (1879), commended Thomas's thought to all students of theology, thereby generating a revival of interest in the Angelic Doctor's works. The following year Thomas was named patron saint of Catholic universities. His feast, formerly on March 7, is on the General Roman Calendar.

29 GILDAS, ABBOT

Gildas (ca. 500–ca. 570) was a monastic leader who influenced the development of monasticism in Ireland through his Irish disciples, a visit to Ireland, and subsequent correspondence with Irish monasteries. Born in Scotland, he became a monk probably after being married and widowed. His famous work, *De excidio Britanniae* ("On the Ruin of Britain"), cited by the Venerable Bede [May 25], described the decadence of contemporary British secular rulers and clerics and placed on them the blame for the victory of the Anglo-Saxon invaders. He founded a monastery on an island in Brittany's Morbihan Bay that became the center of his cult. It is still known as the "island of monks." His feast does not appear on the General Roman Calendar.

30 HYACINTHA MARISCOTTI, FOUNDRESS; MOHANDAS K. GANDHI, HINDU HOLY MAN

Hyacintha Mariscotti (1585–1640) was the foundress of two confraternities in Viterbo to care for the sick, the aged, and the poor. Born of a noble Italian family, she was christened Clarice and educated at the local Franciscan convent. Because of her displays of temper, her parents forced her to enter a convent, where she took the name Sister Hyacintha. For ten years she lived the life of a nun in name only, while surrounding herself with luxuries. Both illness and the influence of a saintly Franciscan confessor eventually helped her change her ways. As mistress of novices, she exhibited great wisdom and common sense. She died on January 30, 1640, and was canonized in 1807. Her feast is celebrated by Franciscans, but is not on the General Roman Calendar.

January 30 is also the day of death of one of the twentieth century's spiritual giants, the Hindu holy man and modern pioneer of nonviolent resistance *Mohandas K. Gandhi* (1869–1948), who was assassinated by a young Hindu fanatic.

31 JOHN BOSCO, PRIEST

John Bosco (1815–88) was the founder of the Society of St. Francis de Sales [January 24], known as the Salesian order. He is the patron saint of Catholic publishers, editors, and young apprentices. Born near Turin, he was brought up in severe poverty. He was ordained a priest in

1841 and soon thereafter began a lifelong devotion to educating and caring for boys and young men, especially of the working class. He opened workshops to train shoemakers, tailors, printers, bookbinders, and ironworkers, thereby becoming a pioneer in vocational training. As other priests came to help, the nucleus of a religious community emerged. The Salesians were formally approved in 1884. He died on January 31, 1888, and was canonized on Easter Sunday, 1934, by Pope Pius XI, who, as a young priest, had known Don Bosco. His feast day is on the General Roman Calendar and is also commemorated by the Church of England.

FEBRUARY

1   BRIGID OF KILDARE, ABBESS

Brigid (d. ca. 525), also known as Brigit, Bridget, and
Bride (of Ireland), is a patron saint of Ireland along with
Patrick [March 17] and Columba [June 9]. What little is
known of her is mixed with myth, Irish pagan folklore,
miracle stories, and cultic elements that are difficult to
disentangle. The legendary exploits, however, are typi-
cally Irish. She distributes butter (a sign of prosperity) to
the poor and changes her bathwater into beer to satisfy
the thirst of some visiting clerics. She established a monastery at Kildare, which later became a double monastery (for men and women) that contributed significantly
to the spread of Christianity throughout the country. Her
feast is not on the General Roman Calendar.

2   PRESENTATION OF THE LORD; ALFRED DELP, PRIEST

On the General Roman Calendar (and on that of the
Greek and Russian Orthodox Churches, the Church of
England, the Episcopal Church in the United States, and
the Evangelical Lutheran Church in America), February 2

is the feast of the Presentation of the Lord, when the infant Jesus was brought to the Temple and Mary was purified following childbirth, to fulfill the requirements of Mosaic law (Luke 2:22–40; Exod. 13:2, 12; Lev. 12:6–8).

This is also the day on which *Alfred Delp* (1907–45), a Jesuit priest, was hanged by the Nazis for his opposition to Hitler. In his final message to friends, he wrote: "If through one man's life there is a little more love and kindness, a little more light and truth in the world, then he will not have lived in vain."

3 BLASE, BISHOP AND MARTYR

Blase (d. ca. 316), also Blaise, was an early bishop of Sebaste in Armenia who was martyred under the emperor Licinius. Little or nothing is reliably known of his life. One legend that has him saving the life of a boy with a fish bone caught in his throat is the origin of the custom of blessing throats on his feast day. He is also patron saint of veterinarians. His feast is still on the General Roman Calendar, although in the 1969 revision it was demoted from a memorial to an optional memorial.

4 RABANUS MAURUS, ABBOT AND BISHOP

Rabanus Maurus (780–856) is credited with composing the hymn *"Veni, Creator Spiritus"* (Lat., "Come, Creator Spirit") and for laying the foundation for another hymn, "King of Kings and Lord of Lords," both of which are still sung today. Born in Mainz, he was educated at the monastery of Fulda and then sent to Tours to study under Alcuin, the English biblical scholar and adviser to the emperor Charlemagne. Under Alcuin's guidance, Rabanus became a part of the Carolingian renewal of biblical studies and liturgy. He wrote scriptural commentaries and developed a spirituality that emphasized an organized prayer life. He was ordained a priest in 815 and elected abbot of Fulda in 822. In 1847, he was elected archbishop of Mainz. His own devotion to the Holy See was so intense that he was known as the "pope's slave." His feast is not observed on the General Roman Calendar.

5   AGATHA, VIRGIN AND MARTYR

Agatha (d. 251) was a martyr widely venerated in Sicily. Although facts are few and her entire life is shrouded in legend, Agatha's cult developed very early in the history of the Church. Her historically dubious biography indicates that she was born into a wealthy family and made a vow of virginity, which the Roman consul attempted to violate; upon her refusal, she was subjected to torture, including the cutting off of her breasts; subsequently, however, she was healed by a vision of the Apostle Peter [June 29]. She is said to have died in prison as a result of her sufferings. She is patron saint of nurses and firefighters. In spite of the dearth of reliable information about her, she continues to be one of the most frequently invoked saints in the Church and her feast remains on the General Roman Calendar.

6 PAUL MIKI AND COMPANIONS, MARTYRS

Paul Miki (d. 1597) *and his companions* were the first martyrs of the Far East. The Japanese ruler Hideyoshi initiated a persecution of Christians when he became alarmed by the success of Francis Xavier's [December 3] mission, which had begun in 1549. To strike terror in the hearts of other Christians, the ruler ordered that twenty-six be crucified and pierced with lances on a hill outside Nagasaki on February 5, 1597. Those martyred included Paul Miki, a Jesuit priest and popular preacher, two Jesuit lay brothers, and six Franciscans, of whom four were Spanish; the fifth was from Mexico City, namely, *Peter Baptist* (1545–97), Mexico's first saint, who is also patron saint of Japan; and the sixth was from Bombay. The other seventeen included sixteen Japanese laypeople and one Korean. Among them were catechists, interpreters, a soldier, a physician, and three boys. They were canonized in 1862. The martyrs' feast day was included on the revised General Roman Calendar in 1969.

7 COLETTE, VIRGIN

Colette (1381–1447) was a Franciscan nun who devoted herself to the reform of Franciscan religious life through the restoration of the Rule of Francis [October 4] and Clare [August 11]. Born in Picardy, she took up the life of a hermit near Corbie abbey. As her reputation for holiness grew, many came to her for spiritual direction. The antipope Benedict XIII (1394–1417) professed her as a Poor

Clare and placed her in charge of all convents she would establish or wish to reform; she founded seventeen and reformed several others. She was canonized in 1807. Her feast does not appear on the General Roman Calendar.

8   JEROME EMILIANI, FOUNDER

Jerome Emiliani (1483–1537) was the founder of the Somoscan Fathers, an order that runs schools and orphanages in Italy. Born in Venice, he became an officer of the Venetian army. In 1518, after a conversion experience he was ordained a priest and devoted his life to the care of suffering people in a time of widespread famine and plague. After his own recovery from the plague in 1531, he founded orphanages, hospitals, houses for former prostitutes, and a small congregation of priests to care for them all, but especially the orphans. He was canonized in 1768 and declared the patron saint of orphans and abandoned children in 1928. His feast is on the General Roman Calendar.

9   APOLLONIA, VIRGIN AND MARTYR;
MIGUEL FEBRES CORDERO,
RELIGIOUS BROTHER

Apollonia (d. ca. 249) was an aged deaconess of Alexandria the form of whose martyrdom has ensured her place in the history of saints. The bishop of Alexandria reported that, during an anti-Christian riot, all of her teeth were broken with blows to the jaw and then she was burned to death. She became known as the patron saint of dentists and of those with toothaches. In Boston there is a dentists' quarterly named after her, *The Apollonian*. Her feast was dropped from the General Roman Calendar in 1969.

Miguel Febres Cordero (1854–1910) was Ecuador's first canonized saint. He joined the Christian Brothers at age fourteen, and before he was twenty he published a Spanish grammar book that was eventually prescribed for all schools in Ecuador. Other books followed as he devoted himself to the religious education of children. He was canonized in 1984. His feast is not on the General Roman Calendar.

10 SCHOLASTICA, VIRGIN

Scholastica (ca. 480–ca. 543) was the sister of Benedict of Nursia [July 11] and is the patron saint of Benedictine nuns. Her own nunnery at Plombariola was only five miles from the famous Monte Cassino. She and her brother would meet annually in a house outside Monte Cassino to discuss spiritual matters. According to the *Dialogues* of Pope Gregory the Great [September 3], at their last meeting she begged her brother to stay longer in order to continue their discussion. He refused on the ground that his Rule prevented it. She thereupon bowed her head in prayer, and a violent thunderstorm prevented her brother from leaving until the following morning. Benedict accused Scholastica of provoking the storm, to which she replied: "I asked a favor of you and you refused it. I asked it of God, and he has granted it." Three days later she died. Her feast is on the General Roman Calendar.

11   OUR LADY OF LOURDES

Between February 11 and July 16, 1858, the Blessed Virgin Mary is said to have appeared to Marie Bernarde (later Bernadette) Soubirous [April 16], a fourteen-year-old girl, eighteen times at the grotto of Massabielle, near her hometown of Lourdes on the northern slopes of the Pyrenees mountains. Although by March twenty thousand pilgrims had gathered to witness the apparition, only Bernadette could see it. She was instructed by the apparition to bathe and drink from a spring that began to flow the following day. Since then the bath at Lourdes has been associated with miraculous healings. The local bishop eventually authorized the cult of Our Lady of Lourdes in 1862. The site of the apparitions attracts over three million pilgrims a year. Of some five thousand reported cures, at least fifty-eight have been declared miraculous by church officials. In 1907 Pope Pius X made the feast of Our Lady of Lourdes a feast of the universal Church. It remains on the General Roman Calendar.

12   BENEDICT OF ANIANE, ABBOT

Benedict of Aniane (ca. 750–821) was a major reformer of Benedictine monasteries in France. Born of a noble Visigothic family in Languedoc, he became a courtier of Pepin III and Charlemagne and then a monk. As Benedict's influence grew, he was enlisted by the Frankish emperor Louis the Pious, successor of Charlemagne, to apply the Rule of St. Benedict [July 11] to all monasteries in his domain. Benedict stressed poverty, chastity, and obedience, the importance of the daily conventual Mass and the keeping of the liturgical hours, the standardizing of the intake of food and drink, and an emphasis on teaching, writing, and artistic work over manual labor on the part of monks who were also clerics. Benedict of Aniane's feast is not on the General Roman Calendar.

13 CATHERINE DE' RICCI, VIRGIN

Catherine de' Ricci (1522–90) was a Dominican nun known for her wisdom, psychological healthiness, and concern for the sick. Born to a wealthy family in Florence and baptized Alexandrina, she is said to have experienced ecstasies each week (from midday on Thursday to about 4:00 P.M. on Friday) over a twelve-year period in which she became physically conformed to the Passion of Christ, including the stigmata. Catherine de' Ricci was canonized in 1746. Her feast is not on the General Roman Calendar.

14 CYRIL, MONK, AND METHODIUS, BISHOP; VALENTINE, MARTYR

Cyril (826–69) and *Methodius* (ca. 815–85) are known as the "apostles of the Slavs" and were named by Pope John Paul II as the patron saints of Europe, alongside Benedict of Nursia [July 11]. Their principal missions were to territories encompassed by the modern-day Czech Republic, Croatia, Serbia, and Slovenia. Cyril was educated in Constantinople. After ordination to the priesthood, he was appointed librarian at the Hagia Sophia, the principal church in Eastern Christendom. He later joined his brother Methodius, who, after a brief government career, entered a monastery in Bithynia.

Both were commissioned by the emperor Michael III ca. 862 to become missionaries in Moravia at the request of the local ruler, Rostislav, who wanted Cyril and Methodius, who had spoken Slavonic since childhood, to teach in the vernacular. In order to put spoken Slavonic in written form, Cyril invented a Slavonic alphabet (from which Cyrillic was derived), based on the Greek alphabet, and then he and Methodius together translated major portions of the Bible and the liturgy.

For mainly political reasons, the German bishops opposed Cyril and Methodius's missionary efforts, especially their advocacy of the use of the vernacular in the liturgy, and refused to ordain them or their disciples. But Pope Hadrian II approved the Slavonic liturgy and ordained Methodius and three of their disciples as priests. Already afflicted with serious health problems, Cyril died at age forty-two, on February 14, 869.

In 870, Methodius was consecrated archbishop of Sirmium. Once again, however, the German bishops and Hungarian clergy opposed him, and he was exiled. In 879 Methodius was called to Rome to answer charges of heresy and disobedience. After he was found innocent, he returned to Moravia in 880 with his appointment as archbishop confirmed and with papal permission to use the Slavonic language in the liturgy restored. During the last four years of his life, he translated the entire Bible into Slavonic, with the exception of Maccabees. He died on April 6, 885. The feast of Cyril and Methodius is on the General Roman Calendar and is celebrated on May 11 in the East.

February 14 is also St. Valentine's Day. *Valentine* was a third-century Roman martyr with a very early cult. It is not clear how his cult became linked with lovers. His feast was suppressed in the 1969 revision of the General Roman Calendar.

15 SIGFRID, BISHOP; CLAUDE LA COLOMBIÈRE, PRIEST

Sigfrid (d. ca. 1045) was bishop of Vaxjo and the "apostle of Sweden." English by birth and a monk of Glastonbury, he was sent by King Ethelred to Christianize the Swedes and the Norwegians, baptizing Olaf, the king of Sweden. During a missionary trip to the more remote areas of the region, Sigfrid's three nephews, who were also his principal helpers, were murdered. On his return Sigfrid persuaded the king not to execute the killers. His cult was established in Norway, Sweden, and Denmark by the thirteenth century. His feast is not on the General Roman Calendar, but he is commemorated by the Church of England.

Claude La Colombière (1641–82) was the confessor of Margaret Mary Alacoque [October 16], who was the recipient of private revelations about the Sacred Heart of Jesus. Born into a wealthy French family near Lyons, he entered the Society of Jesus in 1658 and, even before ordination in 1675, displayed a remarkable talent for preaching. Claude often appealed to the new and growing devotion to the Sacred Heart (with its emphasis on the love of God for all) as a spiritual weapon against Jansenism, a largely French movement that incorporated elements of Calvinism and Lutheranism.

Shortly after his arrival at his first priestly assignment in Paray-le-Monial in Burgundy, Claude paid a call at the Visitation convent there and met Sister Margaret Mary. She told him of her visions, and together they worked for the approval of a new feast in honor of the Sacred Heart of Jesus. Claude was shortly thereafter transferred to Protestant England, where he was eventually arrested for traitorous speech. While he was imprisoned in a damp dungeon, his health deteriorated rapidly. At the request of King Louis XIV, he was saved from execution and banished to France. He never regained his health and died in Paray on February 15, 1682. Claude's feast is not on the General Roman Calendar, but is celebrated on this day by the Jesuits.

16 JULIANA, VIRGIN AND MARTYR

Juliana (d. ca. 305) was an early fourth-century martyr who probably died at Naples or at Cumae, which is near Naples, during the persecution of the emperor Maximian. The principal, though legendary, episode associated with her life is the lengthy argument she supposedly had with the Devil, who tried to persuade her to obey her pagan father and to marry a Roman prefect. Condemned to death, she was beheaded after a furnace and boiling oil did no harm to her. There is evidence of her cult in England at least as early as the seventh century. Her feast is not on the General Roman Calendar.

17 SEVEN FOUNDERS OF THE ORDER OF SERVITES

Today's feast celebrates the sanctity of seven members of well-to-do thirteenth-century Florentine families who founded a new order of friars called the Servites, or the Order of Friar Servants of Mary (O.S.M.) in 1233. Their names are *Buonfiglio* (also Bonfilius) *Monaldi* (also Monaldo), *Giovanni Bonaiuncta* (also Buonagiunta), *Manettus dell'Antella* (also Benedict dell'Antello, or dell'Antela), *Amadeus degli Amidei* (also Bartholomew), *Ricovero Uguccione* (also Hugh), *Geraldino Sostegni* (also Sosthenes Sostegno), and *Alexis Falconieri*. In reaction to the general moral laxity of the city, they gathered in a house outside Florence where they practiced a life of solitude, prayer, and penance. When they were besieged by visitors, they withdrew to the wilderness, where they built a simple church and hermitage. Later, they moderated their extremely austere lifestyle and became friars rather than monks, living in towns rather than in monasteries. A principal devotion fostered by the friars is that of the Seven Sorrows of the Blessed Virgin. The seven founders were canonized in 1887, and their feast appears on the General Roman Calendar.

18 COLMAN OF LINDISFARNE, BISHOP; BLESSED JOHN OF FIESOLE (FRA ANGELICO), PAINTER; MARTIN LUTHER, REFORMER

Colman of Lindisfarne (d. 676) was a leading figure in the seventh-century Irish Church as bishop-abbot of the great monastery of Lindisfarne. He played a key role at the Synod of Whitby, an Anglo-Saxon church council held in 664 to resolve differences between the Roman and Celtic observances, including the dating of Easter, and the relationship of local churches to the See of Rome. After Colman's Celtic side lost the full-scale debate, Colman resigned his post at Lindisfarne and migrated, with all of the Irish monks and about thirty English monks from Lindisfarne, to Ireland, where he founded a monastery on the isle of Inishbofin, ca. 667. Because of a dispute between the Irish and English monks, Colman had to settle the English monks on the mainland at Mayo while the Irish remained at Inishbofin. The new monastery at Mayo flourished. Colman remained abbot of the two communities until his death. His feast is not on the General Roman Calendar.

John of Fiesole (ca. 1400–55), better known as *Fra Angelico,* is the patron saint of artists. Born in a small village near Fiesole, he took up painting early in life, before entering the Dominicans ca. 1420 and taking the name Fra Giovanni. His notable works of art include the *Annunciation, Descent from the Cross,* and the frescoes in the monastic cells at San Marco in Florence. His feast is not on the General Roman Calendar.

The Evangelical Lutheran Church in America and the Episcopal Church in the United States celebrate the feast of *Martin Luther* (1483–1546), the leading figure in the Protestant Reformation, on this day.

19 CONRAD OF PIACENZA, HERMIT

Conrad of Piacenza (1290–1351) was born of a noble family in Piacenza. One day, a fire that he had lit got out of control and burned a neighboring cornfield. Conrad had to sell all of his possessions to pay for the damages. He gave to the poor his remaining wealth, his wife became a Poor Clare nun, and he became a hermit, living a life of great austerity. Crowds were attracted by his sanctity. His last years were spent in a grotto outside Noto, where he died and was buried. Numerous miracles were reported at his tomb, and his cult was approved by Pope Paul III (1534–49). His feast is not on the General Roman Calendar.

20 WULFRIC, PRIEST AND HERMIT

Wulfric (ca. 1080–1154), also Ulric or Ulfrick, of Haselbury was an English hermit. Born in Somerset, he was converted to an austere form of life in the early 1120s. He ministered as a parish priest until 1125, when he undertook the life of a hermit in a corner of the parish church at Haselbury Plucknett. His rigorous penitential practices, including fasting and self-scourging, generated a reputation for sanctity. His cult began to develop about thirty years after his death on February 20, 1154, when various miracles were reported at his tomb. He was never formally canonized, and his feast is not on the General Roman Calendar.

21   PETER DAMIAN, BISHOP AND DOCTOR OF THE CHURCH

Peter Damian (1007–72) was a major reformer of the papacy, episcopate, clergy, and monasteries. Born in Ravenna of a large poor family, he entered in 1035 the Camaldolese Benedictine monastery at Fonte Avellana, which followed an austere program of fasting, abstinence, vigils, and Scripture study. In 1043, Peter was elected abbot. He criticized bishops and monks who violated their high calling and preached against simony and clerical marriage and in favor of a reformed papacy. In 1057 he was appointed bishop of Ostia and a cardinal. He increased his activities on behalf of reform, opposing false claimants to the papacy and fulfilling diplomatic missions. However, Peter remained a monk at heart and successfully persuaded Pope Alexander II to relieve him of his episcopal duties so that he might return to his monastery at Fonte Avellana. He died on February 22, 1072. Peter was never formally canonized, but in 1828 Pope Leo XII approved his cult for the universal Church and also declared him a Doctor of the Church. His feast is on the General Roman Calendar.

22   CHAIR OF PETER, APOSTLE

Today's feast celebrates not only the triumph of Christ's grace in the heart and soul of *Peter* [June 29], but his status as the primary pastor and teacher of the Church. The *chair* is the symbol of his teaching authority, as it is of every bishop. Peter (d. ca. 64) was Jesus' chief apostle, whom later Catholic tradition regards as the first pope. (Previously the popes were regarded as successors of Peter, who was not himself a pope.)

Peter enjoyed a unique status within the college of apostles. He was the first disciple Jesus called; he served as the spokesman for the others; and according to the tradition of Paul [June 29, with Peter] and Luke [October 18] he was the first to whom the Risen Lord appeared. He was prominent in the original Jerusalem community, described by Paul as one of its "pillars," and well known to many other churches. Although there is increasing agreement among historians and biblical scholars that Peter did go to Rome and was martyred there, there is no evidence that he functioned as Rome's first bishop. In the Catholic tradition, the biblical basis for associating the primacy with Peter is embodied in three texts: Matthew 16:13–19 ("You are Peter, and upon this rock I will build my church. . . . I will give you the keys to the kingdom of heaven"); Luke 22:31–32 ("You must strengthen your brothers"); and John 21:15–19 ("Feed my lambs. . . . Tend my sheep. . . . Feed my sheep").

The ministry of pastoral leadership exercised by Peter in the first part of the Acts of the Apostles is the model and the norm for the Petrine ministry exercised by every one of his successors. It involves witnessing to the faith, overseeing the way in which local churches preserve and transmit this faith, providing assistance and encouragement to fellow bishops in their own local and universal ministry of proclaiming and defending the faith, speaking in the name of the bishops and their local churches when the need arises, and articulating the faith of the

Church in the name of the whole communion of local churches that together constitute the universal Church. This feast is on the General Roman Calendar.

23 POLYCARP, BISHOP AND MARTYR

Polycarp (ca. 69–ca. 155), a disciple of John the Evangelist, was bishop of Smyrna (in present-day Turkey) and one of the most important Christian leaders in Roman Asia during the first half of the second century. He defended the faith against the heresies of Marcionism (which rejected the inspired character of the Old Testament) and Gnosticism (which denied the humanity of Christ and held to an understanding of revelation accessible only to an elite few).

Toward the end of his life, Polycarp journeyed to Rome at the invitation of Pope Anicetus (ca. 155–ca. 166) to resolve a dispute over the date for the celebration of Easter. Polycarp urged Anicetus to adopt Asia Minor's practice of observing the feast, regarded as the Christian Passover, the day of the Jewish Passover, regardless of the day of the week on which it fell. Until this time, Rome itself observed no special feast of Easter, considering every Sunday a celebration of the Resurrection. Anicetus denied Polycarp's request, but the discussion remained friendly. They departed in peace, but Rome and the East continued their separate practices.

Soon after, Polycarp returned to Smyrna, where he was arrested, tried (he calmly refused to deny Christ), killed, and burned at the stake. The local Christians collected his bones and also wrote a careful account of his martyrdom—the first of its kind. It was the commemoration of Polycarp's martyrdom that established the custom of celebrating the anniversary of a martyr's death, seen as the day of birth in heaven. His feast is on the General Roman Calendar.

24 ETHELBERT OF KENT, KING

Ethelbert of Kent (d. 616) was the first Christian Anglo-Saxon king, or *bretwalda* ("overlord"). His wife, Bertha, daughter of the king of Paris, was already a Christian when Ethelbert married her; she had agreed to the marriage on condition that she be allowed to practice her religion. Ethelbert offered a friendly welcome to Augustine of Canterbury [May 27] and his monks in 597 when they came, at the behest of Pope Gregory the Great [September 3], to re-Christianize Britain. He offered them a house in Canterbury and allowed them to preach and to make converts. Ethelbert himself was eventually baptized ca. 601 and received a congratulatory letter and gifts from the pope.

His conversion was decisive for the Christianization of Kent and then of all of England. Augustine restored an old church in Canterbury, dedicated it to Christ, and made it his cathedral. Ethelbert built a monastery for the monks, dedicated to Sts. Peter and Paul (later St. Augustine's), outside the walls of the city. He also founded the church in London that became St. Paul's Cathedral and promulgated laws that protected churches and the clergy. He died on February 24, 616. Ethelbert's feast is not on the General Roman Calendar.

25 WALBURGA, ABBESS

Walburga (d. 779) was the abbess of Heidenheim. The sister of Sts. Winnibald and Willibald [June 7], she assisted her uncle Boniface [June 5] in his missionary work in Germany. She was educated at the monastery of Wimborne (Dorset) and then at Tauberbischofsheim (southwest of Würzburg). When Winnibald died, Willibald, the first bishop of Eichstätt, named her abbess of the double monastery (one for men, the other for women) of Heidenheim (fifty miles east of Stuttgart), established by her brother Winnibald. Miraculous cures were associated with her tomb in Eichstätt, from which medicinal oil, known as St. Walburga's oil, is said to have flowed. When her relics were spread to other countries, so was her cult. Her feast is not on the General Roman Calendar.

26 PORPHYRY OF GAZA, BISHOP

Porphyry (353–421), the bishop of Gaza, was renowned for his generosity to the poor. He was born in Thessalonika and came to Macedonia, where, at age twenty-five, he abandoned the world and spent five years as a monk in the desert of Skete. He spent the next five years as a hermit in Palestine, living in a cave near the river Jordan. He became crippled by illness and moved to Jerusalem, where, with the help of a walking stick, he visited the holy places. In 393, when Porphyry was forty years old, the bishop of Jerusalem ordained him a priest. Three years later he was elected bishop of Gaza without his knowledge. He was ordered to go to Caesarea on the pretext that the local bishop wanted to consult with him about biblical matters. At the instigation of the bishop, Porphyry was effectively kidnapped by some of the townspeople of Gaza and forcibly consecrated as their bishop. He spent the remaining thirteen years of his life in active pastoral service of his see, gaining a wide reputation for his generosity to the poor. His feast is not on the General Roman Calendar.

27 GABRIEL POSSENTI, RELIGIOUS

Gabriel Possenti (1838–62) was a Passionist who died at a young age and whose sanctity was often compared with that of Thérèse of Lisieux, The Little Flower [October 1]. Also known as Gabriele dell'Addolorata, the son of the governor of Assisi, he lived a life of self-indulgence until two serious illnesses made him rethink its direction. He entered the Passionist novitiate at Morrovalle in 1856, where he was known for his cheerfulness, his commitment to prayer and penance, and his devotion to Our Lady of Sorrows. He was only twenty-four when he died of tuberculosis on February 27, 1862. He is considered the patron saint of clerics and youth. His feast is not on the General Roman Calendar.

28 OSWALD OF WORCESTER, BISHOP

Oswald (d. 992) was a Benedictine monk, bishop of Worcester, and archbishop of York. Born into a Danish military family, he was the nephew of the archbishops of Canterbury and York. He was formally educated and became a monk at the Cluniac monastery of Fleury-sur-Loire in France; he returned to England as a priest ca. 958, where the king appointed him bishop of Worcester in 961. He founded or supported the foundation of monasteries, especially at Ramsey, and reformed his own cathedral chapter. However, some sources underscore his close cooperation with the king in acquiring considerable tracts of land for his diocese and monasteries, and in accepting the archbishopric of York in 972 while retaining the see of Worcester (at the king's request and with the pope's permission)—an abuse known as pluralism. Nevertheless, Oswald administered both dioceses, built churches, visited parishes and monasteries, and administered justice; he also had a practice of washing the feet of twelve poor men each day at Mass during Lent. Oswald died on Leap Year Day, February 29, 992. His feast is not on the General Roman Calendar.

MARCH

1 DAVID OF WALES, BISHOP

David of Wales (ca. 520–ca. 601), also Dewi and Dafydd, is the patron saint of Wales (and of poets) and the only Welsh saint to have been canonized. His nickname was "Aquaticus" (Lat., "water drinker"), because he was the leader of a group of monks who drank neither wine nor beer, only water. Though he is one of the most famous of British saints, there is no reliable biography of him. He is said to have founded ten or perhaps even twelve monasteries in Wales and England, among them Menevia (now St. David's). More than fifty pre-Reformation churches were dedicated to him in south Wales. His feast is not on the General Roman Calendar, but is celebrated by the Church of England and the Episcopal Church in the United States on this day.

2 CHAD OF LICHFIELD, ABBOT AND BISHOP; JOHN AND CHARLES WESLEY, FOUNDERS

Chad (d. 672), also Ceadda, was the bishop of Lichfield, in service to the Mercians. A pupil of Aidan at Lindisfarne, he became abbot of Lastingham. He was consecrated under dubious circumstances as bishop of the Northumbrians, with his see at York. King Oswiu had become impatient at the absence of Wilfrid [October 12], who had originally been appointed to the see but had gone to France for his consecration. Theodore, the archbishop of Canterbury, refused to recognize Chad's appointment. Chad willingly yielded to Theodore's judgment and retired to Lastingham. Impressed by Chad's humility, Theodore had him reconsecrated as bishop of the Mercians, with his see in Lichfield. Chad proved himself such a dedicated pastor to his people that he was venerated as a saint immediately after his death from plague on March 2, 672. His feast is not on the General Roman Calendar, but is celebrated on this day by the Church of England and the Episcopal Church in the United States.

Lutherans commemorate *John and Charles Wesley* (1703–91 and 1707–88, respectively), leading figures in the establishment of the Methodist Church. The Episcopal Church in the United States celebrates their feast on March 3.

3 KATHARINE DREXEL, FOUNDRESS

Katharine Drexel (1858–1955), also known as Mother Drexel, was the foundress of the Sisters of the Blessed Sacrament for Indians and Colored People (S.B.S.) in 1891. The daughter of a wealthy Philadelphia banker, she was encouraged by Pope Leo XIII himself to follow the example of her generous parents and to devote her fortune (worth more than $80 million today) and her life to the poor. In 1889, at age thirty, she entered the Sisters of Mercy, but felt a special call to do missionary work among African and Native Americans. She undertook the humblest work in the convent and faithfully observed the requirements of the vow of poverty.

In 1891 she started her own religious congregation, the Sisters of the Blessed Sacrament, and established her first American Indian school in Sante Fe, New Mexico, three years later. She would create eleven more schools on Indian reservations, nearly a hundred for African Americans in rural areas and the inner cities of the South, and found in 1915 a teachers college that would eventually grow to become the first and only Catholic university for African Americans, Xavier University in New Orleans. Katharine Drexel died on March 3, 1955, and was canonized on October 1, 2000. Her feast is on the Proper Calendar for the Dioceses of the United States, but is not on the General Roman Calendar. She is the second American-born canonized saint.

4   CASIMIR, PRINCE

Casimir (1458–84) is the patron saint of Lithuania, Poland, and Russia. Born at Kraków, the third son of the king of Poland, he refused his father's orders to take up arms against other Christian countries and to marry the daughter of the emperor Frederick III, preferring instead a life of celibacy and asceticism. He died at age twenty-six of tuberculosis on March 4, 1484. He was canonized in 1521, and his feast was extended to the whole Church in 1621. His feast is on the General Roman Calendar.

5   JOHN JOSEPH OF THE CROSS, RELIGIOUS

John Joseph of the Cross (1654–1734) was born Carlo Gaetano on the island of Ischia off the west coast of Italy, opposite Naples, of which he is patron saint. At sixteen he entered the Franciscans of the strict Alcantarine observance, taking the name John Joseph of the Cross. He was ordained in 1677 and devoted himself particularly to the ministry of the confessional and to spiritual direction. Following a dispute between Italian and Spanish members of the community, the Italians formed their own province, and John Joseph was elected minister provincial. At the end of his term, he returned to the house he had originally entered, seeking a life of obscurity. However, he was constantly followed on the street by people seeking his advice or blessing. He died of a major stroke on March 5, 1739. His feast is not on the General Roman Calendar.

6   CHRODEGANG OF METZ, BISHOP

Chrodegang of Metz (ca. 712–66) was a reformer of the clergy and the author of a Rule for canons (i.e., priests attached to a cathedral and living in common) that was used in Germany, Italy, the British Isles, and throughout the Frankish kingdom. Born near Liège in present-day Belgium of noble Frankish parents, he served in a variety of high offices (including chief minister) under Charles Martel and Pepin III, becoming bishop of Metz in 742. Upon the martyrdom of Boniface [June 5] in 754, he assumed responsibility for church reform in the whole of the Frankish kingdom. His greatest achievement, however, was his reform of the European secular clergy, whose moral conduct had become reflective of society's laxity and general disregard for law.

Chrodegang began his reform at home, with his own clergy in Metz. He obliged them to attend the chanting of the Divine Office and live a common life according to the Rule he drew up, based on that of St. Benedict [July 11]. Chrodegang made Metz not only the center of clerical reform, but also of liturgical renewal. He mandated the use of Roman practices and Roman (Gregorian) chant. The choir school at Metz was renowned throughout Europe for centuries to come. Chrodegang died on March 6, 766. His feast does not appear on the General Roman Calendar.

7   PERPETUA AND FELICITY, MARTYRS

Perpetua and her slave *Felicity* (Felicitas) were North African martyrs who were put to death in 203, during the persecution of Septimus Severus. Their feast was widely celebrated throughout the early Christian world and was recorded in the earliest Roman and Syriac liturgical calendars (late fourth century) as well as in the fifth-century *Martyrology of Jerome* [September 30].

Perpetua (Vibia Perpetua) was a young married noblewoman of twenty-two who was arrested, along with other North African catechumens, a few months after giving birth to a son. Perpetua's husband and her pregnant slave Felicity were arrested with her. *The Passion of Perpetua and Felicitas*, written in part by Perpetua, provides one of the earliest, most valuable, and most revered accounts of Christian martyrdom. In this document Perpetua referred to her prison as a "palace"; she refused the pleadings of her aged father to renounce her faith, nursed her son, is said to have experienced visions, and was baptized while awaiting the start of the games. Her servant *Felicity* gave birth to a girl. On the day of the games, they left for the amphitheater "joyfully as though they were on their way to heaven." The men were attacked by leopards and bears; the women, by a heifer. Injured but not killed, Perpetua guided the gladiator's knife to her throat. It was March 7, 203. Their feast is on the General Roman Calendar. Felicity is patron saint of barren women.

8   JOHN OF GOD, RELIGIOUS

John of God (1495–1550), born John Ciudad, was the founder of the Brothers of the Hospitaller Order of St. John of God (O.H.), also known as the Brothers Hospitallers. Born in Montemor-o-Novo, Portugal, he was taken to Spain by a visiting priest, where he worked for a time as a shepherd and later joined a company of Spanish mercenaries, abandoning his faith and living an immoral life. At about age forty he had a conversion experience and hoped to achieve martyrdom in North Africa, working among Christian slaves. He was dissuaded from doing so by a Franciscan confessor and returned to Gibraltar to spread the faith by going from town to town selling religious books and holy pictures.

Spiritually overcome by a sermon preached by John of Ávila [May 10], he pledged himself to a life of sanctity.

Initially, however, he went to such great extremes in his devotional and penitential practices that he was committed to an asylum for the mentally disturbed. John of Ávila visited him there and directed his energies to the care of the sick and the poor. His mental health improved almost immediately. He subsequently rented a house in Granada and filled it with the sick. Others were attracted to and wished to share in his ministry to those in need. He died on March 8, 1550, his fifty-fifth birthday. He was canonized in 1690. His feast is on the General Roman Calendar.

9 FRANCES OF ROME, RELIGIOUS

Frances of Rome (1384–1440) was the foundress of the Oblates of Tor de' Specchi, a community of women without vows with a mandate to serve the poor. She is the patron saint of motorists and widows. Born Francesca dei Roffredeschi in the Trastevere section of Rome of an illustrious and wealthy family, she was married at age thirteen, in spite of her desire to become a nun.

After the death of two of her six children, Frances founded a society of women devoted to the service of the poor, especially in hospitals. They were known at first as the Oblates of Mary, but later became the Oblates of Tor de' Specchi ("Tower of the Specchi," where their convent was located). After her husband's death in 1436, she herself entered this community and became its superior for four years, until her own death on March 9, 1440, having subsisted for years on dry bread and occasional vegetables. Her feast is on the General Roman Calendar.

10 FORTY MARTYRS OF SEBASTEA

The *Forty Martyrs of Sebastea* (also Sebaste, a city in modern-day Turkey) were a group of soldiers put to death for their faith in 320, during the persecution of the emperor Licinius. The local governor of Sebastea tried to persuade them to renounce their faith and spare their lives. When his entreaties failed, he ordered them to be stripped naked and exposed all night on a frozen lake outside the city. A fire and warm bath were prepared on the bank of the lake to tempt them. Only one of the soldiers weakened, but another, a nonbeliever, immediately took his place and was converted to Christ. All died of exposure. Their feast is not on the General Roman Calendar, but is celebrated on this day by the Greek and Russian Orthodox Churches.

11 EULOGIUS OF CÓRDOBA, MARTYR

Eulogius of Córdoba (d. 859) was an archbishop of Toledo martyred by the Moors. Born into a wealthy landowning family in a city under Muslim occupation, he eventually became a priest and was devoted to the sick. He was imprisoned with the bishop and other clergy of the city for reading the Scriptures to two young women who were about to be martyred. In their honor he wrote his *Documentum Martyrii,* similar to Cyprian of Carthage's [September 16] "Exhortation to Martyrs." On the death of the archbishop of Toledo, Eulogius was chosen as his successor, but he did not live long enough to take possession of the see. He was imprisoned and beheaded on

March 11, 859, for giving refuge to a convert from Islam and for refusing to abjure his faith. His feast is not on the General Roman Calendar.

12 MAXIMILIAN, MARTYR

Maximilian (d. 295), an early example of a Christian conscientious objector, refused to serve in the Roman army. When told he must either serve or die, he replied: "You may cut off my head, but I will not be a soldier of this world because I am a soldier of God." When reminded that there were Christians serving in the army, even as imperial bodyguards, Maximilian answered: "They know what is best for them. I am a Christian and I cannot do what is wrong." He was beheaded in his native town of Theveste (Tebessa) in Numidia (present-day Algeria). His body was buried in Carthage, close to that of Cyprian [September 16]. His feast is not on the General Roman Calendar.

13 EUPHRASIA OF CONSTANTINOPLE, VIRGIN

Euphrasia (d. ca. 420), also Eupraxia, was raised in Constantinople by the emperor Theodosius I, who was a relative of her late father. She was betrothed to a senator at age five, but accompanied her mother to Egypt two years later, where she and her mother each received a nun's habit. Her mother died when Euphrasia was only twelve, and she was recalled to Constantinople by the new emperor in order to marry the senator to whom she had been betrothed. Instead, she was allowed to give her inheritance to the poor, free her slaves, and spend the rest of her life as a nun. Her feast is not on the General Roman Calendar.

14 MATILDA, QUEEN

Matilda (ca. 895–968), also known as Mechtildis and Maud, was married to the German king Henry I, with whom she had five children. While her husband was constantly away at war, Matilda lived a pious life and was generous to the poor and to all in need. Upon his death, her oldest son, Otto, succeeded to the throne and began to criticize his mother's liberality toward the poor. When her favorite son, Henry, allied himself with his older brother, Matilda retired to the country residence where she had been born. Matilda returned to court, however, at the urgent invitation of the nobles, the clergy, and Otto's wife, Edith, and resumed her former works of mercy and almsgiving. She built three convents and a monastery and administered the kingdom in her son Otto's absence. She died at the monastery of Quedlinburg on March 14, 968, and was venerated locally as a saint from the moment of her death. Her feast is not on the General Roman Calendar.

15 LOUISE DE MARILLAC, WIDOW AND FOUNDRESS

Louise de Marillac (1591–1660) was the foundress of the Daughters of Charity of St. Vincent de Paul [September 27].

Born into an aristocratic family, she married and had one son. After her husband's death twelve years later, she met Vincent de Paul, who became her spiritual director. He was at the time encouraging and training devout and wealthy women to care for the sick and the poor. He chose Louise to train girls and widows for this ministry drawn mainly from the lower classes (since the aristocratic women proved unequal to the task). From this small group of women working out of Louise's Paris home, beginning in 1633, there developed the Daughters of Charity of St. Vincent de Paul and all of the other Sisters of Charity communities that were founded and spread all over the world. Louise died on March 15, 1642, and was canonized in 1934. Her feast is not on the General Roman Calendar.

16 ABRAHAM KIDUNAIA, HERMIT

Abraham Kidunaia (sixth century) was a highly venerated Eastern hermit. Born into a wealthy family near Edessa in Mesopotamia, he rejected his parents' plea that he should marry and literally ran off to the desert to live as a hermit. The local bishop ordained him a priest so that he could preach to the local people who had hitherto resisted the faith. Abraham had a church built and destroyed every pagan idol he could find. He was driven out of town, but returned by night to preach once again. They stoned him and left him half dead. This pattern continued for nearly three years. Eventually there was a breakthrough, and they began to listen to him and to be converted and baptized. He died at seventy, and a popular cult developed immediately. His feast is not on the General Roman Calendar.

17 PATRICK, BISHOP

Patrick (fifth century, or possibly ca. 389–ca. 461), the "apostle to" and patron saint of Ireland, is one of the Church's most famous and popular saints, even among those who are not Irish. He is also patron saint of Nigeria. Born in Roman Britain, the grandson of a priest and the son of a public official who was also a deacon, Patrick was captured by Irish pirates while in his mid-teens, sold, and kept as a slave herding livestock for six years. He somehow made his way home after an arduous journey that included near starvation. A much-changed person, he received some rudimentary training for the priesthood, including the study of the Latin Bible.

His appointment as the successor to the first bishop of Ireland, Palladius, encountered some opposition, probably because of his lack of education, but he made his way to Ireland ca. 435, working principally in the north and establishing his see at Armagh—a choice probably determined by the presence of a powerful king nearby who could offer protection. Armagh, where he also founded a school, became the base of his various missionary journeys. His success in making converts, ordaining clergy, and consecrating virgins astonished him. Indeed, his missionary spirit would mark the Irish Church for centuries to come.

These bare, historically verifiable facts are in stark contrast to the popular legends that have grown up around his name, such as his driving the snakes out of Ireland. Even the place of his death and burial is uncertain. St. Patrick's Day is celebrated by people of all ethnic backgrounds by the wearing of the green and parades. His feast, which is on the General Roman Calendar, has always been given as March 17 in liturgical calendars and martyrologies.

18 CYRIL OF JERUSALEM, BISHOP AND DOCTOR OF THE CHURCH

Cyril of Jerusalem (ca. 315–ca. 386) was the bishop of Jerusalem from ca. 350 until his death. He was named a Doctor of the Church in 1882, primarily because of his brilliant catechesis, preserved in a series of twenty-three homilies addressed to baptismal candidates and the newly baptized. Born in or near Jerusalem and well educated there, especially in Scripture, he was ordained a priest in 345 and given the task of instructing catechumens. He became bishop ca. 350 and was soon embroiled in controversy with Acacius, the metropolitan of Caesarea, over the relative importance of their two sees (Acacius regarded Jerusalem as one of his suffragan sees) and over doctrinal matters as well. Charged with insubordination, having sold church goods for the sake of the poor, and with supporting the teaching of the Council of Nicaea (325), Cyril was exiled in 357. Later recalled and then banished and recalled twice more as emperors and pro- and anti-Arian sentiments changed, Cyril would eventually spend sixteen of his thirty-five years as a bishop in exile. His feast is on the General Roman Calendar.

19 JOSEPH, HUSBAND OF MARY

Joseph (first century) was the husband of the Blessed Virgin Mary, the mother of Jesus. In the New Testament Joseph is mentioned as the father of Jesus in John (1:45; 6:42), in Luke (4:22), and in Luke's genealogy of Jesus (3:23). He appears also in the infancy narratives, where he is said to be of Davidic descent. According to Luke, Joseph was born in Bethlehem, but lived with Mary in Nazareth, returning to Bethlehem at one point to register for a census. Matthew, however, indicates that they lived in Bethlehem and moved to Nazareth after their flight to Egypt. Joseph was a carpenter by trade and trained his son as a carpenter as well.

Joseph disappears from the New Testament after the family's pilgrimage to Jerusalem (Luke 2:42–52), which suggests that Joseph died sometime before Jesus' public ministry. The special veneration of Joseph seems to have originated in the East, where the apocryphal *History of Joseph the Carpenter*, a fifth- or sixth-century Greek document, enjoyed widespread popularity. The Copts observed a feast in his honor in the seventh century. The earliest evidence for the cult in the West is in ninth-century Irish martyrologies. He is patron of various causes and countries and of the universal Church. His feast has the rank of a Solemnity on the General Roman Calendar, and it is also celebrated by the Church of England, the Episcopal Church in the United States, and the Evangelical Lutheran Church in America.

20 CUTHBERT, BISHOP

Cuthbert (ca. 634–87) is the most popular saint in northern England. Born of a comfortable Anglo-Saxon family, he became a monk at Melrose in 651 and prior about ten years later. After the Synod of Whitby (664), at which Roman liturgical practices were adopted for the whole of England, Cuthbert became prior at Lindisfarne, but he later relinquished the office to live a solitary life for some nine years. By 685, he was chosen by the king and the archbishop of Canterbury as bishop of Hexham. Almost immediately he and the bishop of Lindisfarne exchanged sees. He was known for his preaching and teaching, his devotion to visiting parishes throughout his diocese, his ministry to the poor, the sick, and the bereaved, his purported gifts of prophecy and healing, and his own ascetical lifestyle. He died after only two years of episcopal ministry on March 20, 687. More than 135 churches in England and some 17 in Scotland are dedicated to Cuthbert. Although his feast is not on the General Roman Calendar, it is celebrated on this day by the Church of England and the Episcopal Church in the United States.

21 NICHOLAS OF FLÜE, HERMIT

Nicholas of Flüe (1417–87), a hermit, is the patron saint of Switzerland. Born into a family of Swiss farmers at Flueli near Unterwalden, he belonged from an early age to a group of laity known as the Friends of God, who lived ascetical lives of prayer and service to one's neighbor. He married and eventually had ten children. In 1467, with his wife's consent, he resigned his civil offices as a magistrate and judge and left his wife and children with the intention of taking up the life of a hermit. It is said that he subsisted on the Eucharist alone thereafter, spending the next twenty years in a small cottage with an attached chapel at Ranft, not far from his home. His reputation as a holy man (known as Brother Klaus) attracted visitors seeking his advice on spiritual and even worldly matters. He died on March 21, 1487, and was immediately hailed as a patriot and a saint. Nicholas is not on the General Roman Calendar.

22   NICHOLAS OWEN, MARTYR

Nicholas Owen (ca. 1550–1606) was a Jesuit lay brother and martyr in Protestant England. Born in Oxfordshire of Catholic (recusant) parents, he was trained as a carpenter, a trade that enabled him to construct hiding places for priests—single-handedly and at night—over a period of twenty-six years. Several of them still exist. He was imprisoned three times, the last time giving himself up in order to deter the authorities from pursuing some priests who had escaped. Nicholas was taken to the Tower and tortured on the rack. When he continued to refuse to divulge information regarding the whereabouts of priests, he was racked one last time, on March 22, 1606, during which his inner organs burst out of his body. He died in agony. He was beatified in 1929 and then canonized by Pope Paul VI in 1970 as one of the Forty Martyrs of England and Wales. Nicholas's individual feast is not on the General Roman Calendar.

23 TURIBIUS OF MONGROVEJO, BISHOP

Turibius of Mongrovejo (1538–1606) was archbishop of Lima and is the patron saint of Peru. Born in Mayorga, Spain, he was chosen archbishop of Lima while serving as a lay professor of civil and canon law at Salamanca University. Arriving in Lima in 1581, he found dangerous conditions, widespread abuses by clergy and conquerors, and an uneducated population in his new diocese, which consisted of thousands of square miles. Turibius built churches, hospitals, and religious houses, approved a new catechism in Spanish and two Indian languages, held councils and synods according to the Council of Trent (1545–63), and in 1591 established the first seminary in the New World. He championed natives' rights and was indefatigable in service to the poor. He is reported to have personally baptized a half million people, including Rose of Lima [August 23] and Martin de Porres [November 3]. He died on March 23, 1606. His cult has been popular in Latin America for more than three centuries, and his feast is now on the General Roman Calendar.

24 CATHERINE OF SWEDEN, ABBESS; OSCAR ROMERO, BISHOP AND MARTYR

Catherine of Sweden (ca. 1331–81) was the daughter of Bridget of Sweden [July 23] and abbess of Vadstena, a monastery founded by her mother. Catherine sought always to emulate her saintly mother; she followed her to Rome in 1350, where Bridget urged the return of the papacy from Avignon to Rome and approval for her monastery. But the years in Rome were very difficult; the city was unsafe and, because Catherine and her mother gave away so much to the poor, their living conditions were stark. Bridget died in Rome.

Upon her return to Sweden, Catherine asked to be received as a novice in Vadstena, but she was immediately acclaimed as abbess. She set about to reorganize the community, but was asked to leave for Rome to promote her mother's cause for canonization. Nothing was resolved after five years, and Catherine returned home to Vadstena, where she died on March 24, 1381. While in Rome, however, she did receive papal approval for the Brigittine order. Catherine's mother, Bridget, was canonized in 1391. The name of Catherine was also added to the *Roman Martyrology*, but she was never formally canonized. Her feast is not on the General Roman Calendar.

Oscar Romero (1917–80), archbishop of San Salvador, was martyred for his defense of the poor and the powerless. He had been denounced by some of his fellow bishops, hated by the military and many in the wealthiest classes, and even distrusted by the Vatican. His weekly sermons, broadcast throughout El Salvador by radio, contained a list of violations of human rights. A few weeks before his assassination he sent a letter to United States president Jimmy Carter appealing for an end to military assistance to the ruling junta.

On March 24, as Archbishop Romero was celebrating Mass in the chapel of the Carmelite Sisters' hospital for cancer patients, where he lived, a single rifle shot was fired from the rear of the chapel. The archbishop was struck in the heart and died almost instantly. Although not yet beatified by his own Church, Oscar Romero is commemorated on this day by the Church of England.

25 THE ANNUNCIATION OF THE LORD

When the feast of the Nativity, or Christmas, was assigned to December 25 before the middle of the fourth century, it was almost inevitable that a feast of the conception of Jesus would be placed nine months beforehand. The basic account of the *Annunciation* appears in Luke 1:26–38. The angel Gabriel appeared in Nazareth to a virgin betrothed to Joseph [March 19], of the house of David. Gabriel proclaimed what has become the first portion of the Hail Mary prayer: "Hail, favored one! The Lord is with you!" (Luke 1:28). Gabriel then predicted the birth of Jesus and his eternal rule over the "house of Jacob." A confused and troubled Mary asked the angel how this was to happen, and Gabriel told her not to be afraid and promised that the Holy Spirit would cause her to conceive (Luke 1:35).

The interchange between Mary and Gabriel provides the opening for the Angelus prayer: "The angel of the Lord declared unto Mary, and she conceived of the Holy Spirit." Mary's response to Gabriel was one of humble submission to God's will: "Behold, I am the handmaid of the Lord. May it be done to me according to your word." It is one of the few direct quotations from Mary in the New Testament and epitomizes her role as a servant of God and a disciple par excellence.

The feast of the Annunciation has the highest liturgical rank, that of a Solemnity, on the General Roman Calendar. It is also celebrated in all of the major Christian liturgical traditions.

26 LUDGER OF MÜNSTER, BISHOP

Ludger (Liuger) *of Münster* (ca. 742–809) was bishop of Münster and is its patron saint; he was the founder of a Benedictine monastery on his family estate at Werden. Born of noble and wealthy parents in Frisia, he was educated at Utrecht and York and ordained a priest ca. 777, after which he built several churches. The churches were destroyed during the Saxon invasions in 784. Two years later Ludger rebuilt the churches, was consecrated bishop of Münster in 804, and built there a monastery for canons under the Rule of Chrodegang of Metz [March 6]. He evangelized Westphalia and Eastphalia and is said to have done more to convert the Saxons by his gentleness than the emperor Charlemagne could accomplish through repressive measures. He died on March 26, 809, at his monastery in Werden. His feast is recorded in liturgical books as early as the ninth century, but is not included on the General Roman Calendar.

27 RUPERT, BISHOP

Rupert (d. ca. 710–20) was the bishop of Worms and of Salzburg. He was Frankish and possibly Irish by birth. Having been expelled for whatever reason from his bishopric at Worms, he was invited by the duke of the

Bavarians to evangelize his territories, which also comprised parts of present-day Austria. Rupert was a successful missionary bishop in the villages along the Danube River as far as Hungary. Upon his return he was given jurisdiction over Juvavum (Salzburg), a Roman town then in ruins. Rupert built a church and a monastery (with himself as its abbot), both dedicated to St. Peter [June 29], a school, and other necessary buildings. He continued his missionary journeys, returning eventually to Salzburg, where he died sometime between 710 and 720. His feast is not on the General Roman Calendar.

28 HESYCHIUS OF JERUSALEM, PRIEST

Hesychius of Jerusalem (d. ca. 450) was a monk in his early life, ordained a priest of Jerusalem in 412, and the author of a now lost history of the Church. He was known for his modesty and gentleness. Indeed, his extant writings display none of the polemical tone one finds in other contemporary works, including those of Jerome [September 30]. In his writings, he avoided minutiae and personal digressions and focused instead on the Risen Christ. In the Eucharist, he insisted, "our bodies become the body of Christ." He is commemorated on this day by the Russian Orthodox Church, but his feast is not on the General Roman Calendar.

29 JONAS AND BARACHISIUS, MARTYRS

Jonas and *Barachisius* (d. ca. 326/27) were two Christian monks who were cruelly martyred by the Persian king

Sapor II at the very time when the Roman Empire under Constantine had ended its own persecution of Christians. Sapor executed great numbers of Christians when they would not sacrifice to the gods. Jonas and Barachisius went to Bardiaboc, where some Christians were being held. They found nine awaiting execution and encouraged them to persevere. After the nine were martyred, Jonas and Barachisius were reported to the same judges who had condemned the nine. They refused to offer sacrifice. After a night of severe torment, they were martyred. The feast of Jonas and Barachisius is not on the General Roman Calendar.

30 JOHN CLIMACUS, ABBOT

John Climacus (ca. 570–ca. 649) was a monk and abbot of Mt. Sinai. Born in Palestine, he was married early in life and became a monk upon the death of his wife. After a period of time in community, he took up the solitary life, during which time he wrote *The Ladder to Paradise,* the work that gave him his name, Climacus (Lat., "ladder"). A volume on monastic spirituality, it touched upon the virtues and vices of monastic life, both communal and eremitical, but did not deprecate the body for the sake of the soul. At about age seventy John Climacus was chosen as abbot of Mt. Sinai, but after four years he returned to his hermitage. He died at about age eighty. His feast is not on the General Roman Calendar, but it is celebrated in the East on the fourth Sunday of Lent as well as on this day by the Greek and Russian Orthodox Churches.

31 STEPHEN OF MAR SABA, MONK; JOHN DONNE, PRIEST; ANNE FRANK, MARTYR

Stephen of Mar Saba (d. 794) was the nephew of John Damascene [December 4], who mentored Stephen at Mar Saba in Palestine until his own death in 749, when Stephen was twenty-four. Stephen felt a strong call to the eremitical life and went through periods of almost total solitude and then more modified ones. Throughout, he showed great compassion not only for other persons, but also for animals, even worms, and displayed an extraordinary gift for assisting those in great difficulty. Stephen died on March 30, 794. His feast is not on the General Roman Calendar, but he is commemorated on this day by the Russian Orthodox Church.

The Church of England, the Episcopal Church in the United States, and the Evangelical Lutheran Church in America commemorate the English poet *John Donne* (1572–1631) on this day. Born and raised a Catholic, he became a priest of the Church of England and one of its most accomplished preachers.

Sometime toward the end of March 1945, a few weeks before Bergen-Belsen was liberated on April 15, *Anne Frank* (1929–45), a young German Jewish girl, died of typhus there. She was one of humanity's most famous martyrs, having provided a unique witness to the Holocaust in her diary, written while in hiding before her capture.

APRIL

1 HUGH OF GRENOBLE, BISHOP

Hugh of Grenoble (1052–1132) was the bishop of Grenoble for fifty-two years and the virtual cofounder of the Carthusians. A canon in the Valence cathedral, he became secretary to the bishop of Die and accompanied him to the synod of Avignon, which reviewed the severe pastoral problems in the vacant diocese of Grenoble. Hugh so impressed the synod that he was elected the new bishop of Grenoble and consecrated in Rome by the pope himself, Gregory VII [May 25]. Hugh dealt with the abuses in the diocese, restored the cathedral, made civic improvements in the town, founded houses of canons regular, and gave a charter to Bruno [October 6] for the Grand Chartreuse, the community that eventually developed into the Carthusian order. He was renowned for his preaching, his skill as a confessor, and his generosity to the poor. After several attempts to resign from his see for a life of solitude and prayer, he died on April 1, 1132, and was canonized only two years later. His feast is not on the General Roman Calendar.

2 FRANCIS OF PAOLA, HERMIT

Francis of Paola (1416–1507) was the founder of the Franciscan Minim Friars and is patron saint of Italian seafarers, naval officers, and navigators (because many of his reported miracles were connected with the sea). Born at Paolo in Calabria, in southern Italy, he lived for a year (at age thirteen) as a Franciscan friar, then took up the life of a hermit in a cave overlooking the sea. At age twenty he was joined by two companions. They called themselves the hermits of Brother Francis of Assisi [October 4]. After the neighbors built for them a chapel and three cells, others joined them. Following Franciscan ideals, they led lives marked by charity toward others, poverty, and penance, including a perpetual Lenten fast. In 1492 Francis changed the community's name to Friars Minim to indicate that its members were "the least" of all religious. Francis died at Tours on April 2, 1507, and was canonized in 1519. His feast is on the General Roman Calendar.

3 RICHARD OF CHICHESTER, BISHOP

Richard of Chichester (1197–1253) was the bishop of Chichester in England. Born at Wych (present-day Droitwich), he was educated at Oxford and Paris, and possibly also Bologna. Upon his return to England, he became chancellor of Oxford, then chancellor of the archdiocese of Canterbury, a position in which he earned a reputation for complete moral integrity. After the death of his friend, the archbishop, in 1240, Richard decided to become a priest and studied theology for two years with the Dominicans in Orleans. Ordained in 1242 (or 1243), he served as a parish priest in two places before being reappointed chancellor by the new archbishop of Canterbury. Two years later he was elected bishop of Chichester. Richard was kindly, accessible, compassionate toward sinners, generous to those stricken by famine, and personally above moral reproach. He also enforced ecclesiastical laws regarding the administration of the sacraments, celibacy, clerical residence, and clerical dress. He died at Dover on April 3, 1253, and was canonized in 1262. Richard of Chichester's feast is not on the General Roman Calendar. He is commemorated on this day by the Episcopal Church in the United States.

4   ISIDORE OF SEVILLE, BISHOP AND DOCTOR OF THE CHURCH

A prolific writer, *Isidore of Seville* (ca. 560–636) is often considered the last of the Fathers of the Church. Born in Seville of a noble family, he served as archbishop of Seville for thirty-six years. He converted many Visigoths from Arianism and organized the Church of Spain through synods and councils, especially the Second Council of Seville (619) and the Fourth Council of Toledo (633). The latter council approved a creed based on Isidore's theology, fixed a uniform liturgy, the Mozarabic Rite, to be observed throughout Spain, and mandated a cathedral school in every diocese. Isidore also devoted himself to education, the completion of the Mozarabic missal and breviary, and an extensive ministry to the poor. He died on April 4, 636. Isidore of Seville was canonized in 1598 and declared a Doctor of the Church in 1722. His feast is on the General Roman Calendar.

5 VINCENT FERRER, PRIEST

Vincent Ferrer (1350–1419) was a renowned Dominican friar and preacher. Born at Valencia, Spain, he became a Dominican in 1367 and quickly distinguished himself as a philosopher and preacher. Ordained ca. 1374 (or perhaps 1379) by Cardinal Peter de Luna, later the antipope Benedict XIII, he taught at Barcelona, studied theology in Toledo, and in 1379 became prior of the Dominican house in Valencia.

His life and ministry overlapped with the Great Western Schism (1378–1417), during most of which Vincent supported the claims of the Avignon popes over those in Rome. When his friend Cardinal Peter de Luna became the antipope Benedict XIII in 1394, he appointed Vincent his adviser and confessor as well as Master of the Sacred Palace, the pope's personal theologian. Over time, Vincent began to see his friend as an obstacle to church unity. He tried unsuccessfully to persuade him to negotiate with Urban VI in Rome. Worn out by his travels and preaching throughout Europe as well as his diplomatic efforts on behalf of church unity, he died at Vannes in Brittany on April 5, 1419. He was canonized in 1455. His feast is on the General Roman Calendar.

6   PETER OF VERONA, MARTYR

Peter of Verona (1205–52) was the first Dominican martyr.
He is also known simply as Peter Martyr. Born in Verona
of Cathar parents (Catharism denied the goodness and
resurrection of the body and the usefulness of the sacraments), he nonetheless became a Dominican at age fifteen
while a student at the University of Bologna, receiving
the habit from Dominic himself [August 8]. He became
prior of various Dominican houses and was famous as a
preacher in Lombardy. He was appointed an inquisitor
for Milan and later for most of northern Italy, directing
his attention mainly toward Cathars. His work aroused
much animosity, and he was assassinated on his way from
Como to Milan on April 6, 1252. Peter was canonized in
1253. His feast is not on the General Roman Calendar.

7   JOHN BAPTIST DE LA SALLE, PRIEST

John Baptist de La Salle (1651–1719) was the founder of
the Brothers of the Christian Schools. Born at Reims in
northern France of a noble and wealthy family, he studied for the priesthood at Saint-Sulpice and was ordained
in 1678. He later received a doctorate in theology in 1681.
He would have settled into a life of relative ease as a
cathedral canon, had he not been approached for help in
opening a free school for the poor in Reims. John Baptist
helped to open not one but two, and pupils flocked to
them. The quality of teachers, however, was low. He was
urged to open his own house for the training of teachers.

By 1684 he had resigned his canonry, donated all of his worldly goods, and dedicated the remainder of his life to education. In May, he and twelve others formed themselves into a community, taking vows and adopting the name Brothers of the Christian Schools. He opened four more schools and several training colleges for teachers. Among his novel approaches were classroom teaching (as opposed to one-on-one instruction), the use of the vernacular rather than Latin, insistence on students' silence during instruction, and a combination of religious education and technical training for future artisans. He died on Good Friday, April 7, 1719. He was canonized in 1900 and declared patron saint of schoolteachers in 1950. His feast is on the General Roman Calendar.

8   JULIE BILLIART, FOUNDRESS

Julie Billiart (1751–1816) was the foundress of the Sisters of Notre Dame de Namur. She was born at Cuvilly in Picardy, France, of a relatively prosperous family, but she had to take up manual labor after her family lost its money. At the same time, she became engaged in various parish ministries as a catechist and a visitor of the sick. After an attempt was made on her father's life when she was in her early twenties, Julie became so frightened that she developed a nervous paralysis that eventually prevented her from walking. She had to be smuggled out of Cuvilly during the French Revolution because of accusations that she was harboring priests and supporting the Church. When the worst of the Reign of Terror was over, she was moved to Amiens, where she met an aristocratic woman, Françoise Blin de Bourdon, who eventually became the cofoundress of Julie's new institute.

With the renewal of the persecution, both women moved to Bettencourt, where Father Joseph Varin assisted them in laying the foundations of the Institute of Notre Dame in 1803, with a dedication to Christian education, the instruction of the poor, and the training of teachers. Father Varin provided them with a provisional Rule, and the first sisters made their vows as religious in 1804. Julie also recovered from her paralysis that same year. By the end of the nineteenth century the community had spread to the United States, Great Britain, and parts of Latin America and Africa, and in the twentieth to other parts of Latin America and Africa, Japan, and China. Julie Billiart died on April 8, 1816, and was canonized in 1969. Her feast is not on the General Roman Calendar.

9   WALDETRUDE, ANCHORESS; DIETRICH BONHOEFFER, MARTYR

Waldetrude (d. ca. 688), also known in France as Waltrude or Waudru, was a married woman whose husband, Vincent Madelgarius, and four children have all been venerated as saints. After the birth of their fourth child, Waldetrude's husband withdrew to an abbey he had founded at Haumont and took the name Vincent. Two years later Waldetrude took a similar path, moving into a small house in semisolitude. Her reputation for sanctity began to attract visitors seeking spiritual direction. Consequently, she founded her own convent at Chateaulieu in the center of what is today the Belgian town of Mons, of which she is patron saint. Her feast is not on the General Roman Calendar.

On this day the Evangelical Lutheran Church in America, the Church of England, and the Episcopal Church in the United States commemorate the Lutheran pastor, theologian, and martyr *Dietrich Bonhoeffer* (1906–45), whose writings warned Christians against a soft understanding of Christian discipleship and who gave personal witness to Christ in the face of the enormous evil of Nazism. He was hanged on April 9 for his alleged involvement in a plot to assassinate Adolf Hitler.

10 MAGDALEN OF CANOSSA, FOUNDRESS

Magdalen of Canossa (1774–1835) was the foundress of the congregation of the Daughters of Charity, also known as the Canossian Sisters of Charity. Born Maddalena Gabriella di Canossa into a wealthy family, she declared her intention to become a nun after surviving a serious illness at age fifteen. She joined the Carmelites for a short time, but did not take to the strict rules of enclosure; she wished to be able to assist the sick, the poor, and abandoned girls. By 1802 she had set up a refuge and school in her home. In 1808 she received permission to take over the buildings of a suppressed Augustinian monastery and use them for a school. The school flourished. She opened a second house in Venice and in 1812 drew up a definitive version of the Rule of her new congregation. Additional houses were opened in various Italian cities. She died in Verona on April 10, 1835, and was canonized in

1988. Magdalen of Canossa's feast in not on the General Roman Calendar.

11 STANISLAUS, BISHOP AND MARTYR

Stanislaus (ca. 1030–79), or Stanislaw, is the patron saint of Poland and the city of Kraków. Born in Szczepanow, Poland, he was ordained a priest and became a canon at the Kraków cathedral. He was appointed bishop of Kraków in 1072 and went on to establish a record as a great preacher, a reformer of his clergy, and a generous benefactor of the poor. At first he was supposedly on good terms with King Boleslaus II, but some conflict developed. When Stanislaus excommunicated the king, Boleslaus ordered the bishop killed; when guards refused to do so, the king killed Stanislaus himself, on April 11, 1709. Because of Stanislaus's murder, Pope Gregory VII [May 25] placed the whole country under interdict until the king fell from power. Stanislaus's feast is on the General Roman Calendar.

12 TERESA OF LOS ANDES, VIRGIN

Teresa of Los Andes (1900–20) was a Carmelite nun who fashioned her spiritual life after those of St. Thérèse of Lisieux [October 1] and St. Teresa of Ávila [October 15]. Born in Santiago, Chile, of pious and well-to-do parents, she made a private vow of virginity at age fifteen, joined the Children of Mary, and taught catechism. At nineteen she entered the Carmelite convent in the town of Los Andes, a run-down house without electricity and adequate sanitary facilities, but whose nuns impressed her as happy in their devotion to a strict observance of the Rule and a simple lifestyle. She took the name Teresa of Jesus and offered her new life of prayer and sacrifice for the sanctification of priests and the repentance of sinners. She contracted typhus and died a few days later, on April 12, 1920, having made her final vows on her deathbed. She was canonized in 1993. Her feast is not on the General Roman Calendar.

13   MARTIN I, POPE AND MARTYR

Martin I (d. 655, pope 649–54) was the last pope to be recognized as a martyr. Born at Todi in Umbria, he became a deacon in Rome, where his reputation for intelligence and charity won him appointment as nuncio to Constantinople, the center of the Byzantine Empire. He was elected pope in 649 and was the first pope in decades to be consecrated as Bishop of Rome without waiting for imperial approval, an act that infuriated the emperor, Constans II, who refused to recognize him as pope. Three months after his election, Martin held a synod at the Lateran Basilica, attended by 105 Western bishops and a number of exiled Greek clergy, which affirmed the doctrine of the two wills in Christ (human and divine) and condemned both Monothelitism (the heresy that held to only one divine will) and the imperial decree that forbade further discussion of it.

In the summer of 653, the emperor put the pope on trial for treason. He was found guilty, condemned to death, and publicly flogged. However, the dying patriarch of Constantinople pleaded for the pope's life and the sentence was commuted to exile. Martin was taken by ship to Chersonesus in the Crimea, where he died on September 16, 655, from the effects of starvation and harsh treatment. Martin's feast is on the General Roman Calendar. It is also celebrated by the Russian Orthodox Church, but on April 14.

14 BLESSED PETER GONZÁLEZ, FRIAR

Peter (Pedro) González (d. 1246) was a Dominican friar who excelled at preaching, especially to Spanish and Portuguese seamen. He is still invoked as patron saint of seamen, but under the name St. Elmo, because he is confused with St. Erasmus, an Italian bishop martyred during the Diocletian persecution who is also patron saint of sailors. Born in Castile of a noble family, Peter was educated by his uncle, the bishop of Astorga, and later decided to enter the Dominicans. He became a popular preacher and served as royal chaplain to the court of Ferdinand III, king of Castile and Léon. Peter tried to elevate the morals of the courtiers and also to mitigate the severity of the king's treatment of the defeated Moors. He died on April 14, 1246; his cult was approved in 1741. He has not been canonized, nor is his feast on the General Roman Calendar.

15 BLESSED DAMIEN DE VEUSTER, PRIEST

Damien de Veuster (1840–89) is better known as Damien of Molokai, "apostle to lepers." Born Joseph de Veuster near Malines, Belgium, he joined the Fathers of the Sacred Hearts of Jesus and Mary, also known as the Picpus Fathers, in 1859, taking the religious name Damien. He sailed to the Hawaiian Islands and was ordained a priest in Honolulu in 1864. In 1873 he responded to the local bishop's call for volunteers to work on Molokai, an island used in part as a leper colony.

There were about eight hundred lepers on the island when Damien arrived, and the number continued to grow. Living conditions were so terrible that Damien referred to the place as a "living cemetery" and a "human jungle." But he was not deterred from his mission. He visited the lepers in their huts and brought them the sacraments as often as possible. He also expanded the hospital and founded two orphanages. His multiple responsibilities were said to have included those of a pastor, physician, counselor, builder, sheriff, and undertaker. Damien contracted leprosy, died on April 15, 1889, and was beatified in 1995. His feast is not on the General Roman Calendar.

16 BERNADETTE SOUBIROUS, NUN

Bernadette Soubirous (1844–79) was the young French girl to whom the Blessed Virgin Mary is believed to have appeared in Lourdes, France, and is the first saint to have been photographed. Born Marie Bernarde Soubirous to a poverty-stricken family, at age fourteen she experienced a series of eighteen visions in six months (February 11–July 16, 1858) at the rock of Massabielle, Lourdes. The Virgin called herself the Immaculate Conception [December 8], a dogma that had just been solemnly defined four years earlier by Pope Pius IX. Her message was simple: do penance for the conversion of sinners and urge people to come to pray at the place of the apparitions. The Blessed Mother also ordered that the church be built over the site and that Bernadette should drink from and bathe in a hidden spring, which, since then, has produced some 27,000 gallons of water per week. Many cures were later attributed to the water.

In 1866 Bernadette joined the Sisters of Notre Dame of Nevers, where she spent the rest of her life as Sister Maria Bernarda. She died on April 16, 1879, at age thirty-five, and was canonized in 1933. Her feast is not on the General Roman Calendar.

17 BLESSED CLARE OF PISA, NUN

Clare of Pisa (1362–1419) was a Dominican nun who has been compared to Bernardino of Siena [May 20] and Teresa of Ávila [October 15] as one of the great reformers of religious life. Born Theodora, or Thora, in either Venice or Florence, of the highly respected Gambacorti family, she was betrothed at an early age. Her husband died during an epidemic when she was only fifteen, and Theodora gave away all of her most expensive clothes to the poor and joined the Poor Clares, taking the name Clare. Her relatives, however, forced her to leave the convent, but her father eventually gave in and allowed her to enter a Dominican convent. It was a lax house, and most of the nuns refused to cooperate with Clare's efforts to reform it. Her father built a new convent for her, and several of the nuns who supported her efforts joined her there. She became prioress of the convent, which became a training center and model of religious life according to a strict observance of the Rule. The nuns led an enclosed life of prayer, manual work, and study. Clare died in 1419. Her feast is not on the General Roman Calendar.

18 BLESSED MARY OF THE INCARNATION, NUN

Mary of the Incarnation (Barbe Acarie, 1566–1618) was responsible for the introduction of the Discalced Carmelite nuns into France, for which she has been known as the "mother and foundress of Carmel in France." Born Barbe Avrillot, the daughter of a high government official in Paris, she married Pierre Acarie, an aristocrat, at age seventeen. They had six children, three of whom became Carmelite nuns and one a priest. Barbe became known throughout Paris for her charitable work. She persuaded the king to allow Carmelite nuns to open a convent in Paris. Several other convents were opened subsequently. When Barbe's husband died in 1613, Barbe entered the Carmelite convent in Amiens as a lay sister, taking the name Mary of the Incarnation. She died on April 18, 1618. Miracles were reported at her tomb, and she was beatified in 1791. Her feast is not on the General Roman Calendar.

19 LEO IX, POPE

Leo IX (1002–54, pope 1049–54) was a leading reformist pope who laid the foundation for the Gregorian reform of the latter half of the eleventh century. Born in Alsace and baptized as Bruno, the son of Count Hugh of Egisheim, he was educated at Toul and became canon of the cathedral there. He was a member for a time of the German emperor's court and was appointed bishop of Toul in 1027, where he served for twenty years as an energetic reformer of clerical and monastic life. When Pope Damasus II died after less than a month in office in August 1049, Bruno accepted the emperor's nomination to the papacy.

Two months later he convened a synod in Rome that denounced simony and violations of clerical celibacy. Several simoniacal bishops were deposed. Leo traveled so extensively throughout Europe to promote the reforms that he was called the "Apostolic Pilgrim." He also held a dozen synods in Italy and Germany and insisted that bishops must be elected by the local clergy and laity, and abbots by their monks.

Unfortunately, Leo's final years in office were marred by his own personal involvement in the military campaign against the Norman invaders in southern Italy (he was held captive for several months) and by the beginning of the schism between East and West. His last days were marked by illness and deep regret. He was acclaimed a saint and in 1087 his relics were enshrined. His feast is not on the General Roman Calendar.

20 AGNES OF MONTEPULCIANO, NUN

Agnes of Montepulciano (ca. 1270–1317) was a Dominican nun known for her simplicity of life and piety. Born of well-to-do parents in a small Tuscan village a few miles from Montepulciano, she entered a local convent of the Sisters of the Sack (so called because of their rough clothes) and adopted an austere lifestyle. When the convent moved to another location near Viterbo, Agnes moved with it. As her reputation for sanctity spread, the people of Montepulciano demanded her return. She did so and opened a new convent under the care of the Dominicans. She became prioress in 1306. She died after a long and painful illness on April 20, 1317, and her tomb, with her incorrupt body, became a popular place of pilgrimage. Agnes of Montepulciano was canonized in 1726. Her feast is not on the General Roman Calendar, but it is celebrated by the Dominicans on this day.

21 ANSELM OF CANTERBURY, BISHOP AND DOCTOR OF THE CHURCH

Anselm (1033–1109), a major theologian and archbishop of Canterbury, gave the Church the most enduring definition of theology, "faith seeking understanding." Born at Aosta in Lombardy, Anselm became a monk at the monastery of Bec ca. 1060, because of the reputation of its abbot, Lanfranc. There he studied Augustine and wrote his famous argument for the existence of God. In 1078 he was elected abbot, keeping all the while in close contact with his mentor Lanfranc, who had become archbishop of Canterbury. Upon Lanfranc's death in 1089, Anselm was the clear choice of the clergy to succeed to the office. But King William II resisted and kept the see open for four years. The king finally relented, but the two men disagreed over papal jurisdiction, lay investiture, and the primacy of the spiritual over the temporal.

When Anselm steadfastly refused to support the anti-pope against Urban II, William exiled him in 1097. In exile he wrote his famous work on the Incarnation, *Cur Deus Homo?* Anselm returned to England in 1100 with the accession of Henry I, but he was exiled again in 1103 over the very same investiture issue. A compromise was reached in 1106, and Anselm was allowed to return to England yet again, where he died on April 21, 1109. There is no formal record of his canonization, but a late twelfth-century Canterbury calendar lists two feast days, one for his death and one for the transfer of his remains. In 1734 he was named a Doctor of the Church. His feast is on the General Roman Calendar.

22 THEODORE OF SYKEON, BISHOP

Theodore of Sykeon (d. 613) was a hermit, miracle worker, and bishop in Asia Minor. Born in the Galatian town of Sykeon, he became a hermit at Arkea, about eight miles from his home, living in a cave underneath a chapel. His reputation as an exorciser of evil spirits rapidly spread, and many came to him for advice and help. He was ordained a priest and went on pilgrimage to Jerusalem. Later, he lived in a cage suspended from the rock over his cave. He eventually established a monastery, a guest house, and a church to accommodate all those who came to him. Then he was chosen, against his will but with the support of the local clergy and landowners, to become bishop of Anastasiopolis, where he served for ten years before his resignation was finally accepted so that he could return to his life of contemplation. Theodore died in 613. His feast is not on the General Roman Calendar.

23 GEORGE, MARTYR; CESAR CHAVEZ, UNION LEADER

George (d. ca. 303) is the patron saint of England and is best known as the legendary slayer of the dragon and savior of the maiden. It is likely but not certain that he was a soldier. The story about the dragon gained immense popularity through the translation and printing of the thirteenth-century *Golden Legend,* a collection of saints' lives and short treatises on Christian feasts. By the late Middle Ages, George had become such a personification of the ideals of Christian chivalry that he was taken as the patron saint of Venice, Genoa, Portugal, and Catalonia as well. His feast is still on the General Roman Calendar and is also celebrated by the Church of England and by the Greek and Russian Orthodox Churches.

Cesar Chavez (1927–93) was the organizer and leader of the United Farm Workers. His nonviolent marches and boycotts always had a religious cast to them, and he was frequently supported by Catholic bishops, priests, and sisters as well as clergy of other religious traditions.

24 FIDELIS OF SIGMARINGEN, PRIEST AND MARTYR

Fidelis of Sigmaringen (1578–1622) was a Capuchin Franciscan friar who was martyred while preaching to the

Zwinglians in Switzerland (Ulrich Zwingli [d. 1531] was a Protestant Reformer who denied that sacraments confer grace and that Christ is truly present in the Eucharist). Fidelis is also one of the patron saints of lawyers. Born Mark Roy at Sigmaringen (Hohenzollern), he was educated at the university of Freiburg-im-Breisgau, where he received doctorates in philosophy and civil and canon law. He was ordained a priest sometime after 1610 and entered the Capuchin branch of the Franciscan order in 1612, taking the name Fidelis (Lat., "faithful"). He served as superior of three different houses and fashioned a reputation as a preacher, confessor, minister to the sick, and ascetic. Fidelis was killed on April 24, 1622, during a mission to Zwinglians in Seewis, Switzerland, in an attempt to reconcile them to the Catholic Church. He was canonized in 1746. His feast is on the General Roman Calendar.

25   MARK, EVANGELIST

Mark (d. ca. 74), who is also identified with the John Mark of the New Testament, was, according to Christian tradition, the author of the Second Gospel. According to the Acts, his mother, Mary, owned a house in Jerusalem in which the earliest Christian community gathered (12:12). After visiting Jerusalem, Paul [January 25; June 29] and Barnabas [June 11] took Mark back with them to Antioch (12:25). Mark assisted them in the proclamation of the gospel in Cyprus (13:1–12), but upon their arrival by ship in Perga, he left them and returned to Jerusalem (13:13).

The first Letter of Peter [June 29], written in all likelihood from Rome, mentions Mark as the "son" of Peter, a term either of simple affection or an indication that Peter was Mark's father in the faith. Mark's presence in Rome with Peter would be consistent with the tradition that Mark took notes that recorded Peter's memories of Jesus' teachings and deeds. This tradition was written down by Papias of Hierapolis, according to the historian Eusebius, who also said that Mark was Peter's "interpreter." Eusebius indicates that Mark was the first bishop of Alexandria. He is said to have been martyred there in the eighth year of Nero's reign. Mark has been venerated as a martyr in both East and West since the fourth century. His feast is on the General Roman Calendar and is also celebrated on this day by all the major Christian liturgical traditions.

26 STEPHEN OF PERM, BISHOP

Stephen of Perm (ca. 1340–96), venerated by Catholics and Orthodox alike, is considered by the Russian Orthodox Church to be its outstanding missionary. Born in the town of Velikij Ustyug, about five hundred miles northeast of Moscow, he became a monk in the monastery of St. Gregory Nazianzen [January 2] in Rostov, where he had received his education. To prepare himself for missionary work among the Zyrani, which he began ca. 1379, he learned their language, created an alphabet, and then translated the Scriptures and liturgy into the vernacular. In 1383 he was appointed the first bishop of Perm and proceeded to establish churches and schools, including a seminary for future priests. He died on April 26, 1396. He was canonized by the Russian Orthodox Church in 1549, but the canonization was later recognized by the Catholic Church as well. His feast is not on the General Roman Calendar, but he is commemorated on this day by the Russian Orthodox Church.

27 ZITA, VIRGIN

Zita (ca. 1218–78), also known as Sitha, Citha, and other variations, is the patron saint of domestic servants. Born at Monsagrati, a few miles from Lucca in Italy, she served as a maid in the Fatinelli household from age twelve until her death. Her fellow servants and the Fatinelli family resented her devotional life, but she eventually won them over by her goodness and constancy. She was generous to the poor and kind to the sick and to prisoners. After her death on April 27, 1278, her cult became popular among those in low stations of life. She became one of the most popular minor saints in medieval England, especially among servants. Her feast is not on the General Roman Calendar.

28 PETER CHANEL, PRIEST AND MARTYR

Peter Chanel (1803–41) is regarded as the protomartyr of Oceania (of which he is patron saint) and the Marists. Born into a peasant family in a small village in eastern France, his intelligence and piety impressed his parish priest and he was encouraged to study for the priesthood himself. He was ordained a priest in 1827. After one year as a curate and three years as a pastor, he joined the recently founded Society of Mary (Marists), a congregation of missionary priests, in 1831.

Peter was sent to preach the gospel in the islands of the South Pacific. Peter and a companion landed by chance on the island of Fatuna, between Fiji and French Samoa. They earned a great measure of respect and appreciation because of their care of the sick, but when the chief's son asked for baptism, the chief was so enraged that he sent a group of warriors to kill Peter. On April 28, 1841, he was clubbed and then killed with an ax, and his body was cut up with knives. Peter was canonized in 1954. His feast was formerly celebrated only in Australia and New Zealand, but it is now on the General Roman Calendar.

29 CATHERINE OF SIENA, VIRGIN AND DOCTOR OF THE CHURCH

Catherine of Siena (1347–80), a reformer of popes, was the first layperson and one of the first two women named a Doctor of the Church (with Teresa of Ávila [October 15]). She is also one of the two primary patron saints of Italy (along with Francis of Assisi [October 4]). In 1999 Pope John Paul II named her co–patron saint of all of Europe, along with Bridget of Sweden [July 23] and Teresa Benedicta of the Cross (Edith Stein) [August 9]. Born Caterina di Giacomo di Benincasa in Siena, the twenty-fourth of twenty-five children, she decided early in life not to marry and joined the third order of Dominicans. After several years of prayer and fasting in virtual solitude, during which she is said to have become mystically espoused to Christ, she felt a call to a more apostolic life and became involved in the nursing of the sick in a local hospital.

Later, she went on frequent preaching journeys to call people to reform and repentance. She had extraordinary success, but evoked opposition from some for her presumption to preach as a laywoman. Beginning in 1376 she urged Gregory XI to return the papacy from Avignon to Rome, and later, as the Great Western Schism (1378–1417) began, she entreated rulers and leaders to recognize Urban VI as legitimate pope, all in the interest of church unity. In 1377–78 she produced her spiritual classic, *The Dialogue.* Catherine suffered a stroke and died on April 29, 1380. She was declared a Doctor of the Church in 1970. Her feast is on the General Roman Calendar.

30 PIUS V, POPE

Pius V (1504–72, pope 1566–72) enforced the decrees of the Council of Trent (1545–63), published the *Roman Catechism,* reformed the Roman Missal and the Roman Breviary, and excommunicated Queen Elizabeth I of England. Born Antonio Ghislieri of poor parents, he became a Dominican at age fourteen. After ordination to the priesthood in 1528, he taught philosophy and theology and then served as inquisitor for Como and Bergamo. So zealous was he that he came to the notice of Cardinal Gian Pietro Carafa, who later, as Pope Paul IV, made him a bishop, then cardinal, then grand inquisitor of the Roman Inquisition in 1558.

He was elected pope on January 7, 1566, with the strong support of Cardinal Charles Borromeo [November 4], who looked upon him as a reformer. His agenda as pope was to implement the decrees of the Council of Trent. He imposed strict standards of lifestyle on himself, the Curia, and the city of Rome. He followed a monastic regimen, including simple, solitary meals and the white Dominican habit. He opposed nepotism, insisted that clerics reside in their dioceses, and supervised religious orders closely.

The pope's background as a grand inquisitor, however, led him to an inordinate reliance upon the Inquisition and its often inhumane methods. He built a new palace for the Inquisition, toughened its rules and practices, and often attended its sessions. Even though many distinguished individuals were tried and sentenced during his pontificate, Pius thought himself too lenient! His excommunication of Queen Elizabeth I of England in 1570 and concomitant declaration that her subjects were absolved from allegiance to her exposed English Catholics to persecution, imprisonment, torture, and execution and also antagonized France, Spain, and the empire. Pius V died on May 1, 1572. His feast is on the General Roman Calendar.

MAY

1 JOSEPH THE WORKER

The principal feast of Joseph, husband of Mary, is celebrated on March 19 (see that entry). This second feast of *Joseph the Worker* was inaugurated by Pope Pius XII in 1955 to counteract a Communist holiday on May 1. The new feast replaced that of the Patronage of St. Joseph, later called the Solemnity of Joseph, which was celebrated since 1913 on the third Wednesday after Easter. The appropriateness of this new feast is grounded in that fact that Joseph was a carpenter by trade (Matt. 13:55) and trained his son Jesus as a carpenter as well (Mark 6:3).

2 ATHANASIUS, BISHOP AND DOCTOR OF THE CHURCH

Athanasius (ca. 295–373) was the outstanding defender of the teaching of the First Council of Nicaea (325) on the divinity of Jesus Christ against the Arians, who held that Jesus was not divine, but only the greatest of creatures. In 328, while still in his early thirties, Athanasius became the bishop of Alexandria, a see comparable in prestige to Jerusalem and Antioch. He took his new responsibilities seriously, making extensive pastoral visits throughout the region. However, he came under heavy personal attack by those opposed to the teaching of the council, who questioned even the validity of his election. Athanasius was summoned to a regional council in Tyre, composed almost entirely of his enemies, and was exiled to Trèves (Trier) in northern Gaul by order of the emperor Constantine in 335.

After the death of the rival bishop of Alexandria, the new emperor, Constantius II, allowed him to return to his see in October 346, where he remained for ten years. During this period, the Arians kept up their campaign against Athanasius. In February 356 a military detachment surrounded the church where Athanasius was holding a vigil service. With the help of monks, he managed to escape and went into hiding in the Libyan desert. He continued to govern his flock from afar and even made a few secret visits to Alexandria. During this period he produced some of his major writings, including his *Life of Antony* [January 17].

From 366 until his death in 373 he functioned once again, and without harassment, as bishop of Alexandria. He died there in 373. Athanasius was proclaimed in 1568 one of the four great Doctors of the Church in the East, alongside Basil the Great [January 2], Gregory Nazianzen, and John Chrysostom [September 13]. His feast is on the General Roman Calendar.

3   PHILIP AND JAMES (THE LESS), APOSTLES

Philip (first century) was one of the original twelve apostles and, with James, is the patron saint of Uruguay. He came from Bethsaida in Galilee (John 1:43–51) and was one of Jesus' first disciples (John 1:43–44), along with Peter [June 29] and Andrew [November 30]. At the Last Supper, Philip asked Jesus to show the Father to the Twelve, eliciting Jesus' response that the one who has seen Jesus has seen the Father (14:8–9). He is listed among those who were in the upper room awaiting the Spirit at Pentecost (Acts 1:12–14).

There are various traditions about the life and death of Philip. One says that he preached the gospel in Phrygia and died in Hierapolis. His supposed remains were taken to Rome and placed in the basilica of the Twelve Apostles. An ancient inscription there indicates that the church was originally dedicated to Philip and James. This explains why the two share the same feast day.

James the Less (first century), to be distinguished from James the Great [July 25], was also one of the original twelve apostles. He was the son of Alphaeus (Matt. 10:3; Mark 3:18; Luke 6:15), and his mother Mary was present at the Cross on Good Friday (Mark 15:40). Almost nothing else is known about him. James the Less is believed to have been clubbed to death upon sentence of the Sanhedrin ca. 62. He is a patron saint of the dying.

4 FLORIAN, MARTYR

Florian (d. 304), one of the patron saints of Poland and of Austria, was martyred in the last and most violent of the imperial persecutions, that of Diocletian, in Lorch (Lauriacum). An army officer and civil administrator at Noricum, in present-day Austria, he gave himself up as a Christian to the local governor. He was scourged and his skin was stripped off before he was thrown with a stone tied around his neck into the Emms River, which flows into the Danube. Many cures were attributed to his intercession, and he was especially invoked against dangers from fire and water; he is patron saint of firefighters. His feast is not on the General Roman Calendar.

5 GOTTHARD OF HILDESHEIM, ABBOT AND BISHOP

Gotthard (or *Godehard*) *of Hildesheim* (ca. 960–1038) was a monastic and episcopal reformer. Born at Reichersdorf in Bavaria, he was educated at the abbey of Nieder-Altaich and later participated in its reform by restoring the Rule of St. Benedict [July 11] there. He was ordained a priest and became a monk at Nieder-Altaich in 990 and was eventually elected its abbot. During his twenty years in that post, he also guided the reform of three other monasteries and provided nine abbots for several houses. His efforts so impressed Emperor Henry II [July 13] that, upon the death of the bishop of Hildesheim, Henry nominated Gotthard to succeed to the see in 1022. Gotthard built and restored churches, established schools, reformed the cathedral chapter, and built a hospice for the sick and the poor. He was canonized in 1131. His feast is not on the General Roman Calendar.

6   MARIAN AND JAMES, MARTYRS

Marian and *James* (d. 259) were North African martyrs, born in Numidia. Marian was a lector, or reader, and James, a deacon. Both were martyred in 259, during the reign of Valerian, at Cirta Julia (later Constantina), the chief city of Numidia. Marian and James confessed their faith and were tortured on the rack and imprisoned. They were executed by beheading. Augustine [August 28] referred to their martyrdom in his *Sermon 284*. Their relics are in the Gubbio cathedral. Their feast is not on the General Roman Calendar.

7   JOHN OF BEVERLEY, BISHOP

John of Beverley (d. 721) was the English saint whom King Henry V invoked on John's feast day during the battle at Agincourt (1415). Born at Harpham in Yorkshire, John became a monk at St. Hilda's double monastery at Whitby, where he was renowned for his concern for the poor and for learning. He was consecrated bishop of Hexham in 687. In his *Ecclesiastical History* Bede attested to various miracles during the bishop's ministry. In 705 John was appointed bishop of York, but little is known of his ministry there. He did found a monastery at Beverley, eventually retired to it in 717, and died there on May 7, 721. His shrine was for centuries one of the most popular pilgrimage sites in England. He was canonized in 1037. John of Beverley's feast is also not on the General Roman Calendar.

8   PETER OF TARENTAISE, BISHOP

Peter of Tarentaise (ca. 1102–74), not to be confused with Pope Innocent V (1276), who was also Peter of Tarentaise, was the archbishop of Tarentaise in Savoy with a special ministry to the sick and the poor. Peter appointed men of high quality as cathedral canons and parish clergy. He visited his largely mountainous diocese regularly, established educational, charitable, and medical institutions, recovered church property, and improved the quality of worship. He was so personally involved in the ministry to the poor and the sick that he developed a reputation for miraculous healings and multiplication of food. Distressed by the general acclaim for his spiritual feats, Peter suddenly disappeared from his diocese in 1155 and was not discovered until a year later in a Swiss Cistercian abbey, living as a lay brother. Persuaded to return to his diocese, Peter resumed his ministry on behalf of the poor. Peter died on September 14, 1174. His feast is not on the General Roman Calendar.

9° PACHOMIUS, ABBOT

Pachomius (d. 346) was the founder of cenobitic, or communal, monasticism. Born in Upper Egypt of pagan parents, he became a Christian upon his discharge from the army in 313. After living as a hermit, he founded his first monastery at Tabennisi in 320 and ruled over nine monastic communities for men and two (or three) for women by the time of his death. Pachomius's military background and organizational skills led him to divide the monks into occupational groups, for example, farmers, bakers, weavers, and potters. Complete obedience was expected of all the monks, and an ascetical lifestyle was followed. Pachomius often spent the whole night in work and prayer. His Rule, translated by Jerome [September 30], influenced those of Basil [January 2] and Benedict [July 11]. Pachomius's feast is not on the General Roman Calendar, but is celebrated in the Coptic Church on this day and in the Greek and Russian Orthodox Churches on May 15.

10 JOHN OF ÁVILA, PRIEST

John of Ávila (1500–69) was the spiritual counselor of Teresa of Ávila [October 15] and facilitated the conversions of Francis Borgia [October 3] and John of God [March 8]. Born in Spain of wealthy Jewish parents, after studies in law, philosophy, and theology he was ordained as a diocesan priest in 1525, gave away most of his inheritance to the poor, and accepted a mandate from the archbishop of Seville to reevangelize Andalusia, the southernmost province of Spain, which had been ruled by the Moors. In spite of his success as a preacher over the course of nine years there, he was brought before the Inquisition because of some of his teachings, including the charge that he unduly favored the poor and excluded the rich from heaven. The accusations were not proved, and John was released from confinement. He produced many sermons and a treatise on Christian perfection and established more than a dozen schools. He was canonized in 1970 and is a patron saint of Spain and of the diocesan clergy. His feast is not on the General Roman Calendar.

11 IGNATIUS OF LACONI, RELIGIOUS

Ignatius of Laconi (1701–81) was a Capuchin lay brother whose sanctity was expressed, like that of Thérèse of Lisieux [October 1], in fulfilling the ordinary obligations of life in an extraordinary way. Born at Laconi (Sardinia) of a poor family, he decided during a serious illness to join the Franciscans as a lay brother. In 1741 he was appointed questor, one who begs for alms, a task he fulfilled on foot in all types of weather and for the rest of his life. He was especially devoted to the sick and to children. Many cures were attributed to him during his lifetime as well as after his death. He was canonized in 1951. His feast is not on the General Roman Calendar.

12 NEREUS AND ACHILLEUS, MARTYRS

Nereus and *Achilleus* (early second century) were Roman martyrs whose ancient and well-established cult was centered on their relics in the cemetery of Domitilla. Former Praetorian soldiers who left military life after their conversion, according to their legendary "Acts" they were beheaded during the reign of Trajan (98–117) for refusing to sacrifice to idols. Their feast is on the General Roman Calendar.

13   OUR LADY OF FÁTIMA

The feast of *Our Lady of Fátima* commemorates the reported apparitions of the Blessed Virgin Mary in Fátima,
a small town in Portugal, to three illiterate peasant children on May 13, 1917, and on five later occasions. She identified herself as Our Lady of the Rosary and urged the
practice of penance, the daily recitation of the Rosary,
and devotion to the Immaculate Heart of Mary. Two of
the three children—Francisco and Jacinta Marto—died
in 1919 and were later beatified by Pope John Paul II in
Fátima itself on May 13, 2000. They were the first children to be beatified who were not martyrs. As of that
date, the surviving child, Lucia de Santos, a Carmelite
nun, was still alive at age ninety-three. Pope John Paul
II attributed his survival of an assassination attempt in
St. Peter's Square on May 13, 1981, to the intercession of
Our Lady of Fátima. Speculation about the nature of the
three secrets alleged to have been revealed to the children
by the Blessed Virgin focused on the third (the first two
were accepted as the forecasting of the end of the First
World War, the start of the Second, and the rise of Com-
munism). It was disclosed on the occasion of the beatification of the two children that the third secret concerned
the attempted assassination of John Paul II in 1981. The
feast is not on the General Roman Calendar.

14   MATTHIAS, APOSTLE

Matthias (first century) was the apostle chosen to re-
place Judas (Acts 1:15–26). The basis of his election by lot

(against Joseph, called Barsabbas, also known as Justus) was that he was a disciple of Christ from the time of Jesus' baptism in the Jordan and a witness of the Resurrection. Nothing certain is known of Matthias's apostolic activity, although he is said to have preached first in Judea and later in Cappadocia near the Caspian Sea. Matthias is said to have suffered martyrdom either at Colchis or in Jerusalem. His feast is on the General Roman Calendar and is also celebrated by the Church of England on this day.

15 ISIDORE THE FARMER

Isidore the Farmer (ca. 1080–1130) is patron saint of Madrid, farmers, and laborers. Born in or near Madrid, he worked as a farm laborer all of his life. He married a peasant like himself and had a son who died at a young age. Thereafter, he and his wife lived as brother and sister. Although his life was lived in obscurity, marked by many devotional practices and generosity to the poor, he achieved great fame after his death. In 1170 his remains were transferred to a beautiful shrine via a process that was equivalent in those days to canonization. Miracles were attributed to his intercession, including the cure of King Philip III ca. 1615. Isidore's incorrupt remains lie in the church of St. Andrew, Madrid. His feast is not on the General Roman Calendar.

16 ANDREW BOBOLA, MARTYR; BRENDAN OF CLONFERT, ABBOT

Andrew Bobola (1591–1657) was a Polish Jesuit martyr who is venerated as "apostle of Lithuania" and a patron saint of Poland. He entered the Jesuit novitiate in Vilna, Poland (now Vilnius, Lithuania) and was ordained as a priest in 1622. Thereafter, he became a church pastor known for his outstanding preaching and his ministry to prisoners and the poor. In 1630 he was transferred to Bobruisk as pastor and superior of the Jesuit house there. He ministered heroically to the sick and dying during a subsequent plague. Andrew became caught up in the midst of the bitter conflict between Catholics and Russian Orthodox at the time because of his successful efforts in bringing large numbers of Orthodox back into communion with Rome. In 1657, he was taken prisoner by Cossacks, tortured, and beheaded. He was canonized in 1938. His feast is not on the General Roman Calendar.

Brendan of Clonfert (ca. 486–575), also Brandon, was founder of several Irish abbeys, including one at Clonfert ca. 559. Mt. Brandon, the westernmost point of Europe, on the Dingle peninsula, is named after him. The legendary story in *The Navigation of St. Brendan* contributed greatly to his popularity and to his reputation as patron saint of sailors and whales.

17   PASCHAL BAYLON, RELIGIOUS

Paschal Baylon (1540–92) was a Franciscan lay brother who is patron saint of eucharistic devotions, congresses, and confraternities. Born at Torre Hermosa on the borders of Castile and Aragon of a poor shepherd family, he tended flocks as a youth (he is also patron saint of shepherds) and in his early twenties joined the reformed Friars Minor of

Peter of Alcántara [October 22]. He devoted himself to the care of the sick and the poor and was known for his devotion to the Mass and the Blessed Sacrament. While carrying letters to the minister general of the Observant Franciscans in France, he suffered injuries inflicted by Protestant Huguenots from which he never fully recovered. He died at age fifty-two. His feast is not on the General Roman Calendar.

18 JOHN I, POPE AND MARTYR

John I (d. 526, pope 523–26) was a Tuscan by birth who became archdeacon of Rome and was elected pope in 523, when aged and infirm. Italy was ruled at the time by an Arian, Theodoric the Goth, who was infuriated by the persecution of Arians in the Eastern empire. He sent John as head of a delegation to Constantinople to persuade the emperor Justin I to end the persecutions. If John failed, Theodoric threatened to exact reprisals upon Catholics in the West. The first pope to travel to the East, John was welcomed with great honors when he arrived in Constantinople in late 525. Justin agreed to all of Theodoric's demands, except that of allowing Arians who had conformed under pressure to return to Arian belief and practice. When John returned to Ravenna, Theodoric was furious, accused the pope of having sold out to the emperor in return for all the adulation he had received, and forced the pope to remain in Ravenna. Already exhausted by his long journey and terrified by the prospect of severe punishment, the elderly pope collapsed and died. He was buried in the nave of St. Peter's Basilica with the epitaph "a victim for Christ." His feast is on the General Roman Calendar.

19 DUNSTAN OF CANTERBURY, ABBOT AND BISHOP

Dunstan (909–88) was abbot of Glastonbury, archbishop of Canterbury, and the restorer of Benedictine life in England; he is the patron saint of goldsmiths, jewelers, silversmiths, locksmiths, and musicians. Born at Baltonsborough, near Glastonbury, of a noble family, he was educated at the local monastery and joined the household of his uncle Athelm, archbishop of Canterbury, and then the court of the king. Expelled from the court, he made private monastic vows and was ordained a priest. He returned to Glastonbury, where he lived as a hermit, practicing the crafts of painting, embroidery, and metalwork. The new king recalled Dunstan to court and then appointed him abbot of Glastonbury, where he restored the Rule of St. Benedict [July 11], beginning in 940. He was made archbishop of Canterbury in 960. He preached and taught frequently, built and repaired churches, and served as judge. Toward the end of his life, Dunstan spent most of his time teaching, correcting manuscripts, and administering justice. Visions, prophecies, and miracles were attributed to him even in his lifetime. He died on May 19, 988. His feast is not on the General Roman Calendar, but it is celebrated by the Church of England, the Episcopal Church in the United States, and the Evangelical Lutheran Church in America.

20 BERNARDINO OF SIENA, PRIEST

Bernardino of Siena (1380–1444) was a Franciscan friar best known for his fostering of devotion to the Holy Name of Jesus and for the popularizing of the "IHS" emblem (a compression of the Greek word for Jesus) surrounded by rays, as if from the sun. Born in a small town near Siena, he became a Franciscan in 1402. He quickly established a reputation as a great preacher. He would travel by foot all across Italy, sometimes preaching for three or four hours at a time. The crowds were often so large that he spoke outside rather than in a church. He also wrote works of theology in both Latin and Italian, and, as vicar general of the Observant Franciscans, established schools of theology for his fellow friars, insisting that ignorance in a friar was as dangerous as riches. In 1442 he resigned his position as vicar general of his order and resumed his preaching, traveling now by donkey rather than on foot. By this time he was regarded as the most influential religious in Italy. He died on May 20, 1444, at Aquila and was canonized only six years later. His feast is on the General Roman Calendar.

21 GODRIC OF FINCHALE, HERMIT

Godric of Finchale (ca. 1069–1170), an English hermit, was the author of the earliest surviving Middle English verse, which he himself set to music, similar in style to Gregorian chant. Born of Anglo-Saxon parents in Walpole (Norfolk), he became by turns a peddler, a pilgrim (to Rome and Jerusalem), a sailor, a sea captain, a bailiff, a writer of music and verse, and then a hermit for fifty years or more. He settled finally at Finchale on land owned by the bishop of Durham. There he followed a regime of austerity and penance in reparation for the sins he committed as a sailor and a merchant. He was never formally canonized, and his cult seems to have been confined to Durham and Finchale. His fame eventually spread, however, through his biography and hymns. His feast is not on the General Roman Calendar.

22 RITA OF CASCIA, WIDOW AND NUN

Rita of Cascia (1377–1457) is patron saint of desperate cases, much like St. Jude [October 28]. Born at Roccaporena in Umbria, she wished to become a nun from her earliest years, but married at the age of twelve in deference to her parents' wishes. The marriage was an unhappy one, but it produced two sons. After eighteen years of inflicting abuse and infidelity, Rita's husband was murdered in a vendetta. Rita became an Augustinian nun ca. 1407 at Santa Maria Maddalena at Cascia, but she was refused the habit three times because she was not a virgin. The Augustinian authorities did not relent until 1413. It is said that she meditated so intensely on the Passion of Christ that a wound appeared on her forehead, as if she had been pierced by a crown of thorns. As her reputation as a mystic grew, she also devoted herself to the care of sick nuns and counseling visiting laypersons. She died of tuberculosis on May 22, 1447, and was canonized in 1900. Her symbol is roses, which are blessed in Augustinian

churches on her feast day. It is not on the General Roman
Calendar, however.

23 JOHN BAPTIST ROSSI, PRIEST

John Baptist Rossi (1698–1764) was a Roman priest who
devoted his life to those on the most distant margins of
society. Born at Voltaggio near Genoa, he studied at the
Roman College and was ordained a priest in 1721. In spite
of his vulnerability to epileptic seizures, he worked tirelessly among the poor, the sick, the homeless, beggars,
and prostitutes. He was also a gifted confessor to people
of all social classes and a compelling preacher, particularly to religious communities. He was canonized in 1881.
His feast is not on the General Roman Calendar.

24 SIMEON STYLITES THE YOUNGER, HERMIT

Simeon Stylites the Younger (ca. 517–92) was one of the so-
called Stylite saints, who lived on top of stone pillars in
the desert, the most famous of whom is Simeon Stylites
the Elder. Born at Antioch, Simeon the Younger lived
atop pillars near his birthplace for some fifty years. By
age twenty he had already acquired a reputation for holiness and was attracting large crowds of visitors. He retired to a more inaccessible location on a mountain. He
was ordained a priest at twenty-three (or thirty-three).
Although many contemporaries questioned the way of
life adopted by the Stylites, they enjoyed popular support

because of their apparent sanctity, the spiritual assistance and cures they rendered, and their success in converting pagans. The feast of Simeon the Younger is celebrated on this day in the Russian and Greek Orthodox Churches, but it is not on the General Roman Calendar.

25 VENERABLE BEDE, PRIEST AND DOCTOR OF THE CHURCH; GREGORY VII, POPE

The *Venerable Bede* (673–735) was the most important historian of the Church in England and a key agent in the preservation of classical and Christian culture. It is fitting that he is the patron saint of scholars. Born near Sunderland, he was educated from age seven, first by Benedict Biscop [January 12], abbot of Wearmouth, and then by Ceolfrith, abbot of Jarrow in Northumbria, both of whose biographies Bede would subsequently write. He entered the monastery at Jarrow and remained there until his death.

Ordained a deacon at the young age of nineteen and a priest at age thirty, he devoted himself to the study of Scripture and other scholarly pursuits. He popularized the use of "A.D." (*Anno Domini*, Lat., "year of the Lord") for the years of the Christian era. His most significant achievement, however, was his *Ecclesiastical History of the English People,* which he completed in 731. It was widely read on the Continent as well as in England and became a classic that is still reprinted and studied. Bede's daily life was uneventful; he rarely traveled, but attended faithfully to his monastic duties and scholarship. Bede's cult was established within fifty years of his death. Pope Leo XIII named him a Doctor of the Church in 1899, the only English saint to achieve this honor. His feast is on the General Roman Calendar and is also celebrated by the Church of England and the Episcopal Church in the United States.

Gregory VII (ca. 1020–85, pope 1073–85), one of the greatest reformer popes in the history of the Church, inspired the so-called Gregorian reform. Born Hildebrand in Tuscany, he served under several popes as chaplain, treasurer of the Roman Church, archdeacon, chancellor, and counselor. Upon the death of Alexander II he was elected pope by acclamation and took the name Gregory, after his patron, Gregory VI, and Gregory the Great [September 3]. He made reform the centerpiece of his pontificate, targeting abuses associated with simony, nepotism, clerical marriage, and lay interference in the appointment and investiture of bishops and abbots. In order to achieve his goals, however, he inflated traditional papal claims over the spiritual and temporal spheres.

His famous *Dictatus papae* (Lat., "Pronouncements of the Pope") stated that the pope alone can wear imperial insignia, that his feet alone can be kissed by all princes, that he has the power to depose emperors, and that he can be judged by no one else. Gregory also restricted the title "pope" to the Bishop of Rome and created the position of papal legate. He died on May 25, 1085. So strong and divisive was his personality that subsequent papal elections were often marked by bitter conflict between Gregorian and anti-Gregorian cardinals. Gregory VII was canonized in 1606. His feast is on the General Roman Calendar.

26 PHILIP NERI, PRIEST

Philip Neri (1515–95) was the founder of the Congregation of the Oratory, also known as the Oratorians. Born in Florence, Philip disavowed a budding career as a merchant and went to Rome after a possible conversion experience in 1533. He spent some time studying the works of Thomas Aquinas [January 28], but then turned to apostolic work among young Florentines employed in banks and shops, whom he encouraged to serve the sick in hospitals and to visit the churches of Rome with him. In 1544, while on one of his frequent visits to the catacombs, he is said to have experienced a vision in which a ball of fire entered his mouth and dilated his heart—a physical condition that allegedly affected him for the remainder of his life.

He was ordained a priest in 1551, lived with a community of diocesan priests at San Girolamo della Carità, and spent long hours in the confessional and in spiritual direction. He and five priest-disciples began using an oratory built over the nave of San Girolamo, to which they would summon the faithful by ringing a small bell. They shared a common life under Philip's direction, but without vows. The group developed into the Congregation of the Oratory, which was approved by his friend Pope Gregory XIII in 1575. Philip and his Oratorians introduced a whole new style of personal spirituality integrated with the pastoral life and ministries of the Church. They encouraged sermons by laypeople, the presentation of plays with biblical themes, and the composition of songs on religious themes. Philip died on May 26, 1595, and was canonized in 1622. His feast is on the General Roman Calendar.

27   AUGUSTINE OF CANTERBURY,
BISHOP

Augustine of Canterbury (d. ca. 604) was the "apostle of
the English" and the first archbishop of Canterbury. He is
one of the patron saints of England. An Italian by birth,
Augustine became a monk and later prior of the monastery of St. Andrew [November 30] on the Celian Hill in
Rome. In 596 he was chosen by his friend Gregory the
Great [September 3] to lead a mission of monks to evangelize the Anglo-Saxons in Britain. The monks landed at
Ebbsfleet, Kent, in 597. They were received cautiously
by Ethelbert [February 24], king of Kent, the most important of the seven Anglo-Saxon kingdoms, who asked
them to remain on the isle of Thanet until he decided
what to do about them. He eventually met with them
in the open air (for fear of spells), gave them a house at
Canterbury, and granted them permission to preach.

Augustine built the first cathedral and school at
Canterbury, dedicating the cathedral as Christ Church,
and founded the monastery of Sts. Peter and Paul (called
St. Augustine's after his death) just outside the walls of the
city but very near the cathedral. He also established the
suburban see of Rochester and later the see of London.
Augustine died on May 26 sometime between 604 and
609. His feast day is on the General Roman Calendar.

28 GERMANUS OF PARIS, BISHOP;
BERNARD OF MONTJOUX, PRIEST

Germanus of Paris (ca. 500–576) is, alongside Geneviève [January 3], patron saint of Paris. Born at Autun in Burgundy, he lived a semimonastic life for fifteen years, was ordained a priest in 530, and then was appointed abbot of the monastic church of St. Symphorien (d. ca. 200) in Autun, where the patronal saint had been martyred for refusing to pay honor to the pagan gods. Germanus proved to be an efficient administrator both of the monastery and the lands it owned as well as a generous benefactor of the poor. When the bishop of Paris was removed from office, Germanus was appointed to succeed him by the other Gallic bishops and the Frankish king, Childebert, who built a cathedral and monastic basilica for the new bishop. The latter building was originally the basilica of St. Vincent and Holy Cross, but was subsequently named Saint-Germain-des-Prés in Germanus's honor.

Germanus played important parts in at least three church councils, two in Paris (562 and 573) and a third in Tours (567). He was devoted to the cult of saints and was renowned for his healing powers. He was especially devoted to the pastoral care of prisoners and slaves of all races. He died in Paris on May 28, 576, and was buried close to his patron, Childebert, in his abbey church. Germanus's feast is not on the General Roman Calendar.

Bernard of Montjoux (d. 1081), also known as Bernard of Aosta and of Menthon, was a priest of the diocese of Aosta who took special care of Alpine travelers, always at risk from snowdrifts and robbers. He founded some houses for them, and a specially trained breed of dogs, Saint Bernards, were named after him. He was declared patron saint of mountain climbers by Pope Pius XI, who had himself engaged in the sport.

29 MAXIMINUS OF TRIER, BISHOP

Maximinus of Trier (d. ca. 347) was regarded by both Jerome [September 30] and Athanasius [May 2] as one of the most courageous bishops of his time. A native of Poitiers, he went to Trier, the imperial capital of the Western empire, for his education, attracted by the reputation of its bishop, Agritius. He eventually succeeded Agritius as bishop in 333 and became celebrated for his staunch opposition to the heresy of Arianism and for the hospitality and assistance he gave to its victims. Although he is known to have written several treatises, none of his writings survive. His feast is not on the General Roman Calendar.

30 JOAN OF ARC, VIRGIN

Joan of Arc (1412–31) is one of the patron saints of France. Born at Domrémy in Champagne, the daughter of a peasant farmer, she was a young girl during the Hundred Years' War between France and England and the civil war within France between the houses of Orléans and Burgundy. As the English armies regained the ascendancy, Joan claimed to have heard the voices of saints urging her to save France. At first no one paid any attention to Joan, but she was taken more seriously when some of her predictions of additional defeats were fulfilled. She was sent to the Dauphin (the future Charles VII), who was impressed that Joan recognized him through his disguise. She also passed review by a group of theologians at Poitiers. Her credentials established, she asked for troops to relieve Orléans in 1429 and was accorded the honor of leading them into battle in full white armor and accompanied by a special banner bearing a symbol of the Trinity and the words, "Jesus, Maria." Orléans was saved, and English forts in the vicinity were captured.

Military reversals and her own capture by the duke of Burgundy changed the situation drastically in 1430. The Burgundians sold her to their English allies, who attributed her military successes to witchcraft and spells. She was imprisoned at Rouen, tried for witchcraft and heresy, and burned at the stake in the marketplace on May 30, 1431. Her gaze fixed on the cross, she died calling on the name of Jesus. In 1456 her case was reopened and the verdict set aside. She was canonized in 1920 by Pope Benedict XV. Her feast is not on the General Roman Calendar.

31 THE VISITATION OF THE BLESSED VIRGIN MARY

This feast commemorates the visit of the *Blessed Virgin Mary* to her cousin Elizabeth [November 5]. According to Luke 1:39–56, Mary, having learned that both she and her aged cousin had conceived, visited Elizabeth and remained with her for three months. Upon her arrival, Mary uttered the song of praise known as the Magnificat. The event is also commemorated as one of the Joyful Mysteries of the Rosary [see October 7].

The feast itself is Franciscan in origin. The general chapter of 1263 introduced it at the request of Bonaventure [July 15], who was minister general of the order. Urban VI (1378–89), the pope whose election precipitated the Great Schism (1378–1417), decided to place this feast on the liturgical calendar for the universal Church with the hope that it might help to end the schism, and Boniface IX (1389–1404) actually prescribed that it be done in 1389. Because of the deep divisions in the Church, however, it was not until the pontificate of Pius V (1566–72) [April 30] that the feast in fact attained universal status, to be celebrated on July 2. In 1969, with the revision of the General Roman Calendar, the date of the feast was changed to May 31 in order to stress its spiritual connection with the feasts of the Annunciation [March 25] and the Birth of John the Baptist [June 24].

JUNE

1   JUSTIN, MARTYR

Justin (ca. 100–ca. 165), one of the first great defenders of the faith, is regarded as the first significant Christian philosopher. (He is the patron saint of philosophers.) Born Flavia Neapolis at Shechem (modern Nablus) in Samaria, of Greek parents, he studied philosophy in Ephesus and Alexandria in search, as he put it, of "the vision of God." He became a Christian ca. 130, having been impressed with the connection between Christ and the Old Testament prophecies as well as with those who suffered martyrdom for their faith.

After his conversion, he continued his role as a philosopher, but now as a Christian. He publicly debated Jews, Gnostics, and other nonbelievers. He went to Rome ca. 150, where he founded a school of philosophy, taught Christian apologetics, and wrote his major works. His writings disclose important information about early church rites and how the second-century Church was seen by contemporary society. Justin was arrested during the reign of Marcus Aurelius and, refusing to sacrifice to the gods, was martyred ca. 165. His feast is on the General Roman Calendar.

2   MARCELLINUS AND PETER, MARTYRS

Marcellinus and *Peter* (d. 304) were Roman martyrs whose names were included in the Roman Canon of the Mass. Marcellinus was a prominent priest of Rome, and Peter was an exorcist. They were arrested, imprisoned, and later beheaded, probably during the persecutions of the emperor Diocletian. The feast of Marcellinus and Peter is on the General Roman Calendar.

3   CHARLES LWANGA AND COMPANIONS, MARTYRS; BLESSED JOHN XXIII, POPE

Charles Lwanga (ca. 1860–86) *and his companions* are regarded as the protomartyrs of black Africa. Charles was one of twenty-two African Catholics who were executed for their faith, including Joseph Mkasa, Denis Sebuggwawo, Matthias Murumba, and Andrew Kagwa. Twenty-four Protestants were also martyred. Born in Buddu County, Uganda, Charles became a catechumen after learning of Christianity from two members of the chief's court. He served as an assistant to Joseph Mkasa, who was in charge of the king's pages. On the night of Mkasa's martyrdom by beheading upon the orders of the new chief, Charles requested and received Baptism. He became head of the pages and instructed them in the Christian faith. When their lives were threatened, he baptized them. Charles and the pages were forced to confess their faith, arrested, and then taken on a brutal sixteen-mile march to Namugongo on Lake Victoria, where they were executed. The martyrs of Uganda were canonized by Pope Paul VI in 1964, and their feast was placed on the General Roman Calendar in 1969.

Pope John XXIII (1881–1963, pope 1958–63) convened the historic Second Vatican Council (1962–65) and is widely regarded as the most beloved pope in history. Born Angelo Giuseppe Roncalli, the third of thirteen children in a family of peasant farmers, he was ordained a priest in 1904 and served as secretary to the bishop of Bergamo and as a lecturer in church history at the diocesan seminary. In 1921 Pope Benedict XV appointed him national director of the Congregation for the Propagation of the Faith. Father Roncalli came to the attention of its librarian, Achille Ratti, the future Pope Pius XI (1922–39). It was Ratti, after his election as pope, who launched Roncalli's diplomatic career in Bulgaria, Turkey, Greece, and then France during World War II.

Cardinal Roncalli was elected pope on October 28, 1958, just shy of his seventy-seventh birthday. Many regarded him as a "transitional pope," but he was to prove them wrong. He was crowned on November 4, the feast day of his hero Charles Borromeo, and, contrary to custom, preached at his own coronation Mass, insisting that he wanted to be, above all, a good shepherd. He announced a new ecumenical council on January 25, 1959, referring to it as a "new Pentecost." He insisted that the council had not been called to refute errors, but to update the Church and to "let some fresh air in."

His encyclicals emphasized the unity of the Church, world peace, social justice, and human rights. No pope in history was so committed to Christian unity as he was.

He established the Secretariat for Promoting Christian Unity (now the Pontifical Council for Promoting Christian Unity) and opened channels of communication with other major Christian leaders and the World Council of Churches. Out of concern for the Jews, he removed the word "perfidious" from the prayer for Jews in the Good Friday liturgy.

Diagnosed with stomach cancer in September 1962, he made his last public appearance from the window of his apartment on Ascension Thursday, May 23, 1963. When he died on the evening of June 3, virtually the whole world mourned his loss. He was beatified on September 3, 2000. The Evangelical Lutheran Church in America also commemorates him on this day.

4   METROPHANES, BISHOP

Metrophanes (d. ca. 325) was the first patriarch of Constantinople and one of the major reasons the emperor Constantine chose Byzantium as the new capital of his empire. Dometius, the father of Metrophanes, after converting to Christianity took his family to live in Byzantium, which was then a small town. Dometius was a close friend of the bishop of Heracles, who ordained him and whom he succeeded as bishop. He, in turn, was succeeded by his older son, and then in 313 by his younger son, Metrophanes. It is not clear whether the see was moved from Heracles to Byzantium, or whether it was divided when Constantine transformed Byzantium into his new capital. In any case, it is clear that Metrophanes was the first bishop of Byzantium (later Constantinople).

Metrophanes had a great reputation for sanctity throughout the East. His feast is not on the General Roman Calendar, but is celebrated by the Greek and Russian Orthodox Churches on this day.

5   BONIFACE, BISHOP AND MARTYR

Boniface (ca. 675–754) was the "apostle of Germany" and is a patron saint of the country. Born Wynfrith (or Winfrid) in Devon, England, he was educated in Benedictine monasteries. As a young monk and schoolmaster, he compiled the first Latin grammar in England. Ordained a priest at age thirty, he was an effective preacher and teacher. He chose to become a missionary, going first to Frisia (the northern part of the Netherlands today) in 716, but resistance from the pagan tribes was so strong that he returned to England. In 719, however, he received a mission directly from Pope Gregory II to preach the gospel in Bavaria and Hesse. On his way there, he learned that conditions had changed for the better in Frisia, so he went there to evangelize for three years. During a visit to Rome in 722 the pope consecrated him a regional bishop with jurisdiction over Germany. It may have been during this visit that Wynfrith, or perhaps even the pope himself, changed his name to Boniface.

With the aid of a papal letter, Boniface received the support of the Frankish king, Charles Martel, to evangelize Hesse, where Boniface converted many and established several monasteries. After being made archbishop in 732 and papal legate to Germany in 739, he reorganized the Frankish Church, conducting five synods, correcting abuses, and establishing the Benedictine Rule for all monasteries. In 752, Boniface, eighty years old, relinquished leadership of the Frankish Church and returned to the evangelization of the Frisians, pressing farther into the area occupied by hostile tribes. While he was reading in his tent at Dokkum, awaiting the arrival of some candidates for Confirmation, his camp was attacked. Boniface forbade any resistance; he and fifty-three companions were massacred.

Boniface left behind a large corpus of letters written to church leaders and former pupils who sought his advice. He was, before all else, a pastor—loving, kind, simple, and devoted to the gospel. His feast was extended to the universal Church in 1874 and is on the General Roman Calendar.

6   NORBERT, BISHOP

Norbert (ca. 1080–1134) was the founder of the Premonstratensians, also known as the Canons Regular of Prémontré or simply the Norbertines. Born of a noble family at Xanten in the Rhineland, Norbert, like other sons of noblemen, became a subdeacon and canon while still living a worldly life. A narrow escape from death in 1115 is said to have brought about a conversion similar to the Apostle Paul's [January 25]. Norbert was ordained a priest the same year and became a celebrated itinerant preacher in northern France, Germany, and present-day Belgium. His efforts to reform the canons at Xanten, and later at St. Martin's in Laon, met with such resistance that, with the blessing of the local bishop in 1121, he made a fresh start with thirteen others in the valley of Prémontré. Their number soon increased to forty, and all made their solemn profession according to the Rule of St. Augustine [August 28] on Christmas Day, 1121. They were not regarded as a new order but as a reform movement within the canons regular of Laon. The movement spread to other countries, attracting both men and women. The order received papal approval and Norbert was made archbishop of Magdeburg in 1126. Norbert died on June 6, 1134, and was canonized in 1582. His feast was extended to the universal Church in 1672 and is on the General Roman Calendar.

7   WILLIBALD, BISHOP

Willibald (d. ca. 786), the bishop of Eichstätt, was the brother of Winnibald, abbot of Heidenheim, and Walburga [February 25], abbess of Heidenheim, and the nephew of Boniface [June 5]. Born in Wessex, he became a monk early in life following an illness that almost killed him. After his education was completed, he became one of the most traveled Anglo-Saxons of his time. In 720 he and other members of his family embarked on a pilgrimage to Rome, Sicily, Cyprus, modern-day Turkey, Syria, and Palestine. He spent a long period in Constantinople and returned to Italy in 730, residing for ten years in the monastery of Monte Cassino, where he contributed to the restoration of the primitive Benedictine Rule.

Around the year 740 Pope Gregory III sent him to Germany to participate in the mission of his uncle Boniface, at Boniface's request. Willibald joined Boniface in Thuringia and was ordained a priest there ca. 741. He then evangelized in Franconia and in 742 was consecrated bishop of Eichstätt. One of his first acts, sometime before 750, was the establishment of the double monastery at Heidenheim, with the same Rule as that at Monte Cassino. Willibald conducted the pastoral affairs of his diocese from the monastery, serving as bishop for forty-five years. His feast is not on the General Roman Calendar.

8   WILLIAM OF YORK, BISHOP;
GERARD MANLEY HOPKINS,
POET AND RELIGIOUS

William of York (d. 1154) was a highly controversial archbishop of York. Born into a noble family with royal connections, William FitzHerbert became canon and treasurer of York Minster at a young age (ca. 1130) and chaplain to King Stephen, who selected him to be the new archbishop of York in 1140. Some of the canons of the cathedral, Theobald, the archbishop of Canterbury, and Bernard of Clairvaux [August 20] and the Yorkshire Cistercians opposed the appointment. Both sides appealed to Pope Lucius II, but Pope Lucius II died and was replaced by a Cistercian, Eugenius III, who accepted Bernard's complaint, suspended and deposed William, and appointed a Cistercian in his place. In the meantime, William retired to Winchester and lived humbly and devoutly as a monk until 1153, when the pope, Bernard, and the Cistercian archbishop of York all died. William was restored to his see and given the pallium in Rome by the new pope, Anastasius IV. Soon after his triumphant return to York in 1154, he died suddenly after Mass on

June 8. William of York's feast is not on the General Roman Calendar.

June 8 is also the day of death of the Jesuit poet *Gerard Manley Hopkins* (1844–89), whose poetry embodied the distinctively Catholic understanding of all created reality as sacramental, that is, as embodying and mediating the presence of God.

9 EPHREM, DEACON AND DOCTOR OF THE CHURCH; COLUMBA OF IONA, ABBOT

Ephrem (ca. 306–73), also Ephraem of Syria, was the author of numerous hymns and works of biblical exegesis for which he was named a Doctor of the Church in 1920, the only Syrian to be so honored. Born in Nisibis (Mesopotamia), he was baptized ca. 324 and joined the cathedral school there, eventually becoming its head. After the Persians captured Nisibis in 363, Ephrem took up the life of a monk in a cave near Edessa. It was during this period that he produced his many hymns (over five hundred survive) and exegetical writings on nearly the whole of the Old Testament and much of the New Testament. Ephrem's feast is on the General Roman Calendar and he is commemorated by the Church of England on this day.

Columba of Iona (ca. 521–97), also Columcille and Columbkille, although Irish by birth, is the most celebrated of the Scottish saints. Born at Gartan in Donegal of a royal clan, he was educated by monks and then founded the monasteries of Derry (546), called Londonderry by its English conquerors, Durrow (ca. 556), and Kells.

For reasons not agreed upon by historians, he left Ireland with twelve companions in 565, setting out for the island of Iona off the southwest coast of Scotland. He established the famous monastery of Iona and devoted himself to the training of its monks, spiritual direction, peacemaking between civil rulers, and copying sacred texts. He died before the monastery's altar, just as his monks gathered for Matins. Columba's feast is not on the General Roman Calendar.

10 BLESSED JOHN DOMINICI, BISHOP

The Dominicans celebrate the feast of *John Dominici* (1376–1419) on this day. One of the leading theologians and preachers of his time, he spearheaded the reform of his order in northern Italy, introducing or restoring the strict Rule of St. Dominic [August 8]. He was the confessor and spiritual adviser of Pope Gregory XII, whom he persuaded to resign the papacy in 1415 in order to bring a definitive end to the Great Western Schism (1378–1417). By then a cardinal-archbishop, it was he who conveyed the pope's resignation to the Council of Constance. His cult was confirmed in 1832.

11 BARNABAS, APOSTLE

Barnabas (first century) was not one of the original twelve apostles, but was regarded as an apostle by Luke [October 18] and the early Fathers of the Church because of his missionary work beyond Jerusalem. He was a Levite from Cyprus (Acts 4:36) whose original name was Joseph. The apostles gave him the name Barnabas, which means "son of consolation (or encouragement)," perhaps because of his pleasant disposition. When he became a follower of Jesus, he sold some property and donated the proceeds to the apostles (Acts 4:36–37). He introduced Paul [June 29] to the leaders of the Church in Jerusalem (Acts 9:27), and he and Paul attended the assembly in Jerusalem that settled the question of circumcision for gentile converts.

Barnabas and Mark later sailed to Cyprus together (Acts 15:39), where according to tradition Barnabas was stoned to death in the Greco-Roman city of Salamis before the year 60 or 61 and after his founding of the Cypriote church. No certain writings of Barnabas survive. The *Letter of Barnabas* is not his, since it was written ca. 130. He is the patron saint of Cyprus, and his feast is on the General Roman Calendar.

12 ONOUPHRIOS, HERMIT

Onouphrios (d. ca. 400) was an Egyptian hermit in whose honor a church (San Onofrio) was erected on the Janiculum Hill in Rome in the fifteenth century. Paphnoutios, a monk who allegedly wandered in the desert, came across Onouphrios, a naked, hairy man with a long white beard, who told him the story of his life and deeds. Onouphrios had been a monk in a large monastery in the Thebaïd, but felt called to a solitary life. For more than sixty years since then, Onouphrios had lived as a hermit. Paphnoutios shared with Onouphrios a message from the Lord to the effect that Onouphrios was to die and he was to bury him. Onouphrios did die, and Paphnoutios did bury him—in a hole in the mountainside. The site allegedly disappeared immediately, which Paphnoutios took as a sign that he should not remain there. The story became popular in the sixth century. The feast of Onouphrios is not on the General Roman Calendar.

13 ANTHONY OF PADUA, PRIEST AND DOCTOR OF THE CHURCH

Anthony of Padua (1195–1231), a Franciscan friar and Doctor of the Church, is considered one of the greatest preachers in the history of the Church. Born in Lisbon of a noble Portuguese family, he joined the Augustinian Canons Regular. In 1220, after meeting a group of friars who were on their way to Morocco to refute the Moors and other heretics and who were subsequently martyred there, Anthony joined the Franciscans and sailed to Morocco hoping to continue the mission of the slain friars, but ill health forced his return. Anthony attended the general chapter of the Franciscans held in Assisi in 1221, at which Francis himself was present. Afterward, Anthony was assigned to a small hermitage near Forli, where he lived in relative obscurity until his considerable theological, spiritual, and homiletical gifts were manifested in a sermon he gave on short notice at an ordination ceremony. As a result, he was sent to preach in different parts of Lombardy, where he attracted people by the thousands. He became one of Francis's favorite disciples and closest friends. After Francis's death, he was elected provincial of northern Italy.

Anthony died at Arcella, near Padua, on June 13, 1231. He was canonized less than a year after his death. Pope Pius XII named him a Doctor of the Church in 1946. His feast is on the General Roman Calendar. Since the seventeenth century Anthony has been frequently invoked as the finder of lost articles. When a novice took his Psalter without permission, Anthony prayed for its return. After a frightening apparition, the novice rushed to restore the book to its rightful owner.

14 METHODIUS OF CONSTANTINOPLE, PATRIARCH

Methodius of Constantinople (d. 847) is the object of great veneration in the East because of the role he played in the final defeat of iconoclasm (a movement, with imperial support, that rejected the use of icons and other sacred imagery as well as the veneration of the saints) and his suffering in prison. Born and educated in Syracuse in Sicily, he entered a monastery in Bythnynia, eventually becoming superior. He later built a monastery on the island of Khios (Chios), whence he was called back to Constantinople by the patriarch Nicephorus because iconoclasm had been revived by the emperor Leo V the Armenian.

After Nicephorus was deposed and exiled, Methodius was sent to Rome by the bishops (after 815) to inform the pope of the situation. He remained there until after the emperor's death. The pope sent a letter to the new emperor, requesting the reinstatement of the patriarch. Upon Methodius's return in 821, he was accused of instigating the papal letter and thrown into prison for at least seven years. When another emperor resumed the attack on veneration of images, Methodius again objected and was thrown back into prison. The emperor died soon thereafter. His widow succeeded to the throne and immediately reversed the work of the iconoclasts. The persecutions stopped, the exiled clergy were called home, and the sacred images were restored to the churches. The iconoclast patriarch was deposed, and Methodius was installed in his place. Methodius's feast is not on the General Roman Calendar, but is celebrated by the Russian Orthodox Church.

15 VITUS AND COMPANIONS, MARTYRS

Vitus (d. ca. 300), martyred during the Diocletian persecution, is the patron saint of those suffering from various diseases associated, correctly or not, with neurological disorders. Thus, the term "St. Vitus's dance" refers to a variety of conditions causing convulsive and involuntary movements. By extension, he is also considered the patron saint of dancers and comedians. According to tradition, Vitus was the son of a Sicilian senator and was raised as a Christian by his tutor and nurse. Vitus was thought to have cured the emperor Diocletian's son of devil possession, but the emperor attributed it to sorcery and had Vitus and two companions arrested, tortured, and condemned to death. Nothing is known of their martyrdom, but Vitus's cult is ancient and is mentioned in the *Martyrology of Jerome* [September 30]. His feast is not on the General Roman Calendar.

16 LUTGARDIS, NUN

Lutgardis (1182–1246), or Lutgard, was a Cistercian nun and one of the leading mystics of the thirteenth century. Born at Tongeren, between Brussels and Maastricht, she was placed in a Benedictine monastery at the age of twelve because her father no longer could pay her dowry. To the nuns she had no apparent vocation to religious life. However, after an alleged apparition of Christ in which he is said to have shown her his five wounds, she renounced all worldly interests. The nuns remained skeptical, but she persevered in her new life of prayer and meditation on the Passion of Christ. Her transformation was such that the other nuns wanted to make her their abbess, but she declined. She remained at the convent for twelve years, having become a nun herself at age twenty, but then moved to a stricter Cistercian house at Aywières, south of Liège, on the advice of her confessor. She would remain there for thirty years, a much-sought-after spiritual director and healer, until her death, on June 16, 1246. Her feast is on the Cistercian liturgical calendar, but not the General Roman Calendar.

17 RAINERIUS OF PISA, HERMIT

Rainerius of Pisa (1117–61) is the patron saint of Pisa. Born in Pisa, Rainerius Scaccieri was the son of a prosperous merchant. In 1140, under the influence of a local monk, he repented of his worldly ways and went on a pilgrimage to the Holy Land, remaining there as a hermit (or barefoot beggar) until 1153. When he returned to Pisa, he was welcomed by the archbishop and people. He took up residence with monks, but without actually becoming one himself. His knowledge of Latin gave him access to the Bible and enabled him to preach on occasion. He enjoyed a reputation for austerity of life, facilitating conversions, and healing. Upon his death, he was buried with great honor in the Pisa cathedral. One of the bells in the famous leaning tower is named after him. His name was entered in the *Roman Martyrology* in the seventeenth century, but his feast is not on the General Roman Calendar.

18 GREGORY BARBARIGO, BISHOP

Gregory Barbarigo (1625–97) was an active seventeenth-century church leader. Born into a noble and wealthy Venetian family, he was ordained a priest in 1655 and ministered heroically to the sick during the plague of 1657. He was appointed bishop of Bergamo the same year, created a cardinal in 1660, and transferred to Padua in 1664. He founded a seminary and a college, to which he donated a printing press, collected a superb patristic library, and was active in efforts to secure reunion with the separated churches of the East. He died on June 15, 1697. His feast is not on the General Roman Calendar.

19 ROMUALD, ABBOT

Romuald (ca. 950–1027) was the founder of the Camaldolese order. Born of a noble Ravenna family, Romuald Onesti fled to a local Cluniac monastery after his father had killed a relative in a duel over property. His austere lifestyle and devotional practices irritated some of the other monks, and after about three years he left and placed himself under the spiritual direction of a hermit near Venice. He later wandered through northern Italy, setting up hermitages, and obtained a mandate from the pope to carry out a mission to the Magyars in Hungary, desiring a martyr's death. Illness upset his hopes, and he returned to Italy.

After prolonged study of the Desert Fathers, he concluded that the way of salvation was along the path of solitude. He founded a monastery at Fonte Avellana, later refounded by his disciple Peter Damian [February 21], and another at Camaldoli. The latter developed into the Camaldolese order. His distinctive contribution to Benedictine monasticism was to provide a place for the eremitical life within the framework of the Rule of St. Benedict [July 11]. The hermits would come together for liturgical worship and certain meals, but otherwise lived in isolation. Romuald died on June 19, 1027. His feast is on the General Roman Calendar.

20 ALBAN, MARTYR

Alban (third century) is the protomartyr of Britain. His death is the earliest recorded execution in that country on the charge of being a Christian. Alban was allegedly a pagan perhaps of Romano-British extraction, who gave shelter to a Christian priest who was being hunted by imperial forces. (It is fitting, therefore, that he is regarded as the patron saint of refugees.) He is said to have been so impressed with the priest's demeanor that he was converted and took instruction in the faith from him. When the soldiers heard of the fugitive's location, they came to Alban's house and found Alban dressed in the fugitive's clerical garments. He surrendered himself in place of his guest and teacher. When the deception was discovered, the magistrate demanded to know Alban's name. He gave it, along with a confession of faith and a refusal to sacrifice to the Roman gods. The magistrate sentenced Alban to death by beheading. Alban's feast is not on the General Roman Calendar, but it is liturgically celebrated in the Church of England and the Episcopal Church in the United States on June 22.

21 ALOYSIUS GONZAGA, RELIGIOUS

Aloysius Gonzaga (1568–91) was a member of the Society of Jesus who died in his early twenties and is the patron saint of young people and of students in Jesuit colleges and universities. Born into a high-ranking family in Castiglione, near Mantua, in Lombardy and destined by his father for a military career, Aloysius decided to become a Jesuit during a family trip to Spain in the company of the empress of Austria in 1581–83. Aloysius renounced his inheritance and entered the novitiate in Rome in November 1585. The vow of obedience and poor health combined to curb his penchant for excessive austerities.

Aloysius was exceedingly scrupulous in prayer, almost masochistic in the exercise of self-mortification, often uncommunicative, uncomfortable with women, and obsessed with the idea and hope of an early death. Some commentators attribute these personality traits to a determined reaction against his privileged upbringing. He died while nursing the sick during a plague outbreak on June 21, 1591. His feast is on the General Roman Calendar.

22 PAULINUS OF NOLA, BISHOP; JOHN FISHER, BISHOP AND MARTYR; THOMAS MORE, MARTYR

Paulinus of Nola (ca. 355–431) was a wealthy noble who retired from public office, gave his fortune to the poor, became the bishop of Nola and, along with his wife, founded an ascetic community. He became a Christian ca. 389 (his wife may already have been one). Following the death of an infant son, they gave away most of their immense fortune to the poor and to the Church. The bishop of Barcelona persuaded Paulinus to accept ordination to the priesthood ca. 393. Paulinus and his wife moved to Italy to settle in Nola, a small town near Naples. He built a church at Fondi, an aqueduct for Nola, and a guest house for pilgrims, debtors, and others who were down on their luck. These occupied the ground floor of his house, while he, his wife, and a few friends followed a semimonastic regime on the upper floor, praying the Divine Office together daily. When the bishop of Nola died in 409, Paulinus was chosen to succeed him. Paulinus died on June 22, 431. His feast is on the General Roman Calendar.

John Fisher (1469–1535) was chancellor of Cambridge University, bishop of Rochester, a cardinal, and a vigorous defender of the Catholic faith in England at the time of the Reformation. Born at Beverley in Yorkshire, he was educated at Cambridge from the age of fourteen and ordained a priest in 1491. In 1504, at age thirty-five, he became both chancellor of the university and bishop of Rochester. He had reluctantly accepted the episcopal appointment, but once in office he executed his pastoral responsibilities with great energy and care.

Fisher was a famous preacher and scholar. His theological works were influential at the Council of Trent (1545-63), and he wrote four volumes against Martin Luther. When King Henry VIII began contemplating divorce and remarriage, it was Fisher who argued for the validity and indissolubility of his first marriage. He later protested Henry's new title as "Supreme Head of the Church of England," suggesting that it be qualified with the words "so far as the law of Christ allows." Fisher was arrested as a traitor, condemned to death on June 17, 1535, and beheaded five days later. He was canonized in 1935. His feast, along with that of Thomas More, is on the General Roman Calendar.

Thomas More (1478–1535) was the most famous victim of King Henry VIII's persecution of Catholics who refused to accept royal supremacy over the Church in England. He is the patron saint of Catholic lawyers. The son of a lawyer and judge, More joined the household of the archbishop of Canterbury at age thirteen. He was a member of Parliament for four years (1504–8). Thomas More's reputation for intelligence, wit, integrity, and loyalty brought him to the attention of Henry VIII, who promoted him to a series of public offices. His reputation as a man of learning and of letters was definitively established with the publication in 1516 of his Latin classic, *Utopia*, which was later translated into several European languages.

In the late 1520s, when the marriage issue was still under papal review, the king asked Thomas for his opinion of the marriage question. More at first declined for lack of expert knowledge, but when the king persisted, More acknowledged that he did not share the king's view. Nevertheless, Henry chose Thomas More as his lord chancellor in 1529—a post in which More excelled because of his fairness and integrity. As he became increasingly concerned, however, about the king's real intentions regarding the Church of England, he resigned the chancellorship on May 16, 1532.

Thomas More refused to attend Anne Boleyn's coronation as queen. Then in March 1534 the Act of Succession required all of the king's subjects to recognize the offspring of the second marriage as successors to the throne, the nullity of his first marriage, and the validity of his second. Opposing the Act of Succession was considered tantamount to treason. Upon his second refusal to take the oath, More, along with John Fisher, was arrested and consigned to the Tower of London on April 13, 1534. While in the Tower, he wrote such works as *Dialogue of Comfort Against Tribulation* and *Treatise on the Passion of Christ*.

More's trial was held on July 1. In his own defense he argued that his indictment was based on an act of Parliament that was against the laws of God and the Church; nonetheless, he was condemned to death. He was beheaded on July 6. His death and that of John Fisher

sent shock waves throughout Europe. Both were beatified in 1886 and canonized in 1935. They are among the
few English saints whose cult is worldwide. Along with
Fisher's, Thomas More's feast is on the General Roman
Calendar.

23 ETHELDREDA, ABBESS

Eltheldreda (d. 679), also Aethelthryth or Audrey, the
foundress and abbess of Ely, was one of the best-known
Saxon women saints. (The word "tawdry" is derived from
a corruption of "Audrey" and was applied to the cheap
necklaces and other items that were offered for sale at
her annual monastery fair.) Born probably at Exning in
Suffolk, she was the daughter of the king of East Anglia
and the sister of three saints. She was married twice, but
according to her biography she remained a virgin in both
marriages. She became a nun at Coldingham, where her
aunt was abbess, in 672, and then founded a double monastery (i.e., one for men and one for women) at Ely a year
later. She died of the plague in 679. Her feast is celebrated
by the Church of England on this day, but it is not on the
General Roman Calendar.

24 BIRTH OF JOHN THE BAPTIST

John the Baptist (first century) was the prophet who prepared the way for Jesus Christ and who baptized him in
the Jordan River. He is the patron saint of Jordan, the city
of Florence, monks, and highways. This celebration of
his birth is primarily concerned with the events recorded

in the first chapter of the Gospel of Luke (1:5–80). John was a cousin of Jesus, of priestly descent, and the son of Zechariah and Elizabeth [November 5].

Nothing more is known of John's life until the fifteenth year of Tiberius (28 CE) when, as Luke reports (3:1), he began his public ministry of preaching repentance and of baptizing in the Jordan. Matthew 3:7–10 and Luke 3:7–9 record John's diatribes against sinners, and all of the Gospels report John's proclamation of a stronger one to come after him (Matt. 3:11–12; Mark 1:7–8; Luke 3:15–18; John 1:24–28). His basic message about Jesus was that "He must increase, while I must decrease" (John 1:30). The Synoptics also report that John baptized Jesus. One finds in the Gospels a contrast between the ministries of John and Jesus. John insisted on ascetical practices (Matt. 3:4; Mark 1:6), while Jesus was more lenient (Mark 2:18; Matt. 11:16–19). Jesus, however, respected John (Matt. 11:11; Luke 7:28), applied Malachi 3:1 to him (Matt. 11:10; Luke 7:27), and identified him as Elijah (Matt. 11:14; Mark 9:11–13). John was executed by Herod Antipas, ruler of Galilee, who resented John's denunciation of his immoral behavior (Matt. 14:3–12; Mark 6:17–29; Luke 3:19–20). This feast, which is on the General Roman Calendar, is one of the oldest feasts of the Church.

25 PROSPER OF AQUITAINE, THEOLOGIAN

Prosper of Aquitaine (ca. 390–ca. 460) was an influential fifth-century theologian. Little is known of his life, however. Prosper Tiro was probably a layman from Provence in southwestern France, where he spent most of his adult life. He was an intellectual disciple of Augustine [August 28] and was in correspondence with him. The extracts he drew from Augustine's writings were used at the Council of Orange (529). Like Augustine, Prosper was thoroughly involved in the controversy provoked by Pelagianism, a heresy that held that salvation can be obtained by human effort alone, without the grace of God. Although heavily indebted to Augustine, Prosper softened Augustine's views on grace, free will, and predestination, insisting that grace was a free gift of God available to all because of divine mercy. Prosper served as secretary to Pope Leo the Great (440–61) and died in Rome sometime between 460 and 463. His feast is not on the General Roman Calendar.

26 JOHN AND PAUL, MARTYRS

John and *Paul* (d. before 410) were Roman martyrs of the fourth century. Although their cult is both early and well established, little is known of their lives. Their feast, however, is recorded both in the *Martyrology of Bede* [May 25] and in the Sarum liturgical calendar in wide use throughout England. The popularity of their biography, or Acts, however unreliable it may be, contributed to the spread of their cult. According to it, John and Paul were brothers and soldiers of the emperor Constantine who continued to serve him after their military service and until the time of his death. Constantine's successor, his nephew Julian the Apostate, was unsympathetic to their Christian ways. He is said to have commanded them to renounce their faith. When they refused, they were executed in their house on the Celian Hill, owned by the wealthy Roman Pammachius, a close friend of Jerome [September 30], and their bodies were buried in the garden. The feast of John and Paul is not on the General Roman Calendar.

27 CYRIL OF ALEXANDRIA, BISHOP AND DOCTOR OF THE CHURCH

Cyril of Alexandria (ca. 376–444) was one of the leading theologians of the fifth century, the patriarch of Alexandria, and a Doctor of the Church (1882). Born in Alexandria, he was the nephew of the patriarch of Alexandria, Theophilus, whom he succeeded in 412. Cyril's principal theological adversary was Nestorius, the patriarch of Constantinople, who held that there were two persons in Christ, one divine and one human, which were bound together by a merely moral union. For that reason, the Blessed Virgin Mary should not be called the Mother of God, but only the mother of Christ. The Council of Ephesus (431), over which Cyril presided, ruled against Nestorius. The result was a schism that produced a separate Nestorian Church, which did missionary work in China and India before being overwhelmed by the Mongol invasions of the fourteenth century.

The Council of Chalcedon (451) also appealed to Cyril's teachings. Perhaps too little attention has been paid to the rich spiritual dimension of Cyril's theology and too much to the more systematic and controversial aspects. The focal point of his spirituality was his doctrine of the image of God in the human person, wherein lies human dignity and happiness. Cyril's feast is on the General Roman Calendar.

28 IRENAEUS, BISHOP AND MARTYR

Irenaeus of Lyons (ca. 130–200) was one of the greatest bishops and theologians of the second century. Born in the East, Irenaeus studied at Rome and then was ordained a priest of Lyons, the principal diocese in Gaul. During a persecution of Christians, Irenaeus was sent to Rome with a letter for the pope, Eleutherius, urging leniency toward a heretical sect of Christians in Phrygia (in Asia Minor) for the sake of peace and unity. On his return ca. 178, he was chosen to succeed the bishop who had been killed during the persecution.

Irenaeus was also a significant theologian, whose work was not fully appreciated until the early twentieth century, when one of his principal works was discovered. He was a strong and effective opponent of Gnosticism, and he appealed to the principle of apostolic succession to show that saving revelation is available to everyone. He saw all of human history and Jewish history as an educational process by which the human race was schooled in divine revelation and formed in grace. Jesus Christ was the climax and personification of this whole process. Irenaeus died in Lyons in 200. He is usually venerated as a martyr, but there is no reliable evidence to support that belief. His feast is on the General Roman Calendar.

29 PETER AND PAUL, APOSTLES

Peter (d. ca. 64) was the first disciple chosen by Jesus and was the leader of the twelve apostles. A native of Bethsaida, near the Sea of Galilee, his original name was Simon. He was the son of Jonah (Matt. 16:17) and the brother of Andrew [November 30], who introduced him to Jesus. Peter and his brother were fishermen, like their father, working their father's trade possibly in a consortium with Zebedee and his sons. Peter was the first disciple whom Jesus chose, on which occasion he gave him a new name, Cephas, or Peter, which means "rock" (Matt. 16:18), and designated him a "fisher of men" (Mark 1:17; also Luke 5:10).

Peter enjoyed a special status and role within the company of Jesus' disciples, especially in Matthew's Gospel. On the other hand, Peter was not without human flaws and weaknesses. Just as Paul is remembered as the one who persecuted the Church before his own conversion on the road to Damascus, Peter is remembered for all time as the apostle who denied the Lord. John [December 27], "the beloved disciple," noted that Peter's insights were inferior to his own (John 20:6–9; 21:7). Jesus prayed for Peter that his faith might be strengthened (Luke 22:31–32).

Peter's role in the early Church is described in Acts. He functioned as the chief witness of Jesus (2:14–36). He defended the gospel before legal courts (4:7–12), and he himself functioned as a judge within the Christian community (5:1–10) and an arbiter of conflict (15:7–11). There is increasingly reliable evidence that Peter did travel to Rome and was martyred there. But not until the late second or early third century did the tradition identify Peter as the first Bishop of Rome. Clement of Rome [November 23] describes Peter's trial in Rome (*1 Clement* 5:4), and the historian Eusebius reports an ancient story about his crucifixion, upside down, just as he had requested (*Ecclesiastical History* 2.25.5, 8). Peter was invoked as a saint of the universal Church from very early times and is considered the patron saint of the Church and the papacy. His feast, along with that of Paul, is on the General Roman Calendar and is celebrated also on this day throughout the East, in the Anglican Communion, and by the Evangelical Lutheran Church in America.

Paul (ca. 1/5–ca. 62/67) was the most prominent early Christian missionary, known as the "apostle to the Gentiles." He is patron saint of Greece and Malta as well as the lay apostolate and the Cursillo movement. Born in Tarsus and raised as a Pharisee, he was originally named Saul. He had a conversion experience while on the way to Damascus (commemorated in the feast of the Conversion of Paul on January 25), was baptized and given the name Paul, and then became a Christian missionary to the Gentiles (see the entry for January 25).

Paul was first introduced to Peter by Barnabas [June 11] in Jerusalem (Acts 9:25–29; Gal. 1:18–19). He came into contact with Peter again at Antioch, where they had an intense argument (Gal. 2:11–21). Peter had preached the gospel to the Gentiles and at first enjoyed meals with his gentile converts in accordance with the decision reached by the council of Jerusalem (Acts 15:19). But after a group of conservative Jewish Christians came to Antioch from Jerusalem, Peter began to draw back and separate himself

(Gal. 2:12). Peter's example affected others as well. So Paul opposed him, saying, "If you, though a Jew, are living like a Gentile and not like a Jew, how can you compel the Gentiles to live like Jews?" (2:14).

Paul's movements following his three missionary journeys are uncertain, but he did end up in Rome, where he was detained and kept under house arrest for two years. Though he was eventually released, he was evidently arrested again because he was executed in Rome at Tre Fontane sometime in the 60s. He was buried on the present site of the basilica of St. Paul's Outside the Walls.

Peter and Paul, the two greatest missionaries of the early Church, are forever linked because of the tradition that they "founded" the church in Rome through their martyrdom there. The joint commemoration of the two saints in Rome is attested from the year 258. The two were liturgically rejoined in the reform of the General Roman Calendar in 1969.

30 FIRST MARTYRS OF THE CHURCH OF ROME

This feast commemorates those who were martyred during the persecution of Nero, who reigned 54–68. Peter and Paul also died during this persecution, and this feast follows immediately upon theirs on June 29. It was introduced in 1969 with the reform of the General Roman Calendar partly in compensation for the several Roman martyrs whose feasts are no longer on the universal calendar.

The Roman historian Tacitus reports that on July 19, 64, a great fire broke out in the city. By the time it was completely over, two-thirds of the city was in ruins. Nero announced that Christians had been responsible and ordered their arrest and execution. Some were crucified; some were covered with wax and set afire; and some were sewn into animal skins to be devoured by animals. The cruelty and horror of the spectacle appalled even those who had been hardened by previous imperial spectacles.

JULY

1   BLESSED JUNIPERO SERRA, PRIEST

Junipero Serra (1713–84) was a Spanish Franciscan priest who established the first mission in present-day California in 1769. Born in Majorca, Spain, he entered the Franciscans in 1730 and was ordained a priest in 1737. After teaching for a time, he went to New Spain (present-day Mexico and Texas) in 1749, where he did missionary work for the next twenty years. He expanded his ministry into upper California in 1769 and established nine of the twenty-one Franciscan missions along the Pacific coast, serving as their president until his death. He is credited with having baptized some six thousand converts.

His cause for canonization became the source of controversy between the Catholic Church and leaders of the Native American community, who objected to the Franciscan missionaries' treatment of those whom they sought to convert. Serra himself, however, defended the local people against abuse and exploitation and stressed their equality before God. He died at Monterey on August 28, 1784. His feast is on the Proper Calendar for the Dioceses of the United States, but is not on the General Roman Calendar.

2   BERNARDINO REALINO,
     FRANCIS REGIS, AND FRANCIS
     JEROME, PRIESTS

Bernardino Realino (1530–1616) was an Italian Jesuit who served as a parish priest in Lecce in Apulia for forty-two years. His work was that of an ordinary pastor: celebrating the Eucharist, preaching, hearing confessions, ministering to the sick, educating children in the faith, providing spiritual direction, and visiting prisoners. He was so highly respected and deeply beloved by the townspeople that the mayor came to him on his deathbed and made him promise that he would be Lecce's patron saint in heaven. Bernardino Realino was canonized in 1947.

Francis Regis (1597–1640), also John Francis Regis, was a French Jesuit who spent most of his priestly life as a missionary among those who had lapsed from the faith during the Wars of Religion between Calvinists (Huguenots) and Catholics. He visited prisons, collected food and clothing for the poor, and established homes for the rehabilitation of prostitutes. He was canonized 1737. He is patron saint of social workers and of marriage. *Francis Jerome* (1642–1716) was an Italian Jesuit who spent forty years of his priesthood in parish work in Naples, where he was an indefatigable preacher. He also had a special ministry to slaves and criminals as well as to the sick. He was canonized in 1839.

The feast of all three is celebrated on this day by the Jesuits, but is not on the General Roman Calendar.

3   THOMAS, APOSTLE

Thomas (first century), called Didymus, "the twin" (John 11:16; 20:24; 21:2), was one of the twelve apostles, best known for his doubts about the reports of Jesus' Resurrection (20:24–29). Thus, he is also known by the epithet "doubting Thomas." He was the first apostle to insist that he was ready to die with Jesus (11:16). At the Last Supper he admits that he does not know where Jesus is going, to which Jesus replies that he is the Way, the Truth, and the Life (14:4–6). Thomas's confession of faith, upon seeing the Risen Lord, is the only instance in the New Testament in which Jesus is explicitly addressed as God: "My Lord and my God" (20:24–29).

There is much uncertainty about Thomas's missionary activities after Pentecost. One tradition, supported by the historian Eusebius (d. ca. 339), indicates that he preached to the Parthians in what is now Iran. The strongest tradition links him with southern India and indicates that he founded the Church there after preaching in Syria and Persia. The Syrian Christians of Malabar, known as Thomas Christians, claim that they were evangelized by him and that he was killed by a spear and buried at Mylapore, near Madras. Indian Christians, however, insist that he is still buried in India at what they call San Tome, the place of his martyrdom, on which site was built the Cathedral of St. Thomas.

In the Syrian churches and in Malabar, July 3 was believed to be the date of Thomas's death, in the year 72. With the reform of the General Roman Calendar in 1969, the Catholic Church, along with the Church of England, celebrates his feast today, while the Greek and Russian Orthodox Churches celebrate it on October 6. He is patron saint of India, the East Indies, Pakistan, surveyors, construction workers, carpenters, and architects.

4 ELIZABETH OF PORTUGAL, QUEEN

Elizabeth of Portugal (1271–1336) was queen of Portugal by marriage to King Denis, or Diniz. Born in Zaragoza, Spain, the daughter of the king of Aragon, she was always known in her own country as Isabella. Her marriage was not a happy one, and she diverted her energies to prayer and the care of the sick, orphans, the poor, pilgrims, and prostitutes. After her husband's death in 1325, she became a Franciscan tertiary and lived in great simplicity. Toward the end of her life she prevented a war between Portugal and Castile, but the effort exhausted her and she died at Estramoz on July 4, 1336. She was canonized in 1625. Elizabeth is one of the patron saints of Portugal. Her feast is on the General Roman Calendar.

5 ANTHONY MARY ZACCARIA, PRIEST

Anthony Mary Zaccaria (1502–39) was the founder of the Barnabite order. Born at Cremona in northern Italy, he served as a doctor in his hometown until he decided to change from physical to spiritual healing. He was ordained a priest in 1528. Two years later, together with two Milanese noblemen, he founded an order of priests to regenerate the love of the liturgy and a Christian way of life by frequent preaching, with emphasis on the writings of St. Paul [June 29] and the faithful administration of the sacraments. The order, approved in 1533, adopted the name Clerks Regular of St. Paul and later added "the Beheaded" to the title.

At first the order encountered opposition from the local clergy because of the reforms it tried to introduce, but Rome stood behind it. Anthony himself organized conferences for the clergy, established associations for married people, preached in the open air, and ministered to the sick. In the last year of his life, Anthony began negotiations to make the church of St. Barnabas [June 11] in Milan the headquarters of his order. This is why its members became known popularly as Barnabites. Anthony died on July 5, 1539, at age thirty-seven. His feast is on the General Roman Calendar.

6   MARIA GORETTI,
      VIRGIN AND MARTYR

Maria Teresa Goretti (1890–1902) was killed by a rapist at the age of twelve. Born of a peasant family in Corinaldo, near Ancona, in Italy, she was left to take care of the house while her mother worked in the fields following her father's death. A young man in the neighborhood made sexual advances and, when she resisted an attempted rape, he stabbed her repeatedly. Maria died the next day, July 6, 1902, in the hospital at Nettuno, but not before voicing a word of forgiveness for her attacker. Her killer was sentenced to thirty years in prison. He later repented, expressed remorse for what he had done, and lived to see his victim beatified in 1947 and canonized in 1950 as a martyr for chastity. She became the patron saint of the Children of Mary and of teenage girls. Her feast is on the General Roman Calendar.

7 BLESSED BENEDICT XI, POPE

Benedict XI (1240–1304, pope 1303–4) was born Niccolò Boccasini in Treviso of an ordinary working-class family. He joined the Dominicans at seventeen. He was a lecturer in theology and preacher, a provincial in Lombardy, master general of the order, cardinal, and bishop of Ostia before becoming pope.

Benedict's pontificate was marked by a weak acquiescence to the demands of the king of France, Philip IV. A quiet, scholarly man, even as pope Benedict remained a friar at heart, following an austere spiritual regime and abating none of his humility and moderation. He revoked a bull by his predecessor, Boniface VIII, restricting the rights of Dominicans and Franciscans to preach and to hear confessions and made conciliatory gestures to ease the dispute between supporters and detractors of Boniface. The factional conflict that erupted, however, forced Benedict XI to leave Rome for Perugia in April 1304. The pope became ill with acute dysentery and died in Perugia on July 7, 1304. Benedict XI was beatified in 1736. His feast is not on the General Roman Calendar, but it is celebrated on this day by the Dominicans.

8 AQUILA AND PRISCA, MARTYRS

Aquila and *Prisca* (first century), also known as Priscilla, were husband and wife and disciples of Paul [June 29]. They had to leave Italy for a short time because of an imperial edict, rendered in the year 49 or 50, prohibiting Jews from living in Rome. Paul visited them in Corinth and discovered that Aquila was a tentmaker like himself, so he lodged with them and they worked together (Acts 18:1–3). When Paul left Corinth, Aquila and Prisca went with him, but stopped at Ephesus while he went on to Syria. In Ephesus they instructed Apollos, a Jew from Alexandria (18:18–19, 24–26). The *Roman Martyrology* states that they died in Asia Minor, but there is also a tradition that they were martyred in Rome, perhaps because of the existence of the church of St. Prisca on the Aventine Hill, known as "in the title of Aquila and Prisca." Their feast is not on the General Roman Calendar.

9 MARTYRS OF GORKUM; ROSE HAWTHORNE, NUN

This feast commemorates a group of nineteen martyrs put to death by Dutch Calvinists in a deserted monastery at Ruggen, in the Netherlands, in 1572. The group included eleven Franciscans, including their guardian *Nicholas Pieck,* two Norbertines, a Dominican, an Augustinian, and four diocesan priests. They had been arrested and imprisoned at Gorkum from June 26 to July 6, then taken by ship to Briel. When they refused an offer of freedom in return for denying Catholic teaching on the

Eucharist and the papacy, they were hanged at Ruggen, near Briel. The martyrs were canonized in 1867. Their feast is not on the General Roman Calendar.

This is also the day of death of *Rose Hawthorne* (1851–1926), who became a Dominican nun after the death of her husband, George Lathrop. She was the daughter of the American writer Nathaniel Hawthorne (1804–64) and the foundress of the Servants of Relief for Incurable Cancer. Her biography inspired Dorothy Day [November 29] to launch the Catholic Worker movement.

10 VERONICA GIULIANI, ABBESS

Veronica Giuliani (1660–1727) was a Franciscan nun who has been described as the most representative figure of Baroque mysticism. Born Orsola Giuliani in Urbino of a comfortable middle-class family, she became a Capuchin nun at Città di Castello in Umbria in 1677 against her father's wishes. She took the name Veronica and had a difficult novitiate because of the severity of her superiors. She is said to have had numerous mystical experiences in which she received the stigmata, including those of a crown of thorns on her head. She served as mistress of novices for thirty-four years and abbess for ten, leaving behind a ten-volume spiritual diary. Veronica died on July 9, 1727, and was canonized in 1839. Her feast is not on the General Roman Calendar, but it is celebrated by the Franciscans on this day.

11 BENEDICT OF NURSIA, ABBOT

Benedict of Nursia (ca. 480–ca. 550) is the founder of Western monasticism, the author of the famous Rule that bears his name, and a patron saint of Europe (declared as such by Pope Paul VI in 1964). Little is known about his life, apart from Gregory the Great's [September 3] *Dialogues*. Born at Nursia in central Italy, he studied for a time in Rome, but was so distressed by the immorality of society that he left the city ca. 500 to become a hermit at Subiaco. Disciples later joined him, and he organized them into twelve deaneries of ten monks each. He stayed at Subiaco for about twenty-five years and then moved with a small group of his monks to Monte Cassino, near Naples. It was there that he wrote the final version of his Rule.

Benedict's Rule emphasized authority and obedience, and stability and community life. The monks' primary occupation was the praying of the Divine Office in common, complemented by the reading of sacred texts and manual work of various kinds. Benedict insisted that an abbot should be elected by all of the monks and that he should be wise, discreet, flexible, learned in the law of God, and a spiritual father to his community—just as he himself was. The flexibility of his Rule allowed it to be adapted readily to the needs of society, so that monasteries shaped by it became centers of scholarship, agriculture, medicine, and hospitality. Benedict died at Monte Cassino ca. 550. His feast is on the General Roman Calendar.

12 JOHN GUALBERT, ABBOT

John Gualbert (ca. 995–1073) was the founder of the Vallombrosian monks. Born Giovanni Gualberto in Florence of a noble family, he spared the life of his brother's murderer and soon after entered the Benedictine monastery of San Miniato. He left four years later to seek a more austere way of life untouched by contemporary abuses in the Church, namely, clerical concubinage, nepotism, and simony. Gaulbert decided to establish his own monastery and chose Vallombrosa, a site about twenty miles east of Florence. As his community grew, he adopted a modified form of the primitive Rule of St. Benedict [July 11], laying greater stress on silence, poverty, and strict enclosure. He died on July 12, 1073, and was canonized in 1193. His feast is not on the General Roman Calendar.

13 HENRY II, KING

Henry II (973–1024) was a Holy Roman emperor and benefactor of the Church. The son of the duke of Bavaria, whom he succeeded in 995, he was educated by Wolfgang, the saintly bishop of Regensberg, and in 1002 succeeded his cousin, Otto III, as emperor of the Holy Roman Empire. He repaired and endowed the dioceses of Hildesheim, Magdeburg, Strassburg, and Merseburg and in 1006 founded the diocese of Bamberg, building a cathedral and monastery there. He was also a supporter of the Cluniac reform of monasticism, centered at the abbey of Gorze, and of the papacy's claim over the Papal

States in Italy. He died on July 13, 1024, and was canonized in 1146 (others put the date at 1152). His feast (formerly celebrated on July 15) is on the General Roman Calendar. His wife, Cunegund, was canonized in 1200.

14 CAMILLUS DE LELLIS, PRIEST; BLESSED KATERI TEKAKWITHA, VIRGIN

Camillus de Lellis (1550–1614) was the founder of the Order of Camillians and is co–patron saint (with John of God [March 8]) of hospitals, nurses, nurses associations, and the sick. Born at Bucchioanico, Italy, at seventeen he fought with the Venetian army against the Turks. He contracted an incurable disease of the leg and in 1574–75 lost all of his money through gambling. He had a religious conversion and tried to enter the Franciscans, but was denied because of his health. Instead, he became a member of the staff of the hospital of San Giacomo in Rome, where he himself had previously been a patient. He began by caring for the incurably sick, but was so appalled by the state of medical care at San Giacomo that, with the support of his spiritual director, Philip Neri [May 26], he left and established his own hospital. He was ordained a priest in 1584 and drew up a simple Rule committing himself and his helpers to the service of plague victims, the sick in hospitals and homes, and prisoners.

In 1591 the order was approved. After opening a new house in Naples, Camillus and twenty-five others made their solemn profession, adding to the vows of poverty, chastity, and obedience a fourth vow of "perpetual physical and spiritual assistance to the sick, especially those with the plague." Their habit was black, with a large red cross on the breast and on their capes. In 1595 and again in 1601 some members of the congregation served the wounded on battlefields in Hungary and Croatia—the first recorded examples of medical field units. Camillus died in Rome on July 14, 1614, and was canonized in 1746. His feast is on the General Roman Calendar.

Kateri Tekakwitha (1656–80), also known as the "Lily of the Mohawks," is the first Native American to have been beatified. Born Tekakwitha (Kateri, or Catherine, was her Christian name), the daughter of a Christian Algonquin and a pagan Mohawk chief, in present-day Auriesville, New York, she was orphaned at age four. A bout of smallpox left her disfigured and partially blind. She made a vow early in life not to marry, which ran counter to the culture of her people and created great personal difficulty for her. She met a missionary, Father Jacques de Lamberville, a Jesuit, who baptized her on Easter Sunday, 1676. Finding life in her village stressful, she walked two hundred miles to settle in a Christian mission in Sault St. Louis, near Montreal, where she made her First Holy Communion in October 1677. For the next three years she led a devout Catholic life, attending Mass twice a day, fasting on Wednesdays and Saturdays, teaching children, and caring for the sick and the aged. She died on April 17, 1680, and was beatified in 1980. Her feast is on the Proper Calendar for the Dioceses of the United States, but not on the General Roman Calendar.

15   BONAVENTURE, BISHOP AND DOCTOR OF THE CHURCH

Bonaventure (1221–74), known as the Seraphic Doctor, was one of the greatest theologians in the history of the Church. A Franciscan, he is sometimes referred to as the second founder of the order. Born Giovanni di Fidanza of a noble family near Orvieto, he became a Franciscan in 1243 and took the name Bonaventure. His intellectual gifts were quickly recognized, and he was sent to Paris to study under another celebrated Franciscan theologian, Alexander of Hales. In 1253 Bonaventure became master of the Franciscan school in Paris. As a theologian he was more Augustinian than Aristotelian, emphasizing an affective over a rational approach. For Bonaventure, the purpose of human knowledge, including theology, is not to speculate, but to love.

In 1257, at age thirty-six, he was elected minister general of the Franciscan order. Although Bonaventure strongly defended Franciscan ideals, he differed with Francis himself on the need for study and, therefore, on the need for possessing books and buildings. He confirmed the existing practice of Franciscans teaching in universities and also their work of preaching and spiritual direction. Nevertheless, Bonaventure lived a life of austere simplicity. Reluctantly accepting a bishopric, he took a leading part in the Second Council of Lyons (1274) and died in Lyons on July 15, 1274. He was canonized in 1482 and declared a Doctor of the Church in 1588. His feast is on the General Roman Calendar, and he is com-

memorated on the liturgical calendar of the Church of
England.

16 OUR LADY OF MOUNT CARMEL

July 16 is one of several feast days on the General Roman
Calendar in honor of the *Blessed Virgin Mary*. Mount
Carmel, about three miles south of Haifa in present-day
Israel, is the place traditionally associated with the begin-
nings of the Carmelite order ca. 1200, when a group of
lay hermits formed a community on its western slope.
Between 1206 and 1214 they received a "formula of life"
from the patriarch of Jerusalem commending daily Eucharist, continual prayer (especially the psalms) with
silence otherwise, manual labor, and other traditional
forms of eremitical asceticism. From the very beginning
the Carmelites identified themselves with the Blessed
Virgin Mary. In time, the feast of Our Lady of Mount
Carmel, celebrated on this day, became the patronal feast
of the order.

17 HEDWIG OF POLAND, QUEEN

Hedwig (1374–99), or Jadwiga, was queen of Poland. The
daughter of Louis Angevin, the king of Hungary and
Poland, she was only ten when crowned. At age twelve
she married Jagiello, the grand duke of Lithuania and
Ruthenia. Jagiello kept his marriage promise to assist in
the evangelization of Lithuania. A diocese was established
in the capital, Vilnius, and both Jagiello and Hedwig sent

chalices, holy pictures, and vestments for the new cathedral and other churches. She endowed a college in Prague for the education of Lithuanian priests and worked for the reunion of Latin and Orthodox Christians, importing monks from Prague, who used the Slavonic rite to help build bridges between the two churches. In June 1399 a daughter was born prematurely, but died three weeks later. Hedwig herself died four days after that, on July 17. In later years, as Poland was partitioned, she became a symbol of Polish nationalism. She was not beatified until 1986 and then canonized in Kraków in 1997 by John Paul II, the first Polish pope. Her feast is not on the General Roman Calendar.

18 PAMBO, HERMIT

Pambo (ca. 303–ca. 390), or Pamo, was an Egyptian hermit who was a disciple of Anthony [January 17] and who was held in high regard by Athanasius [May 2], not only because of the quality of his life, but also for his vigorous defense of the teachings of the Council of Nicaea (325). Pambo was ordained ca. 340. He led a life typical of contemporary desert monks: hard manual labor, long fasts, physical penance, and sustained periods of prayer. He looked upon the capacity for silence as a basic first step toward a deeper spirituality. The constant theme in his teaching was: "Guard your conscience toward your neighbor, and you will be saved." His feast is not on the General Roman Calendar, but he is one of the saints commemorated on this day by the Russian Orthodox Church.

19 MACRINA THE YOUNGER, VIRGIN

Macrina the Younger (ca. 327–79) was the older sister of
Basil [January 2] and Gregory of Nyssa [January 10]. Born
in Caesarea in Cappadocia, the oldest of ten children, she
was betrothed to be married at age twelve, but after her
intended spouse died, she vowed never to marry and remained at home to assist in the education of her brothers and sisters. When Basil returned from his studies in
Athens, Macrina took him aside and persuaded him
eventually to renounce his property and prospects and
become a monk. Basil later provided an estate for his
mother and sister in Pontus, where they lived a communal life with other women who came to join them. The
mother died ca. 373 and Macrina gave away all of their
possessions, living thereafter on the fruits of her own
labor. Macrina died nine months after Basil in 379. Her
feast is not on the General Roman Calendar, but she
is one of the saints commemorated on this day by the
Russian Orthodox Church.

20 FRUMENTIUS, BISHOP; BARTOLOMÉ
   DE LAS CASAS, MISSIONARY

Frumentius (ca. 300–ca. 380) is regarded as the "apostle of
the Ethiopians" (sometimes "the Abyssinians"). He was
called "Abuna" ("Our Father"), a title still given to the
primate of Ethiopia. Born in Tyre, Palestine, Frumentius
and another young man, Aedesius, accompanied a merchant on a voyage to Arabia. On their return, in a port
on the Ethiopian coast, the ship's crew and most of the

passengers were killed. Frumentius and Aedesius were taken to the king's court, where they were given minor roles of service. When they king died, they were given their freedom, but they decided to remain at the request of the queen regent. Frumentius seems to have begun using his influence to promote the growth of Christianity in the country. When the new king came of age, Frumentius returned to Alexandria, where the bishop, impressed by his work, made him bishop of Axum, the capital of a kingdom in northern Ethiopia, and sent him back to continue preaching the gospel. Frumentius came to be known in Ethiopia as Bishop Salama ("Bishop of Peace"). Frumentius's feast is not on the General Roman Calendar.

On this day, the Church of England commemorates *Bartolomé de Las Casas* (1474–1566), a Dominican missionary to the Americas known as "apostle to the Indies." He has never been beatified by the Catholic Church, much less canonized. He was the son of a landowner in present-day Dominican Republic, became critical of the Spaniards' treatment of the indigenous people, joined the Dominicans, and became one of the most vigorous advocates on behalf of those abused by Spain.

21 LAWRENCE OF BRINDISI, PRIEST AND DOCTOR OF THE CHURCH

Lawrence of Brindisi (1559–1619) was an Italian Franciscan and is a Doctor of the Church. Born Giulio Cesare Russo in Brindisi, in the kingdom of Naples, of a well-to-do family, he became a Capuchin friar in Verona at age sixteen, taking the name Lawrence. After ordination in 1582 he became a highly respected preacher in Padua, Verona, and other northern Italian towns. He was elected provincial of Tuscany and then of Venice. In 1596 he was called to Rome to serve as definitor general of the Franciscan order, with special responsibility for the conversion of the Jews. After his term in Rome he established, along with other friars, Capuchin houses in Vienna, Prague, and Graz and spent considerable time and energy caring for plague victims. In 1601 he actually led a German imperial army into battle against the Turks, armed only with a crucifix. The following year he was elected minister general of the order, now some nine thousand strong in Italy, France, Belgium, Switzerland, and Spain. His writings consist mainly of sermons, but also include a commentary and works against Lutheranism. He died in Lisbon, on July 22, 1619. His feast is on the General Roman Calendar.

22 MARY MAGDALENE, DISCIPLE

Mary Magdalene (first century) was a witness of the Resurrection and is patron saint of repentant sinners, hairdressers, and the contemplative life. Known also as Mary of Magdala, she was, according to Luke 8:2, healed of seven demons by Jesus. She was also among the women who accompanied and supported Jesus and the twelve apostles and was present at the Crucifixion and burial (Matt. 27:56; Mark 15:40; John 19:25). In Matthew, John, and the appendix to Mark's Gospel, she, not Peter, is the primary

witness to the Resurrection. Peter is the primary witness in the tradition of Paul and Luke (1 Cor. 15:5; Luke
24:34). These facts underscore the complementary roles
of women, Peter, and the other disciples as witnesses to
the Risen Christ. Later traditions erroneously equated
Mary with both the sinful woman of Luke 7:36–50, who
anointed Jesus, and Mary of Bethany, who also anointed
Jesus (John 11:1–12:8; Luke 10:38–42). Contrary to the popular novel *The DaVinci Code* (2003), there is no biblical or
historical evidence that she was married to Jesus and bore
him a child, although she was indeed one of his closest
disciples. Her feast is on the General Roman Calendar.

23 BRIDGET OF SWEDEN, RELIGIOUS

Bridget of Sweden (1303–73), or Birgitta, was the founder of
the Brigittine order (Order of the Most Holy Savior) and
is the patron saint of Sweden and of nuns. In 1999 Pope
John Paul II named her a co–patron saint of all of Europe along with Catherine of Siena [April 29] and Teresa
Benedicta of the Cross (Edith Stein) [August 9]. The
daughter of a wealthy governor of Uppland, Bridget
married at age fourteen and bore eight children, one of
whom was Catherine of Sweden [March 24]. She entered
the Cistercian monastery at Alvastra after her husband's
death in 1343. Three years later she founded a double monastery at Vadstena for sixty nuns and twenty-five men,
who lived in separate enclosures but shared the same
church for worship. In 1349 Bridget went to Rome to obtain approval for her new order and to receive the Jubi-

lee indulgence of 1350. Her daughter Catherine followed her the next year. The city was unsafe, and Catherine unsuccessfully implored her mother to return to Sweden. Instead, Bridget spent the rest of her life in Italy or on various pilgrimages, including one to the Holy Land. She died in Rome on July 23, 1373, and was canonized in 1391. Bridget's feast is on the General Roman Calendar.

24 DECLAN, BISHOP; THOMAS À KEMPIS, PRIEST

Declan (early fifth century), an Irish bishop in the Waterford area, was one of four bishops ministering in Ireland before the arrival of Patrick [March 17]. According to his biography, Declan was born of noble blood near Lismore. He was consecrated bishop and founded the church of Ardmore, where there are remains of a monastery and a hermitage as well as a holy well, where cures have been reported. In his old age, Declan retired to a hermit's cell, but returned to the main settlement at Ardmore to die. His feast is not on the General Roman Calendar.

The Episcopal Church in the United States commemorates *Thomas à Kempis* (ca. 1380–1471), a priest who authored the classic *The Imitation of Christ,* which has been translated into more languages than any other book apart from the Bible. It stresses personal piety over learning and the inner life over active service in the world. He has been neither beatified nor canonized.

25 JAMES (THE GREAT), APOSTLE; CHRISTOPHER, MARTYR

James the Great (or the Greater; first century), the son of Zebedee and the older brother of John [December 27], was one of the twelve apostles and one of the three closest disciples of Jesus, along with Peter [June 29] and John. He may also have been the cousin of Jesus through his mother, who, in turn, may have been the sister of the Blessed Virgin Mary (cf. Matt. 27:56; Mark 15:40; John 19:25). He is called "the Great" (or "Greater") to distinguish him from a younger apostle of the same name [May 3]. Born in Galilee, James was, like his father and brother, a fisherman whom Jesus called among his first disciples (Matt. 4:21; Mark 1:19; Luke 5:10). The list of apostles in Mark 3:17 indicates that Jesus gave James and John the nicknames "sons of thunder," perhaps because of their zeal or perhaps because of their temperament. On one occasion, when a Samaritan village refused to welcome Jesus, they urged Jesus to call down fire from heaven to destroy it (Luke 9:51–56).

We do not know if James left Jerusalem after Pentecost to preach the gospel elsewhere, but an early tradition says that none of the apostles left the city until after James's death. James was beheaded during the persecution of Herod Agrippa I between the years 42 and 44 (Acts 12:1–3) and was buried in Jerusalem. He was the first of the Twelve to be martyred. James's feast is on the General Roman Calendar and is also observed by the Church of England, the Episcopal Church in the USA, and the Evangelical Lutheran Church in America. The Greek and Russian Orthodox Churches celebrate his feast on April 30.

Christopher was a third-century martyr who is best known as the patron saint of motorists. His name, from the Greek, means "Christ-bearer." He was put to death in Lycia during the persecution of Decius (249–51). In the Fourteen Holy Helpers, a group of saints known for their assistance to people in need, Christopher's specialty was the care of travelers and protection against sudden death. There were many legends about him. In one, a child asked Christopher to carry him across a river on his shoulders. When Christopher admitted that he was too heavy to carry, the child revealed that he was Jesus and that he carried the weight of the whole world. His feast was removed from the universal calendar of the Catholic Church in 1969, but it may still be observed locally.

26 JOACHIM AND ANNE, PARENTS OF MARY

Neither *Joachim* nor *Anne* (first century) is even mentioned in the New Testament. The belief that they were the father and mother of the Blessed Virgin Mary is based on the *Gospel of James* (also known as the *Protevangelium of James*), an unreliable second-century apocryphal document that became popular in the Middle Ages. Joachim and Anne are portrayed as old and childless. He retired to the desert to fast and pray. Still at home, Anne also bewailed her fate. Suddenly she was visited by an angel who told that she would conceive and bear a child and that the child would become famous throughout the world. Joachim also received the same message in the desert.

The feast of Anne and Joachim was first observed in the East toward the end of the sixth century, but it was not until the mid-fourteenth century that it was generally kept in the West. Anne's cult is especially strong in Canada. She is the country's patron saint, along with Joseph [March 19]. The feast of Joachim and Anne is on the General Roman Calendar.

27 PANTALEON, MARTYR

Pantaleon (d. ca. 305), or Panteleimon, a name that means "the all-compassionate," was venerated in the West as one of the Fourteen Holy Helpers and in the East as the "Great Martyr and Wonder-worker." He is a patron saint of physicians, second only to Luke [October 18]. Born in Nicomedia of a pagan father and Christian mother, he studied medicine and was appointed physician to the emperor Galerius, in whose court he abandoned his faith. He was later reconverted by another Christian. Unfortunately, his life is clouded by legends of miraculous cures, the raising of a dead child to life, and various feats of strength. After his reconversion he was condemned to death during the persecution of Diocletian and, after many tortures, was beheaded. Alleged relics of his blood exist in Constantinople, Madrid, and Ravello. Those at Ravello are said to liquefy on his feast day in a manner similar to the blood of Januarius [September 19] in Naples. His feast is not on the General Roman Calendar.

28 PROCHORUS, NICANOR, TIMON, AND PARMENAS, DEACONS

Prochorus, Nicanor, Timon, and *Parmenas* were four of the seven men listed in Acts (6:1–6) as the Church's first deacons. The work of two of the Seven, namely, Stephen (6:8–8:2) [December 26] and Philip (8:5–40; 21:8), makes it clear that the Seven did not limit themselves to serving at table, but functioned for the Hellenistic Christians in the way that the Twelve did for the Jewish Christians. Prochorus is said to have become bishop of Nicomedia and been martyred at Antioch. Tradition says that Nicanor went to Cyprus, where he was martyred under Vespasian (69–79). Timon is thought to have become bishop of Bostra in Arabia and eventually been martyred by fire in Basrah. Parmenas is said to have preached for years in Asia Minor and become bishop of Soli on Cyprus before being martyred at Philippi ca. 98 under Trajan. Their feast is not on the General Roman Calendar, but is observed by the Greek and Russian Orthodox churches.

29 MARTHA, DISCIPLE

Martha (first century) is the sister of Lazarus [December 17], who was raised from the dead by Jesus, and of Mary, with whom Jesus compared her. Martha is mentioned in three biblical situations. In the first, Jesus visits her home in Bethany. Martha busies herself with household chores, while Mary sits at Jesus' feet listening to his words. When Martha asks Jesus to encourage Mary to help her in the kitchen, he replies that Mary "has chosen the better part" (Luke 10:38–42). The second occasion is the raising of her brother Lazarus from the dead (John 11:1–44). Again, it is Martha who takes the active role, going out to meet Jesus while Mary remains at home. Jesus assures Martha that her brother will rise again, saying, "I am the resurrection and the life . . . everyone who believes in me will never die," whereupon Martha confesses him as the Messiah. The third situation is just before the Passion, when Martha, Mary, and Lazarus entertain Jesus at dinner in Bethany (John 12:1–8). Martha "served," while Mary anointed his feet. Martha, however, is not mentioned after the Resurrection, and there is no indication of when or where she died. Her feast is on the General Roman Calendar.

30 PETER CHRYSOLOGUS, BISHOP AND DOCTOR OF THE CHURCH

Peter Chrysologus (ca. 380–ca. 450) was archbishop of Ravenna. Born in Imola in northeastern Italy, he was a deacon there before the emperor Valentinian III appointed him archbishop of Ravenna, the capital of the Western empire, sometime between 425 and 430. The title "Chrysologus" (Gk., "Golden-worded") may have been given him in the ninth century or later, so that the Western Church would have a preacher of equal status to the East's John Chrysostom (Gk., "Golden-tongued") [September 13.] A large number of his sermons survive and are suggestive of careful preparation, warmth, and zeal. Unlike many of his contemporary bishops, he eschewed polemical tirades against pagans and Jews. The sermons are also valuable for the picture they give of Christian life in fifth-century Ravenna. He died on December 3 (others say July 31), ca. 450, and was declared a Doctor of the Church in 1729. His feast is on the General Roman Calendar.

31 IGNATIUS OF LOYOLA, PRIEST

Ignatius of Loyola (1491–1556) was the founder of the Society of Jesus, better known as the Jesuits. Born Iñigo López de Loyola, the youngest of eleven children, in the ancestral castle in the Basque province of Guipúzcoa, he left home in 1506 to become a page in the household of a distinguished noble. His early life was marked by gambling, womanizing, and fighting, but it changed suddenly after Ignatius went to Pamplona and, in the army of the local duke, was severely wounded in a siege of the city. He went to Confession and promised that, if he lived, he would devote his life as a knight to the Apostle Peter [June 29]. During extended recuperation Ignatius read about the lives of the saints and is said to have had a vision of Our Lady that filled him with intense joy.

As soon as he was well enough, he set out for Barcelona to board a ship to Jerusalem as a humble pilgrim, but after stopping at a monastery in Montserrat, he decided instead to live as a hermit at nearby Manresa, where he developed his *Spiritual Exercises,* one of the classics of Western spirituality, based on his own experiences and noted for its practical orientation. The *Exercises* lay out a program (usually for thirty days, in solitude) of examination of conscience, contemplation, meditation based on vivid representations of biblical events, and discernment of God's will in one's life.

Ignatius felt drawn to the monastic life, but decided that his vocation was to the active apostolate. After a short pilgrimage to Jerusalem, he returned to Spain, where he studied Latin, theology, and the humanities at the university in Alcalá and continued to give spiritual direction. He and a mixed group of disciples were forbidden by the local Inquisition to wear clerical dress or hold meetings. So Ignatius moved to Paris in 1528, where he studied philosophy and was joined by other followers who were to become the core of his group, or company, including the great missionary-to-be Francis Xavier [December 3]. They took vows of poverty and chastity and also one to go to Jerusalem to convert the Muslims or, failing that, to place themselves at the service of the pope. Their plans to travel to Jerusalem were postponed because of the outbreak of war between the Turkish empire and Venice.

Ignatius and two companions went to Rome toward the end of 1537, where the three heard confessions, preached, and taught catechism to children. Ignatius drew up an initial constitution, or "formula," for his company in 1539. The apostolate was to focus on preaching, hearing confessions, teaching, and caring for the sick, but it involved none of the traditional elements of a religious order, such as praying the Divine Office in common or other prescribed prayers and penances. The element of direct obedience to the pope was also a novel feature. Papal approval was granted a year later (1540) and the company was given the name "Society of Jesus." Ignatius was elected superior in 1541.

Ignatius spent the rest of his life in Rome, administering the Society and caring for the poor, the sick, orphans, and prostitutes. He was convinced of the need for an educated clergy and of the importance of an educated laity as well. The first of many colleges and universities founded by the Jesuits were opened in Padua in 1542, Bologna in 1546, and Messina in 1548. The first college in Rome opened in 1551 and, when it added courses in theology and philosophy leading to ordination, became the beginning of the famous Gregorian University. Ignatius died suddenly on July 31, 1556, and was canonized in 1622. His feast is on the General Roman Calendar.

AUGUST

1   ALPHONSUS LIGUORI, BISHOP AND DOCTOR OF THE CHURCH

Alphonsus Liguori (1696–1787) was the founder of the Redemptorists (Congregation of the Most Holy Redeemer) and one of the greatest moral theologians in the history of the Church. Born Alfonso Maria de'Liguori, the son of a Neapolitan noble, he practiced law successfully until, after losing an important case through his own fault and seeing it as a sign of God's will, he decided to enter the priesthood. Ordained in 1726, he soon established a reputation as an effective preacher and understanding confessor. In 1732 Alphonsus founded the Congregation of the Most Holy Redeemer for priests dedicated to preaching the gospel, especially to the rural poor in the kingdom of Naples. Because of internal divisions about authority, however, the new order did not flourish until after his death. Alphonsus continued to preach and hear confessions with great success throughout the kingdom, especially in villages and hamlets, until 1752 when his health failed. He was especially gentle with the scrupulous (i.e., those with an unhealthy sense of anxiety and guilt), because he himself suffered from scrupulosity.

In 1745 he published the first of his thirty-six theological and devotional works, the most important of which was his *Moral Theology*. In 1762 Alphonsus was consecrated bishop of Sant'Agatha dei Goti (between Benevento and Capua), a diocese of some thirty thousand people. He organized parish missions and urged his priests to be simple in the pulpit and compassionate in the confessional. During the famine of 1763 he sold everything he had to buy food for the starving. Alphonsus died in 1787. He was canonized in 1839, declared a Doctor of the Church in 1871, and made patron saint of confessors and moral theologians in 1950. His feast is on the General Roman Calendar.

2   EUSEBIUS OF VERCELLI, BISHOP

Eusebius of Vercelli (d. 371) was a fourth-century bishop noted for his strong opposition to Arianism. He is thought to have contributed to the formulation of the Athanasian Creed. Born on the island of Sardinia, where his father was said to have died in chains as a Christian martyr, he was taken to Rome as an infant by his mother. He was ordained a lector and served in that capacity at Vercelli, in Piedmont, where he so impressed the local clergy and laity that he was chosen their bishop ca. 344.

In 355 a council was held in Milan to seek an end to the division between Arians and Catholics faithful to the teaching of the Council of Nicaea (325). When the bishops were asked to sign a condemnation of Athanasius [May 2], the foremost exponent of Nicene orthodoxy, Eusebius refused, placed the Nicene Creed on the table, and insisted that all the bishops sign that before even considering the case against Athanasius. The emperor sent for Eusebius and two other bishops and ordered them to condemn Athanasius. He threatened them with death but, upon their refusal, sent them into exile instead. When Constantius died in 361, the new emperor, Julian, allowed the exiled bishops to return to their sees. Eusebius continued his efforts throughout the East to heal the Arian conflict, to assure the wavering, and to reconvert those who had gone over to the Arian side. Little is known of his final years, except that he died, probably at Vercelli, on August 1, 371. His feast is on the General Roman Calendar.

3   LYDIA, DISCIPLE

Lydia (first century) was a devout Jew from Thyatira (in present-day western Turkey) who was converted by Paul [June 29] in the city of Philippi and the first one he baptized there (Acts 16:11–15). She was also his first "European" convert. She was the founding member of the Christian community that met in her house (16:40), having previously invited Paul and his companions, although complete strangers, to come and stay there (16:15). This fact underscores the important point that women, especially those who owned their own homes, exercised a leadership role in the early Church. Lydia was not formally canonized by the Eastern Church in Constantinople until 1982. Her feast is not on the General Roman Calendar.

4   JOHN VIANNEY, PRIEST

John Vianney (1786–1859), better known as the Curé d'Ars, is the patron saint of parish priests. Born near Lyons, he spent his early years as a shepherd boy on his father's farm. It was during the French Revolution that he began to study for the priesthood, at age twenty. Just as his popular image portrays, he was not a good student and had particular difficulty with Latin, in which all courses were taught. He was dismissed from the seminary and had to be privately tutored, but because of Vianney's evident piety and goodness he was approved for ordination in 1815.

In 1817, he was appointed parish priest of Ars-en-Dombes, a remote village with a population of fewer than 250. He would remain there for the rest of his life, refusing all ecclesiastical promotions and honors. His sermons were often about hell and the Last Judgment, and he railed publicly against dancing and other forms of amusement. Nevertheless, he was perceived as a compassionate priest and came to be revered as a confessor and spiritual counselor. Visitors came—about 300 a day between 1830 and 1845—as his reputation for miracle working spread, including the report that he had multiplied loaves of bread to supply food for an orphanage he had founded. John Vianney died on August 4, 1859, at age seventy-three. He was canonized in 1925. His feast is on the General Roman Calendar.

5   DEDICATION OF ST. MARY MAJOR

Today's feast on the General Roman Calendar celebrates the dedication of the basilica of *St. Mary Major,* known in Italian as Santa Maria Maggiore, one of Rome's four major basilicas (along with St. Peter's, St. John Lateran, and St. Paul's Outside the Walls). Founded in the fourth century by Pope Liberius on the Esquiline Hill, the present church was built by Pope Sixtus III in the fifth century. Relics of the manger in Bethlehem are reputed to be held there. The basilica was formerly called Our Lady of the Snows because, according to legend, the pope built it on a site where the Blessed Virgin Mary left her footprints in an August snowfall.

6   TRANSFIGURATION

The *Transfiguration* refers to the appearance of Jesus to his disciples in glorified form (Matt. 17:1–9; Mark 9:2–10; Luke 9:28–36). Jesus took Peter [June 29], James [July 25], and John [December 27] with him onto a mountain. (Tradition locates it on Mt. Tabor, but many scholars prefer Mt. Hermon.) He appeared there before them in a luminous form with Moses and Elijah at his side. Peter proposed that they build three tabernacles, or tents. A heavenly voice declared Jesus to be the "beloved son" and enjoined the disciples to heed him. Jesus then appeared in his usual form and commanded his disciples to keep silence.

Some view the episode as a misplaced account of a resurrection appearance. Others view it as a mystical experience that Jesus' disciples had in his presence. Whatever its origin, the episode of the Transfiguration serves at the very least as a literary device to place Jesus on the same level as the Law (represented by Moses) and the Prophets (represented by Elijah) and as a foreshadowing of his future glory. He is the authentic source of divine truth for those who would listen to him. The feast is on the General Roman Calendar and is also celebrated by the Russian and Greek Orthodox Churches, the Church of England, and the Episcopal Church in the United States.

7   SIXTUS II, POPE, AND COMPANIONS, MARTYRS

Sixtus II (d. 258, pope 257–258) is one of the Church's most highly venerated martyrs. His companions in martyrdom were seven Roman deacons: *Agapitus, Felicissimus, Januarius, Vincent, Magnus, Stephen,* and *Lawrence* [August 10]. More correctly known as Xystus, Sixtus was elected Bishop of Rome just as the emperor Valerian abandoned his policy of toleration toward Christians, first ordering them to participate in state-sponsored religious ceremonies and forbidding them from gathering in cemeteries and then ordering the execution of bishops, priests, and deacons and imposing assorted penalties on laypersons. On August 6, 258, while the pope was seated in his episcopal chair addressing the congregation at a liturgical service in the private (and presumably safe) cemetery of Praetextatus, imperial forces rushed in and seized and beheaded the pope and four deacons. Two other deacons were executed later the same day, and the seventh, Lawrence, was put to death four days after that.

Before his death, however, Sixtus had successfully devoted his energies to healing the breach between Rome and the churches of North Africa and Asia Minor created by the issue of the rebaptism of heretics and schismatics who wished to enter or be reconciled to the Church and, in particular, by the intransigent approach taken by his predecessor, Stephen I. Since there is strong evidence that Sixtus II was martyred on August 6, his feast was originally celebrated on that day. It was moved to August 7 in the 1969 revision of the General Roman Calendar.

8   DOMINIC, PRIEST

Dominic (ca. 1170–1221) was the founder of the Order of Preachers, or Black Friars, better known as the Dominicans. Born Dominic de Guzmán in Old Castile, Spain, he was at first educated by a priest-uncle, then studied theology at the cathedral school of Palencia. During a famine there, he sold his books and furniture to raise money for the poor. Because of this gesture, Diego de Azevedo, the prior of the reformed cathedral chapter of Osma, persuaded Dominic to join his group, which lived a common life under the Rule of St. Augustine [August 28]. Dominic became a canon of Osma ca. 1196 and later succeeded Diego when he was appointed bishop of Osma. Diego and Dominic conducted a preaching mission among Albigensian heretics in the area of Toulouse, in southern France. The Albigensians, also known as Cathari, regarded matter as evil and believed that perfection required a restrained diet and abstinence from sexual intimacy. Diego and Dominic remained among them, adopting an austere lifestyle and traveling bare-foot as they preached from place to place. Diego died on December 30, 1207, leaving Dominic now completely in charge of preaching.

Dominic's familiarity with the Cathar way of life may have influenced his conception of the religious order he would later found. In late 1214 or early 1215 the new papal legate appointed him head of the preaching mission centered at Toulouse, where the local bishop wished to establish a permanent institute of preachers for his diocese. The first Dominican community began its common life under vows at Toulouse in 1216. Bertrand de Garrigues [September 6] was chosen as superior, and Dominic remained in charge of preaching. Dominican houses were founded in Paris, Milan, Bergamo, Verona, Piacenza, and Brescia. In 1219 the pope confirmed the order and Dominic as master general.

The order's commitment to begging (thus it is called a mendicant order) was confirmed. It was to own only its churches and monasteries. Superiors were to be elected, and friars could receive dispensations from observances that impeded their pastoral work. There was to be an emphasis on study and presence in universities, especially Paris and Bologna, which became pivotal centers of Dominican pastoral activity. Dominic died in 1221 and was canonized in 1234. Dominic's feast is on the General Roman Calendar.

9   TERESA BENEDICTA OF
    THE CROSS, MARTYR

Teresa Benedicta of the Cross (1891–1942), whose original name was Edith Stein, was a convert from Judaism who was gassed to death by the Nazis during World War II. In 1999 Pope John Paul II named her a co–patron saint of all of Europe, along with Bridget of Sweden [July 23] and Catherine of Siena [April 29]. Born at Breslau (then in Germany, now Wroclaw, Poland) of Jewish parents, she was a self-proclaimed atheist as a young woman. She studied at the universities of Göttingen and Freiburg, with special emphasis on philosophy. The autobiography of Teresa of Ávila [October 15] had a profound effect on her, and she was baptized a Catholic on January 1, 1922.

As Hitler rose to power in Germany, she joined the Carmelites, taking the name Teresa Benedicta of the Cross. With the escalation of anti-Semitism in Germany, she left Cologne for the Netherlands, where she wrote her major work, *The Knowledge of the Cross*. Edith and her sister Rosa, also a convert from Judaism, were arrested on August 2, 1942. Edith Stein was executed at Auschwitz on August 9. She was canonized in Rome on October 12, 1998.

10 LAWRENCE, DEACON AND MARTYR

Lawrence (d. 258) was Rome's most famous postapostolic martyr. His name appears in the First Eucharistic Prayer, or Canon, of the Mass. There is no doubt of Lawrence's existence and martyrdom, mentioned in an ancient martyrology, but few details of his life are historical. A deacon, he was martyred, like Pope Sixtus II (257–58) [August 7], during the persecution of Valerian and was reputed to have been prominent in almsgiving. Most scholars believe that he was beheaded four days after Sixtus II's own beheading and was buried in the cemetery of Cyriaca on the Via Tiburtina. His feast is on the General Roman Calendar.

11 CLARE OF ASSISI, VIRGIN

Clare of Assisi (ca. 1193–1253) was the close friend and spiritual associate of Francis of Assisi [October 4] and the foundress of the Poor Clares, or Minoresses. Born in Assisi, at age eighteen she was so moved by the Lenten sermons of Francis in the church of San Giorgio in Assisi that she renounced all of her possessions and took the habit of a nun. She was formed in the religious life at Benedictine convents and then accepted Francis's offer of a small house for herself and her companions adjacent to the church of San Damiano, which Francis had restored, in Assisi. He appointed Clare abbess ca. 1215, much against her will. She would govern her convent for the next forty years. The way of life of those in the new order was marked by poverty and austerity and sustained itself entirely by alms. Clare's nuns soon spread to other countries in Europe. By the late twentieth century they were established in the Middle East, Asia, Africa, Oceania, and the Americas. Clare, however, never left her own convent in Assisi. She was canonized in 1255, only two years after her death. Her feast is on the General Roman Calendar.

12 EUPLUS, MARTYR

Euplus (d. 304), or Euplius, was martyred in Catania, Sicily, during the persecution of the emperor Diocletian. He is said to have stood outside the governor's court and taunted the authorities to arrest him. "I am a Christian and willing to die for it," he is reported to have shouted. When brought inside, he was carrying a forbidden book of the Gospels, which he admitted belonged to him. He was imprisoned for three months and then interrogated again. Asked if he still had the forbidden writings, he replied that he did, but now they were in his heart. The exasperated governor ordered him to be tortured until he agreed to offer sacrifice to the gods. When Euplus continued to refuse, he was beheaded. His feast is not on the General Roman Calendar.

13 PONTIAN, POPE AND MARTYR; HIPPOLYTUS, PRIEST AND MARTYR

Pontian (d. 235, pope 230–35) was the first pope to have abdicated, or resigned, his office, and *Hippolytus* (ca. 170–ca. 236) was not only the first of thirty-nine antipopes, but also the only antipope to be recognized as a saint. Both were martyred. Pontian was a Roman by birth. All except the last few months of his pontificate had been peaceful because the tolerant emperor Severus was still reigning. After succeeding Severus as emperor in March 235, Maximinus Thrax launched a violent campaign against Christian leaders. He arrested Pontian and the antipope Hippolytus, who had been a strong critic of popes Zephrynus (198/9–217) and Callistus (217–22) [October 14] and was the leader of a schism in the Roman church. Both Pontian and Hippolytus were imprisoned in Rome and then exiled to Sardinia, the so-called island of death, to work in the mines. Since deportation was normally for life and few survived it, in order to allow a successor to assume the leadership of the Roman community as soon as possible, Pontian abdicated on September 28, 235, the first precisely recorded date in papal history.

In fact, neither Pontian nor Hippolytus survived the harsh treatment and conditions on Sardinia. Pontian died less than a month after his resignation. It has been suggested that Pontian and Hippolytus were reconciled while in prison or in exile and that when Pontian abdicated, Hippolytus also renounced his claim to be Bishop of Rome and urged his followers to end their schism. Unity was thereby restored to the Roman church. The feast of Pontian and Hippolytus is on the General Roman Calendar.

14 MAXIMILIAN MARIA KOLBE, PRIEST AND MARTYR

Maximilian Kolbe (1894–1941) was put to death in a Nazi concentration camp when he volunteered to take the place of another prisoner who had been designated for execution. Born Raimund Kolbe in Russian Poland near Lodz, he entered the Franciscans in 1910, taking the name Maximilian Maria. After studies in Rome, he was ordained a priest in 1918, but returned to Poland when he contracted tuberculosis. In 1917 he had organized the Knights of Mary, dedicated to advancing devotion to the Blessed Virgin. Over the next years, he traveled to India and Japan, spreading the message of the Knights of Mary via the printing press. He was recalled to Kraków in 1936 and made superior of more than 760 friars at Niepokalanów. He also started more magazines and papers and conducted regular radio broadcasts.

When the Germans invaded Poland in 1939, and Maximilian's monastery became a refugee camp for some three thousand Poles and fifteen hundred Jews. After being arrested by the Germans, Maximilian was sent to Auschwitz on May 28, 1941. Near the end of July, men from Maximilian's block were selected for death as a reprisal for an escape attempt. When Francis Gajowniczek was picked, he cried out in despair. Kolbe stepped forward and took his place. Maximilian went to the death chamber, helping the others prepare to die with dignity. He was beatified in 1971 and canonized in 1982 in the presence of the man he had saved. His canonization was the source of some controversy within the Jewish community because of indications of anti-Semitism in some of his writings and publications. His feast is on the General Roman Calendar.

15   ASSUMPTION OF MARY

Great portions of the universal Church, in both East and West, annually celebrate the feast of the *Assumption of Mary* into heaven on this day. Although the feast is relatively ancient in origin, the dogma was not formally proclaimed by the Catholic Church until Pope Pius XII did so in 1950. The definition holds that, "when the course of her earthly life was finished," the Blessed Virgin Mary "was taken up body and soul into the glory of heaven."

The definition does not take a position on the long-disputed question of whether Mary actually died.

In proclaiming the dogma of the Assumption, Pope Pius XII intended to send a message to a world newly emerging from the horrors of World War II. His pronouncement deplored the destruction of life, the desecration of the human body, and the prevalence of moral corruption. He pointed to Mary's Assumption as "the exalted destiny of both our soul and body." The feast of the Assumption is on the General Roman Calendar and is one of the four Solemnities (the highest liturgical rank for a feast) devoted to Mary; the others are Mary, Mother of God [January 1], Annunciation [March 25], and Immaculate Conception [December 8].

16 STEPHEN OF HUNGARY, KING

Stephen of Hungary (ca. 975–1038) united and Christianized the Magyars, who had settled in Hungary at the end of the ninth century. Born Vajk, the son of the third Magyar duke of Hungary, he was baptized István, or Stephen, at about age ten, when his father became a Christian. Stephen married at age twenty and succeeded his father as leader of the Magyar people two years later, in 997. He consolidated his political power over rival leaders and established Christianity as the religion of his country. He imposed a narrow and strict form of Christianity on the nation; at the same time, he was devoted to the poor and often distributed alms to them in disguise. After his death on August 15, 1038, miracles were attributed to him at his tomb. He was canonized in 1083. In August 2000, the ecumenical patriarch, Bartholomew I of Constantinople, "recognized" Stephen as a saint for the Orthodox Church as well. His feast is on the General Roman Calendar.

17 JOAN OF THE CROSS, FOUNDRESS

Joan of the Cross (1666–1736) was the foundress of the Sisters of St. Anne of Providence. Born Jeanne Delanoue, the youngest of twelve children, at Saumur in Anjou, France, she managed her family's religious goods shop after her parents had died. Her attitude, however, was dominated by greed and insensitivity to the beggars who came looking for food. On the eve of the Epiphany 1693, an elderly, unkempt woman who was on pilgrimage from shrine to shrine showed up at her door, claiming to be on intimate terms with God; Joan allowed her to stay. Joan subsequently began listening to sermons and fasting. After a three-day conversion experience, Joan dedicated her life to the poor. She took in and cared for many poor people; her residence became known as Providence House. In 1704 she and two other young women became the nucleus of a new religious congregation to be known eventually as the Congregation of St. Anne of Providence. Joan took the religious name Joan of the Cross. She began the first local hospice and, by the time of her death, had founded twelve communities, hospices, and schools and was already recognized as a saint. She died on August 17, 1736, and was canonized in 1982. Her feast is not on the General Roman Calendar.

18 HELEN, EMPRESS

Helen (ca. 250–330) was the mother of the first Christian emperor, Constantine. Born at Drepanum (later Helenopolis) in Bithynia, she married the Roman general Constantius Chlorus, who divorced her in 292 to marry the stepdaughter of the emperor and eventually become an emperor himself. She became a Christian ca. 312 when she was already over the age of sixty. She dressed simply, was generous to the poor and to churches, reached out to those in prison, and made a pilgrimage to the Holy Land, where she devoted herself to the building of basilicas (on the Mount of Olives and at Bethlehem) and shrines, the endowing of convents, the collecting of relics, and the care of the poor, orphans, and prisoners. She is also believed to have found the True Cross there ca. 320, but there is no evidence to support that claim. Her feast is not on the General Roman Calendar, but it is celebrated in the East (along with that of her son, Constantine).

19 JOHN EUDES, PRIEST

John Eudes (1601–80) was the founder of the Congregation of Jesus and Mary (Eudists). Born of a farming family at Ri in Normandy, he was educated by Jesuits and in 1623 joined the newly established French Oratorians in Paris, was ordained in 1625, and remained in that community for twenty years, earning a reputation as one of the great preachers of France. In 1637 he published *The Life and Kingdom of Jesus in Christian Souls*, which contained the essence of his devotional thought. For him, Jesus is the source of all sanctity and Mary is the model of the Christian life. He also promoted devotion to the Sacred Heart and urged the establishment of a feast day (which was not approved until 1765). It was a time of weak religious practice among Catholics and of a poorly educated and weakly motivated diocesan clergy. In 1643, he left the Oratory and founded a society of diocesan priests, without vows, calling it the Congregation of Jesus and Mary. The new group was dedicated to the education and spiritual formation of future diocesan priests in seminaries. John Eudes died on August 19, 1680, and was canonized in 1925. His feast is on the General Roman Calendar.

20 BERNARD OF CLAIRVAUX, ABBOT AND DOCTOR OF THE CHURCH

Bernard of Clairvaux (1090–1153) was one of the greatest monastic leaders and theologians in the history of the Church. He has sometimes been referred to as the last of the Western Fathers of the Church. Born to an aristocratic family at Fontaines, near Dijon, he became a monk at age twenty-two at a poverty-stricken, reformed monastery at Cîteaux, located a few miles south of his family's estate. It had the strictest monastic Rule of the time. Three years later he was made abbot of a new foundation at Clairvaux, a post he would hold for the next thirty-eight years. At first, and by his own admission, he was too strict on the monks, but later relented. The monastery prospered, establishing other foundations in France, Britain, and Ireland. By the time of his death there were some seven hundred monks at Clairvaux itself.

In spite of his commitment to a life of solitude and seclusion from the world, Bernard was extremely active in the affairs of the Church. He secured approval for the new order of Knights Templar, whose Rule he had written, dedicated to supporting the Crusades and to the care of the sick and of pilgrims, and preached an exhausting campaign against the Cathari (Albigensians) in southern France. He rallied the Church in support of Innocent II against the antipope Anacletus and mediated an armed conflict between the duke of Lorraine and the city of Metz. Some of his writings have become classics. He made a profound impact on the development of Western monasticism, especially through his emphasis on mystical prayer within the ordinary monastic framework. Bernard died on August 20, 1153. At the time of his death there were some four hundred Cistercian houses in Europe. Because of his eloquence, he has been called *Doctor mellifluus* (Lat., "Mellifluous Doctor"). His feast is on the General Roman Calendar.

21 PIUS X, POPE

Pius X (1835–1914, pope 1903–14) was the pope best known, unfortunately, for the war he waged against Modernism, an ill-defined grab bag of liberal but not necessarily unorthodox opinions, in the course of which campaign he set back Catholic theological, biblical, and historical scholarship at least fifty years. On the other hand, he was also the pope who encouraged frequent Communion and determined that First Communion should be received at the "age of discretion," usually around seven.

Born Giuseppe Melchior Sarto of a poor family at Riese in upper Venetia, he was ordained in 1858. After service as a country curate and then as a pastor, he was appointed in 1875 as the bishop's chancellor and in 1884 was consecrated bishop of Mantua, a run-down diocese that he successfully revived. In 1893 he was appointed patriarch of Venice and named a cardinal. Cardinal Sarto was elected pope on August 4, 1903, taking the name Pius X.

In adopting as his papal motto "To restore all things in Christ" (from Eph. 1:10), he made it clear that he intended to be a pastoral rather than political pope. However, he found himself immersed in politics almost immediately. He appointed as his own secretary of state Cardinal Merry del Val, an ultraconservative Spaniard who began reversing Pope Leo XIII's more accommodating approach to secular governments. Pius X's popularity in the United States plummeted when, in 1910, he refused to receive ex-president Theodore Roosevelt because Mr. Roosevelt was scheduled to speak at the Methodist church in Rome. He condemned the ecumenical French social movement *Le Sillon* and opposed trade unions that were not exclusively Catholic.

Pius X devoted much of his energy toward the repression of dissent in the Church. The decree *Lamentabili sane exitu* (July 1907) condemned sixty-five doctrinal propositions, and *Pascendi Dominici gregis* (September 1907) characterized Modernism as the "synthesis of all heresies." Three years later he imposed an oath against Modernism on all clerics. He also explicitly encouraged a network of informants known as the Sodalitium Pianum (League of

St. Pius V), whose members reported perceived deviations from orthodoxy to Rome.

Pius X's pontificate had another, brighter side as well. The Roman Curia was reorganized, a new Code of Canon Law was created (but not promulgated until the next pontificate), seminaries were reformed, the Pontifical Biblical Institute was established, laity were encouraged to cooperate with their bishops in the apostolate, Gregorian chant was restored in the liturgy, the Breviary recited by priests was revised and shortened, and frequent Communion was encouraged. Pius X died on August 20, 1914, and was canonized in 1954 by another Pius, Pius XII. His feast is on the General Roman Calendar.

22 QUEENSHIP OF MARY

The feast of the *Queenship of Mary* was first instituted by Pope Pius XII in 1954 and was formerly celebrated on May 31. It is now observed as a memorial rather than a major feast on this day, August 22, which is the octave of the Solemnity of the Assumption [August 15]. The two feasts are connected by the traditional belief that, after her Assumption into heaven, Mary was crowned Queen of Heaven.

23 ROSE OF LIMA, VIRGIN

Rose of Lima (1586–1617) is the first canonized saint of the Americas. Born in Lima, Peru, she was baptized Isabel de Flores. An Indian maid was struck by the infant's beauty and declared in a phrase, still common in Spanish, that she was *como una rosa* (Sp., "like a rose"), and her mother agreed that this is how she was to be known. As an adolescent she took Catherine of Siena [April 29] as her model, not only for her mystical experiences, but also for her acts of severe penance, including vomiting after meals (a sickness known today as bulimia) and self-flagellation.

At age twenty she became a Dominican tertiary and slept on a bed of broken tiles in a tiny hermitage she built behind her house. She set up a small infirmary in one of the rooms of the family home to care for destitute children and sick elderly people. This ministry, rather than her acts of mortification, probably accounted for her extraordinary popularity in Lima by the time of her death, on August 24, 1617, at age thirty-one. She was the first canonized saint of the New World and was proclaimed patron saint of Peru and all of South and Central America, the West Indies, and the Philippines. Her feast is on the General Roman Calendar.

24 BARTHOLOMEW, APOSTLE

Bartholomew (first century) was one of Jesus' original twelve apostles, according to four lists in the New Testament (Matt. 10:3; Mark 3:18; Luke 6:14; Acts 1:13). Nothing certain is known of him, however. Some scholars identify him with Nathanael of John 1:45–51, because both are closely associated with Philip [May 3]. If the identification with Nathanael is correct, Philip brought Bartholomew (Nathanael), a native of Cana of Galilee (John 21:2), to acknowledge Jesus as the Messiah (John 1:45–46), and Jesus referred to him, in turn, as an Israelite "in whom there is no guile" (1:47). If the identification is not correct, we know nothing of Bartholomew from the New Testament other than that he was one of the Twelve.

Bartholomew is also thought to have preached the gospel in Phrygia, Lycaonia, Mesopotamia, and Persia and to have been martyred by being skinned alive and beheaded at Albanopolis, in Greater Armenia. His feast is on the General Roman Calendar. Sadly, it is also the day on which a mass slaughter of French Huguenots occurred in Paris and elsewhere in France, known as the St. Bartholomew's Day Massacre.

25 LOUIS IX, KING

Louis IX (1214–70) was king of France and a model Christian ruler. Born at Poissy, the son of Louis VIII, he became king upon his father's death in 1226, but his mother served as queen-regent until 1235. Louis married Margaret of Provence in 1234 (he was fourteen and she, thirteen) and thereby became the brother-in-law of Henry III, king of England. He ruled France at a time of great cultural achievement, symbolized in the building of great Gothic cathedrals and the development of universities. He himself was generous to the poor, often distributing food to them in person, founded a hospital for the destitute and the sight-impaired, established three monasteries, and was impartial but often merciful in the execution of justice. At the same time, he had many of the faults of his contemporaries, particularly in his attitude toward Jews, Muslims, heretics, homosexuals, and even lepers. In 1269, he decreed that all Jews should wear a distinctive red badge on their chest and back, a precursor of the yellow star they were forced to wear during the Nazi era. On a crusade in 1270, Louis caught typhoid fever and died on August 25. He was canonized in 1297. His feast is on the General Roman Calendar

26 ELIZABETH BICHIER DES AGES, FOUNDRESS

Elizabeth Bichier des Ages (1773–1838) was the foundress of the Daughters of the Cross. Born Jeanne Elisabeth Marie Lucie Bichier des Ages at Le Blanc, between Poitiers and Bourges in France, she led a life of prayer and care of the poor. Father Andrew Fournet devised a Rule of life for her and suggested that she found a community of nuns to continue her work among the poor. By 1811 there were twenty-five nuns, and five years later the local bishop approved their Rule. They took the name Daughters of the Cross. By 1830 there were sixty convents. Elizabeth's community was part of the first phase of the extraordinary expansion of French religious orders in the nineteenth century dedicated to social service. She died on August 26 and was canonized in 1947. Her feast is not on the General Roman Calendar.

27 MONICA, WIDOW

Monica (332–87) was the mother of Augustine [August 28]. Most of the information about her comes from her son's *Confessions* (Book IX). Born probably at Tagaste in North

Africa, she married Patricius, who lived a dissolute life marked by a violent temper, heavy drinking, and infidelity. Monica's mother-in-law lived in the same house and compounded her difficulties. But Monica's patience eventually won them over. Her husband was baptized a year before his death. Monica had three sons, including Augustine. Augustine went to Italy in 383 with his female companion of many years and their son, stopping first in Rome and then continuing on to Milan. Monica followed him to Milan, where he had settled; there she was befriended and influenced by its bishop, Ambrose [December 7]. Ambrose helped Augustine toward not only his conversion to Christianity, but a deep moral conversion as well. After a period of preparation with Monica and a few chosen friends, Augustine was baptized in 387. The party then set off for Africa, but Monica died on the way, at Ostia. Various associations of Christian mothers have taken Monica as their patron saint. Her feast is on the General Roman Calendar and is also celebrated by the Church of England.

28 AUGUSTINE OF HIPPO, BISHOP AND DOCTOR OF THE CHURCH

Augustine of Hippo (354–430) was one of the most distinguished theologians in the history of the Church and may have exercised more influence on the shape and character of Western theology, both Catholic and Protestant, than any other. Patron saint of theologians, he was born Aurelius Augustinus at Tagaste in Numidia, North Africa, to Monica [August 27], a Christian, and Patricius, who was a pagan until just before his death. Augustine was raised a Christian, but, in accordance with contemporary custom, baptism was delayed until adulthood. He took a concubine at age seventeen or eighteen, following his formal education as a rhetorician and lawyer in Carthage, and had a son of his own, Adeodatus, ca. 373.

At age eighteen or nineteen Augustine experienced a kind of conversion through reading Cicero's *Hortensius*. He became enthralled with wisdom, or "philosophy," particularly Plato's as interpreted by Plotinus. When he turned to Scripture, he found it insufficiently philosophical and stylistically unsatisfactory. He then joined the Manichees, a religious sect that not only rejected the Old Testament, but also renounced most of the ordinary pleasures of life associated with eating, drinking, and sexual expression. In 383 he, his companion, and their son sailed for Rome in order to seek professional advancement. After teaching rhetoric there for a year, he was appointed professor of rhetoric in Milan. His mother, Monica, had followed him to Rome and then to Milan. She attempted to arrange a socially advantageous marriage for him, but Augustine refused.

In Milan, Augustine came under the influence of its bishop, Ambrose [December 7], who showed that it was possible to interpret the Bible in a way consistent with Platonic ideas. After a long interior conflict, vividly described in his *Confessions,* Augustine abandoned Manichaeism, changed his mind about the nature of evil, and turned his attention to stories of monks and nuns in Italy and Egypt. He was particularly affected by the *Life of Antony* by Athanasius [May 2]. In 386 he retired from teaching and withdrew to a country villa near Milan with family, friends, and former students to take up what he expected to be a permanent communal life centered on leisurely philosophical discussion. There he wrote rebuttals of Manichaeism and read Paul's Letters. After a conversion experience in which all doubt disappeared, he returned to Milan, took a catechetical course offered by Ambrose, and at age thirty-three was baptized. After a year in Rome, he returned to Tagaste, where he established on his family's estates a quasi-monastic community of educated laymen.

In 395 he became bishop of the port city of Hippo and remained so for the rest of his life. During his episcopate he engaged in many pastoral and ecclesiastical activities and produced a number of major works, including sermons, the *Confessions, On the Trinity,* and the *City of God.* His writings were especially influential in the development of the doctrines of creation, grace, and the sacraments. Augustine died on August 29, 430, during the fourteen-month siege of Hippo by the Vandals. He is one of the four original Western Doctors of the Church, proclaimed in 1298, along with Ambrose, Jerome [September 30], and Gregory the Great [September 3]. His feast is on the General Roman Calendar and is also observed by the Church of England, the Episcopal Church in the United States, and the Evangelical Lutheran Church in America.

29 BEHEADING OF JOHN THE BAPTIST, MARTYR

John the Baptist (first century) was the prophet who prepared the way for Jesus Christ and who baptized him in the Jordan River. He is the patron saint of monks and of the city of Florence. This feast commemorates his death by beheading. Another feast, on June 24, celebrates his birth.

John had condemned the Jewish ruler Herod Antipas for his marriage to Herodias, which was technically both adulterous and incestuous. She was not only his niece, but also the wife of his brother, who was still alive. At Herodias's insistence, Herod imprisoned John (Matt. 4:12; Mark 1:14; Luke 3:19–20). During a banquet, Herodias's daughter Salome danced provocatively in front of Herod, and he rashly promised to grant her any wish (Matt. 14:1–12; Mark 6:14–28; Luke 9:7–9). Herodias took revenge on John the Baptist by telling her daughter to ask for his head on a dish. Herod reluctantly acceded. John was beheaded. The mention of John in the Canon, or Eucharistic Prayer, of the Mass is evidence of a very early cult. This feast is on the General Roman Calendar and is also celebrated by the Greek and Russian Orthodox Churches and by the Church of England.

30 MARGARET WARD, MARTYR

Margaret Ward (1558–88) is one of the few women among the known Catholic martyrs of the British Isles to have been canonized. Born in Congleton, Cheshire, she lived in London as a housekeeper. She was herself imprisoned for aiding a priest's escape from prison. For eight days she was suspended by her hands while beaten, before being brought before the court. She was offered her release if she would disclose the priest's hiding place, beg Queen

Elizabeth I's pardon, and agree to attend services at the established Church. When she refused, she was hanged at Tyburn on August 30, 1588, together with a priest and four laymen. She was beatified in 1929 and canonized in 1970 as one of the Forty Martyrs of England and Wales [October 25]. Her individual feast is not on the General Roman Calendar.

31 JOSEPH OF ARIMATHEA AND NICODEMUS

Joseph of Arimathea (first century) was a righteous, respected, and wealthy member of the Sanhedrin (or at least a member of the local council) who had become a clandestine disciple of Jesus and took responsibility for his burial out of respect for Jewish law, which mandated burial as a duty to be performed even for enemies. Fittingly, he is the patron saint of funeral directors and pallbearers. *Nicodemus* (first century) was a Pharisaic leader, presumably a prominent member of the Sanhedrin, who was at least partially sympathetic to Jesus. In the Fourth Gospel, Nicodemus protests to the chief priests and Pharisees that Jesus must have an opportunity to respond to the accusations against him (John 7:50–51) and participates in Jesus' burial, "bringing a mixture of myrrh and aloes weighing about one hundred pounds" (John 19:39). The feasts of Joseph of Arimathea and Nicodemus are not on the General Roman Calendar.

SEPTEMBER

1 GILES, ABBOT

Giles (d. ca. 710), also Aegidius, was a popular saint in the Middle Ages whose monastery, Saint-Gilles, near Arles in Provence, became an important pilgrimage center on the route to both Compostela in Spain and the Holy Land. Little else is known about him. He is patron saint of the disabled, lepers, and nursing mothers, based in part on the tenth-century legend that he gave shelter to a female deer that had once nursed him and that had later been wounded and crippled by the king during a hunt. It is said that when the king searched for the hind, he found only Giles with the arrow in him, not the deer.

In England 162 ancient churches were dedicated to him and at least 24 hospitals. His churches were often found at road junctions so that travelers could visit while their horses were being shod by blacksmiths, of whom he is also a patron saint. His feast was widely celebrated in England and throughout Europe and is still celebrated today by the Church of England, but it is not on the General Roman Calendar.

2   JOHN THE FASTER, PATRIARCH; MARTYRS OF PAPUA NEW GUINEA

John the Faster was the patriarch of Constantinople (John IV) from 582. He was renowned for his ascetical lifestyle and his lack of personal ambition. At a synod in 588, however, he assumed the title Ecumenical Patriarch, which had been applied to his predecessors by the emperor Justinian. Pope Pelagius II refused to endorse the acts of the synod because of his conviction that the title infringed upon papal primacy. His successor, Gregory the Great [September 3], insisted that there is no universal patriarch in the Church, including even the pope. However, John the Faster ignored the protests and passed on the title to his successors.

The Church of England and the Episcopal Church in the United States commemorate the *Martyrs of Papua New Guinea* (d. 1942) on this day. During World War II eight missionaries and two Papuans were betrayed by non-Christians to the Japanese invaders and were executed. This feast, which is also celebrated in many dioceses of the (Anglican) Church of Australia, honors those of various Christian traditions who risked their lives in the care of the wounded and in the service of the native population.

3   GREGORY THE GREAT, POPE AND DOCTOR OF THE CHURCH

Gregory the Great (ca. 540–604, pope 590–604), only the second pope in all of church history to be called "the Great" (Leo I [440–61] was the first), was the first pope to have been a monk and was one of the papacy's most influential writers. His *Pastoral Care,* which defined the episcopal ministry as one of shepherding souls, became the textbook for medieval bishops. The son of a Roman senator, he entered the service of the state as a young man and became prefect of Rome, but in 573 he sold his extensive properties, founded seven monasteries, and distributed much of his wealth to the poor. Although only a junior deacon at the time of Pope Pelagius II's death in 590, he was unanimously elected to the papacy.

His early letters disclose his unhappiness over having been forced to leave the contemplative life to assume the burdensome responsibilities of the papacy. Indeed, those responsibilities were far heavier than usual because of the general breakdown of civil order at the time. Gregory found himself drawn as deeply into temporal and political affairs as into spiritual and ecclesiastical concerns. He immediately organized the distribution of food to the starving, and, in order to expand the reservoir of resources, he also reorganized the papal territories in Italy, Sicily, Dalmatia, Gaul, and North Africa.

When the imperial exarch in Ravenna proved incapable of doing anything about the Lombard threat, the pope took the lead and fashioned a truce with the duke of Spoleto. When the exarch broke the truce and the Lombards moved against Rome, Gregory saved the city by bribing the Lombard king and promising yearly tributes. As a result of all these efforts, Gregory became virtually the civil as well as the spiritual ruler of Rome. He negotiated treaties, paid the troops, and appointed generals and governors. At the same time, he carefully attended to the need for reform in the government of the Church. He imposed a detailed code, for example, for the election and conduct of bishops in Italy and enforced clerical celibacy. He also secured better relationships with the churches of Spain and Gaul.

Given his own monastic background, Gregory was a vigorous promoter of monasticism and of the liturgy, particularly of liturgical music. Indeed, his name was so closely identified with plainsong that it came to be known as Gregorian chant. Gregory died on March 12, 604. His feast is on the General Roman Calendar.

4   ROSE OF VITERBO, VIRGIN; ALBERT SCHWEITZER, HUMANITARIAN

Rose of Viterbo (1234–52) had a short and spiritually undistinguished life when viewed in the light of current theological and ascetical criteria. Born of poor parents in Viterbo, Italy, she is said to have had a vision of the Blessed Virgin Mary at the age of eight and thereafter began preaching in the streets in support of the pope and on the side of the Guelfs against the occupying Ghibellines. She constantly denounced the emperor Frederick II, whose allies sought her death. She fled to Soriano and in 1250 predicted the emperor's death, which occurred a few days later. She was refused admittance to the convent of St. Mary of the Roses in Viterbo because she lacked a dowry, and when she moved to a house nearby, the nuns had the house closed down. Rose returned to her parents' home in Viterbo and died there on March 6, 1252, at age seventeen. She was canonized in 1457. Her feast is not on the General Roman Calendar.

The Evangelical Lutheran Church in America commemorates *Albert Schweitzer* (1875–1965), renowned theologian, biblical scholar, physician, and missionary to Africa. He won the Nobel Peace Prize in 1952 for his work on behalf of the "brotherhood of nations." Many regard him as the twentieth century's greatest humanitarian.

5   BERTINUS, ABBOT;
BLESSED MOTHER TERESA OF
CALCUTTA, FOUNDRESS

Bertinus (d. ca. 698) was a monk of the abbey of Luxeuil, founded by the Irish missionary Columban [November 23]. Bertinus was sent to assist the new bishop of Thérouanne, where a people known as the Morini lived, who posed great obstacles to the mission. The Morini had been evangelized a century earlier, but had since lost their faith and become exceedingly belligerent toward the Church. In spite of the difficulties, Bertinus and his companions persevered in their work of evangelization and began to make progress. A new monastery was built along the river, which soon proved inadequate for the number of those who sought entrance. A second monastery was built on a donated plot of swampland, and Bertinus became its abbot. The monastery was initially dedicated to St. Peter [June 29], but was later renamed in honor of Bertinus himself, as Saint-Bertin. Bertinus is known to have lived to a great age. His feast is not on the General Roman Calendar.

Mother Teresa of Calcutta (1910–97) is one of the twentieth century's most highly respected and venerated figures. In the early Church, she would have been popularly proclaimed a saint upon her death. Born in Albania, she was the foundress of the Missionaries of Charity, a congregation that ministers to the poorest of the poor and to those nearest to death. She won the Nobel Peace Prize in 1979 as well as prestigious awards from the governments of India and the United States for her extraordinary humanitarian work around the world. She was beatified on October 19, 2003.

6   BLESSED BERTRAND DE GARRIGUES, FRIAR

Bertrand de Garrigues (d. ca. 1230) was one of the original members of the Order of Preachers and a close associate of its founder, Dominic [August 8]. Born in Garrigues sometime in the second half of the twelfth century, he joined the Cistercian mission against the heretical Cathari, or Albigensians, whose influence continued to spread, especially throughout southern France. In 1208 Pope Innocent III gave approval for a crusade against the heretics, but unfortunately it spawned more violence and bloodshed than conversions. Through prayer and preaching, Dominic tried to limit the damage being done by the crusade and to bring about a reconciliation with the Albigensians. Bertrand was impressed with Dominic's approach and began working with him. By 1215 they were joined by five other preachers, and by the following year their number had increased to sixteen. The group met at Prouille, where Dominic had already founded a community of nuns, to lay the foundations for the Order of Preachers. Dominican houses were founded in Paris, Rome, and Bologna. At the second general chapter of the order in 1221, the year of Dominic's death, Bertrand was appointed prior provincial in Provence, and for the remaining nine years of his life he preached throughout the south of France, generally expanding the work of the order. He died ca. 1230. His feast is not on the General Roman Calendar.

7   SOZON, MARTYR; MARK KÖRÖSI, STEPHEN PONGRÁCZ, AND MELCHIOR GRODECZ, MARTYRS

Sozon (date unknown) was a shepherd, perhaps in Cilicia, who had a vision of Christ while asleep under a tree in which he was told to leave his sheep and follow the Lord to death. He went to the nearby town of Pompeiopolis during a pagan festival, walked into the temple, and shattered the golden idol with his shepherd's crook. Sozon later was sentenced to be burned. His feast is on the Greek and Russian Orthodox calendars.

The Jesuit liturgical calendar commemorates three priests martyred in Košice (then in northern Hungary) in 1619: *Mark Körösi, Stephen Pongrácz,* and *Melchior Grodecz,* the first a diocesan priest and the other two, Jesuits. The three priests were invited by the Catholic king's deputy in Košice to minister to the beleaguered Catholics in the city, then a stronghold of Hungarian Calvinists. After a Calvinist prince occupied the city, the three priests were arrested, imprisoned, and subjected to the most brutal forms of torture before being killed. They were beatified in 1905 and canonized in 1995.

8   BIRTH OF MARY

Nothing is known of the circumstances of the birth of the *Blessed Virgin Mary*. Her parents, traditionally known as Joachim and Anne [July 26], are not mentioned in the Bible. The belief that they were Mary's father and mother is based on the *Gospel of James,* an unreliable second-century apocryphal document that was popular in the Middle Ages when devotion to Our Lady became more widespread. An ancient tradition in the West identifies Nazareth as her birthplace, but another favors Jerusalem, even specifying the neighborhood of the pool of Bethsaida, where a crypt under the church of St. Anne is venerated as the actual location.

This feast originated in the East and was probably modeled on that of the Birth of John the Baptist [June 24], which was known at least from the beginning of the sixth century. In some parts of the West, the feast of the Birth of Mary was observed before the middle of the seventh century. It finally reached Rome during the pontificate of Sergius I (687–701), who ordered that four feasts of Our Lady—her Birth, the Annunciation [March 25], the Purification, or Presentation, in the Temple [November 21], and the Assumption [August 15]—should be celebrated in Rome and marked by processions.

9   PETER CLAVER, PRIEST

Peter Claver (1580–1654) was a Spanish Jesuit priest whose ministry to African slaves brought forcibly to the New World earned him the title the Saint of the Slaves. He is the patron saint of Colombia and of missionary endeavors among people of color. Born into a working-class family at Verdú in Catalonia, Spain, he was educated at the university in Barcelona and became a Jesuit in 1602. Under the influence of Alphonsus Rodríguez [October 31], a porter at the Jesuit college on Majorca, Peter was inspired to serve as a missionary in the New World. He was sent to Cartagena, Colombia, in 1610 and was ordained a priest six years later. At the time, Cartagena was major center for the African slave trade. Peter devoted his energies to the spiritual and physical care of the slaves, bringing them food, medicine, and other necessities. It is said that he baptized more than three hundred thousand by 1615. Peter died on September 8, 1654, and was canonized along with his friend Alphonsus Rodríguez in 1888. His feast is not on the General Roman Calendar, but is on the Proper Calendar for the Dioceses of the United States.

10   NICHOLAS OF TOLENTINO, FRIAR

Nicholas of Tolentino (1245–1305) was an Augustinian friar who is the patron saint of mariners. Born in the March of Ancona, Italy, he joined the Augustinian friars just before his eighteenth birthday. Even prior to his ordination to the priesthood in 1269, he had earned a reputation as a healer. Nicholas was soon recognized as an eloquent preacher, gentle confessor, and devoted minister to the sick, the dying, the poor, and prostitutes. Almost immediately after his death on September 10, 1305, a commission was established to gather evidence to support his canonization. The tribunal investigating his cause accepted as authentic thirty of his reported miracles, all of which were performed to relieve some manifestation of human distress. Nicholas is also the patron saint of babies, mothers, animals, and the souls in purgatory. His feast is not on the General Roman Calendar.

11 PROTUS AND HYACINTH, MARTYRS

Protus and *Hyacinth* were Roman martyrs of unknown date, who are mentioned in the fourth-century list of martyrs, the *Depositio Martyrum,* in the early sacramentaries, including the *Gelasian Sacramentary*, and in the Naples calendar of stone. Pope Damasus I (366–84) [December 11] thought they were brothers, perhaps because they were buried close to one another. The *Martyrology of Jerome* [September 30] refers to them as "teachers of the Christian Law." One tradition identifies them as eunuchs who were slaves of Eugenia, Christian daughter of the prefect of Egypt. They were said to have accompanied her when she fled from her father and were beheaded for their faith along with Basilla, a Roman woman whom they had converted. Another tradition has them as servants of Basilla herself. The cult of Protus and Hyacinth was early and widespread. Their feast is mentioned in the oldest English martyrologies and liturgical calendars. However, it is not on the General Roman Calendar.

12 AILBE, BISHOP; STEPHEN BIKO, FREEDOM FIGHTER

Ailbe (d. ca. 526), or Ailbhe, is the patron saint of the diocese of Imlech (Emly) in County Tipperary, Ireland. Unfortunately, much of the material about his life is unreliable. What does seem certain is that he preached, mainly in southern Ireland, with such power and authority that many were not only converted to Christianity, but inspired by his example of Christian living as well. There seems little or no basis to the belief that Ailbe preached in Ireland before Patrick [March 17] did. His feast is not on the General Roman Calendar.

This is also the day of death of *Stephen Biko* (1946–77), a leader in the fight against apartheid in South Africa, who was imprisoned and later died of injuries from beatings and maltreatment.

13 JOHN CHRYSOSTOM, BISHOP AND DOCTOR OF THE CHURCH

John Chrysostom (347–407) was the most prolific of the Fathers of the Church and is the patron saint of preachers. His surname "Chrysostom" (Gk., "golden mouth") was given him in the sixth century and has largely supplanted his baptismal name. He is one of the four great Greek Doctors of Church, named in 1568; the other three are Athanasius [May 2], Basil the Great [January 2], and Gregory Nazianzen [January 2]. Born in Antioch and educated in oratory and law as well as Christian doctrine and Scripture, Chrysostom was baptized at age eighteen and became a monk ca. 373. In 386 he was ordained a priest and became a special assistant to the bishop in the ministry to the numerous Christian poor in Antioch. He acquired a reputation as a compelling preacher and as a commentator on the Letters of Paul and the Gospels of Matthew and John, emphasizing always their literal meaning and practical application.

In 397 he was appointed patriarch of Constantinople and initiated a program of reform—of the court, the clergy, and the people generally. The reforms alienated many of the clergy, but met with broad support among the laity. The upper classes, however, were not pleased by his blunt denunciations of their extravagances and luxurious living. At the same time, however, he reduced his own household expenses, gave the surplus to the poor, and provided hospitals for the sick.

The empress Eudoxia regarded his denunciations of the court as directed at herself and Chrysostom suffered two banishments. He died at Comana in Pontus on September 14, 407. His commentaries on the Bible and his treatise on the priesthood are among his most enduring writings. His feast is on the General Roman Calendar and is also celebrated by the Church of England. He is particularly revered in the East, which celebrates his feast on November 13.

14 TRIUMPH OF THE CROSS

This feast, formerly known in the West as the Exaltation of the Cross (and still known by that name in the East), celebrates the finding of the True Cross of Christ under a Roman landfill by the emperor Constantine's mother, Helen [August 18], ca. 320, and the subsequent dedication of a basilica built by Constantine on the site of the Holy Sepulchre and Calvary on September 14, 335. It is also known as "Holy Cross Day." This feast is on the General Roman Calendar and is also celebrated by the Greek and Russian Orthodox Churches, and by the Church of England, the Episcopal Church in the United States, and the Evangelical Lutheran Church in America, for whom it is known as Holy Cross Day.

15 OUR LADY OF SORROWS

This feast celebrates the spiritual martyrdom of the *Blessed Virgin Mary*, particularly in the Passion and death of her son Jesus Christ. By the fourteenth century her sorrows were fixed at seven: the presentation of Jesus in the Temple [February 2], the flight into Egypt, Jesus' being lost in Jerusalem, the encounter with Jesus on the way to Calvary, the Crucifixion, the taking of the body down from the cross, and Jesus' burial. This feast is on the General Roman Calendar, but is not observed by any other churches.

16 CORNELIUS, POPE, AND CYPRIAN OF CARTHAGE, BISHOP, MARTYRS

Cornelius (d. 253, pope 251–53) was the pope who insisted that those baptized by heretics or schismatics need not be rebaptized upon entering or returning to the Catholic Church. After the death of Pope Fabian [January 20] in January 250, the Roman clergy postponed the election of a new pope because of the violent persecution under the emperor Decius. During the interregnum of fourteen months the Roman church was governed as it had been during the first century of its existence, that is, collegially, with the presbyter Novatian acting as spokesman.

The following spring the emperor left Rome to fight the Goths. During his absence, the persecution subsided and the election could be held. Novatian fully expected that he would be elected, but the clergy voted instead for Cornelius. Novatian reacted bitterly to the result and had himself ordained a bishop, setting himself up as a rival (antipope) to Cornelius. What was clearly at the basis of Novatian's opposition was Cornelius's readiness to readmit to communion, albeit after suitable penance, those Christians who had lapsed during the persecution. Novatian flatly opposed reconciliation, under any conditions. Cornelius's election was upheld by Cyprian, who had some influence over the African clergy in Rome, and by Dionysius (d. 264/5), bishop of Alexandria. Cornelius excommunicated Novatian at a synod held in Rome in 251. The synod also affirmed the pope's policy of readmitting, after appropriate contrition and "the medicines of repentance," those Christians who had lapsed during the Decian persecution.

When the new emperor, Gallus, resumed the persecutions in June 252, Cornelius was arrested and died the following June (more likely as a result of the hardships of his imprisonment than by beheading). Both his name and that of Cyprian are included in the Eucharistic Prayer (Canon of the Mass), immediately after the names of Popes Linus, Cletus (Anacletus), Clement [November 23], and Sixtus [August 7].

Cyprian (ca. 200–58) was one of the most prominent and influential bishops of the early Church. Born in Carthage and trained as an orator, rhetorician, and lawyer before his conversion to Christianity, he was ordained a priest and in 248 was elected bishop of Carthage by the laity, clergy, and neighboring bishops. Almost immediately he was confronted with the persecution conducted by the emperor Decius, and he fled to safety, ruling and encouraging his flock by letter. A number of Christians apostatized by sacrificing to idols or buying certificates that falsely stated that they had sacrificed. Cyprian reconciled those who lapsed, but only after a period of penance. The antipope Novatian held out for a more severe approach, but Cyprian's more moderate position was approved by the Council of Carthage in 251.

Cyprian tangled with a later pope, Stephen I (254–57), over the issue of the rebaptism of heretics and schismatics. Along with most of the churches of North Africa, Syria, and Asia Minor, Cyprian held that they had to be rebaptized; Stephen insisted, along with the churches of Alexandria and Palestine, that they did not. After several synods upheld Cyprian's view, tensions mounted. Dionysius, bishop of Alexandria, who agreed with Cyprian's position, nonetheless urged him to adopt a more conciliatory approach for the sake of church unity. The situation might have deteriorated even further if Pope Stephen had not died in the midst of the controversy and had Cyprian himself not been martyred a year later under the emperor Valerian. Cyprian's greatest legacy is his body of writings, focusing on the unity of the Church, the office of bishop, the primacy of the pope, and the sacraments. The feast of Cornelius and Cyprian is on the General Roman Calendar.

17 ROBERT BELLARMINE, BISHOP AND DOCTOR OF THE CHURCH; HILDEGARD OF BINGEN, ABBESS

Robert Bellarmine (1542–1621) was the most influential ecclesiologist (theologian who specializes in the doctrine of the Church) between the time of the Council of Trent (1545–63) and the Second Vatican Council (1962–65). Born at Montepulciano in Tuscany, he entered the Society of Jesus in 1560, taught classics for several years, and was ordained a priest in 1570. Having lectured for seven years at Louvain in modern-day Belgium, he was appointed in 1576 as professor of "controversial theology" in a recently established chair at the Roman College (now the Pontifical Gregorian University), which had been founded by Ignatius of Loyola [July 31] in 1551. His lectures provided the basis for his celebrated three-volume work *Disputations on the Controversies of the Christian Faith Against the Heretics of This Age,* which was so comprehensive that it was thought mistakenly to have been the product of a team of scholars rather than of one author.

Bellarmine became rector of the Roman College in 1592 and provincial of Naples in 1594, and then was recalled to Rome in 1597 to serve as the pope's theologian; the following year he was appointed cardinal. His private life, however, remained one of simplicity and even austerity. His view that the pope may act regarding temporal matters only when they affect the spiritual order alienated Pope Sixtus V (1585–90), but he was later made archbishop of Capua and then prefect of the Vatican Library (1605). Bellarmine died at age seventy-nine on September 17, 1621. He was named a Doctor of the Church in 1931, a year after his canonization by Pope Pius XI. His feast is on the General Roman Calendar.

On this day the Benedictines, the Church of England, and the Episcopal Church in the United States celebrate the feast of *Hildegard of Bingen* (1098–1179), a Benedictine abbess and visionary. Born in present-day Germany, she was educated from age eight by a recluse, Blessed Jutta von Spanheim, an anchoress who lived in a small cottage attached to the abbey church founded by St. Disibo. As others joined Jutta there, a monastic community took form under the Rule of St. Benedict [July 11], with Jutta as abbess. Hildegard joined this community at age fifteen and led an uneventful life until she began to experience visions and revelations seventeen years later. Jutta died in 1136, and Hildegard succeeded her as abbess. She began a long process of dictating the content of her visions to establish a written record. The three-volume work was entitled *Scivias* (an abbreviation of the Latin *sci vias Domini*, "Know the ways of the Lord"), with illustrations drawn by Hildegard herself. When the community grew too large for the convent, she moved it near Bingen sometime between 1147 and 1152. From there she corresponded with rulers and other prominent people, including the pope and the emperor. She also wrote poems, plays, and hymns as well as works of medicine and natural history, commentaries, and lives of the saints. Hildegard of Bingen was over eighty when she died on September 17, 1179. She has never been formally canonized, and her feast is not on the General Roman Calendar.

18 JOSEPH OF CUPERTINO, PRIEST

Joseph of Cupertino (1603–63), a Franciscan, is known as the "flying friar" because of his reported levitations. It is not surprising that he is the patron saint of aviators. Born Giuseppe Desa of a poverty-stricken family in Cupertino near Brindisi, he was ordained a Franciscan priest in 1628, in Grotella. He was reputed to have the power of healing and of flying through the air by no apparent physical force. There were seventy instances of levitation recorded during his seventeen years at Grotella alone. His superiors were so disturbed by his behavior that they forbade him to celebrate a public Mass, attend choir, walk in processions, or eat in the refectory for thirty-five years. He died on September 18, 1663, at the Franciscan friary at Osimo and was buried there. His canonization followed in 1767, not for his levitations, it was insisted, but for his patience, gentleness, and humility. His feast is not on the General Roman Calendar.

19 JANUARIUS, BISHOP AND MARTYR

Januarius (d. ca. 305) is best known for the annual liquefaction of his blood in Naples on three of his feast days. He is not only the patron saint of Naples, but also of blood banks. Born Gennaro in either Naples or Benevento, he was bishop of Benevento when the persecution of the emperor Diocletian was unleashed in 303. When he went to visit four imprisoned Christians in Nola, he himself was arrested. He was tortured, heavily manacled, made to walk with other prisoners in front of the governor's chariot from there to Pozzuoli, and then thrown to the wild beasts. When the animals ignored them, the prisoners were beheaded and buried near the town. Januarius's blood, which is in a vial in the cathedral at Naples, is reported to liquefy each year on three feast days associated with him: today, December 16 (the day on which he supposedly averted a threatened eruption of Mt. Vesuvius in 1631), and the Saturday before the first Sunday of May (commemorating the transfer of his relics). His feast is on the General Roman Calendar.

20 PAUL CHŎNG HASANG, ANDREW KIM TAEGŎN, AND COMPANIONS, MARTYRS

Paul Chŏng Hasang (d. 1839), a layman, and *Andrew Kim Taegŏn* (d. 1846), the first native-born Korean priest, are among 103 Korean martyrs canonized by Pope John Paul II in the Catholic cathedral in Seoul on May 6, 1984. These 103 martyrs died in persecutions that occurred between 1839 and 1867. Other lay leaders who originally established the Church in Korea after 1784 and who died for their faith before the 1839–67 persecutions are not included in the list of those who were canonized in 1984— much to the disappointment of many Korean Catholics who are proud of the lay origins of their Church.

From age twenty, *Paul Chŏng Hasang* devoted himself to the revitalization of the Church in Korea and made no fewer than nine trips to Beijing, China, to recruit priests. He was a nobleman whose father and brother had died for the faith at the beginning of the nineteenth century and whose mother and sisters were martyred shortly after his own martyrdom in 1839. He was one of the sixty-seven lay Catholics who died for their faith after being held for weeks and months in wretched conditions of overcrowding, filth, and torture between May 20, 1839, and April 29, 1841.

In January 1845 *Andrew Kim Taegŏn* was sent to Macao with two other Korean youths for seminary training. He returned to Korea in 1845, reentering the country only with great difficulty by way of Manchuria, and made contact with a few catechists. He then left again to escort two priests and a bishop into the country. The bishop ordained Andrew on August 17 in Shanghai, making him the first native-born Korean priest. Andrew was arrested the following June and was condemned to death. He was only twenty-six when he was beheaded at Saenamt'o, at the River Han near Seoul, on September 16, 1846. Paul's and Andrew's feast, along with that of more than one hundred other Korean martyrs, is on the General Roman Calendar.

21 MATTHEW, APOSTLE AND EVANGELIST

Matthew (first century) is one of the twelve apostles and the Evangelist traditionally regarded as the author of the

First Gospel, whose message is that in Jesus Christ the Reign, or Kingdom, of God has drawn near and will remain with the Church until the end of time. Matthew's name occurs in all lists of the Twelve: Matthew 10:3; Mark 3:18; Luke 6:15; and Acts 1:13. Matthew and Levi (Mark 2:14; Luke 5:27–28) may be two names for the same person, in which case Matthew is the son of Alphaeus and the brother of James [May 3] (not James, the son of Zebedee [July 25]), or else two different persons confused in the traditions. In any case, both Matthew and Levi are referred to as "tax collectors." Nothing is known for certain about what Matthew did after the Resurrection. He is venerated as a martyr, but nothing is known of his martyrdom. Matthew's feast is on the General Roman Calendar and is also celebrated on this day by the Church of England, the Episcopal Church in the United States, and the Evangelical Lutheran Church in America.

22 THOMAS OF VILLANOVA, BISHOP

Thomas of Villanova (1486–1555) was archbishop of Valencia and an Augustinian friar before that. Born in Fuentellana, he took his surname from the town of Villanueva de los Infantes, where Thomas himself was raised. He studied at the famous Complutensian University at Alcalá, which was founded as an instrument of intellectual renewal in the Church. He was made professor of philosophy at age twenty-six, but after four years he left the university and joined the Augustinian friars in Salamanca. He was ordained a priest in 1518 and served as prior in a number of houses after 1519 and for a period of some twenty-five years. In 1544 the emperor Charles V nominated him for the archbishopric of Valencia.

He traveled to the diocese on foot, wearing his old monastic habit and a battered hat that he had worn for years. Seeing his poverty, the canons gave him money to furnish his episcopal residence, but he gave it away to the local hospital. His subsequent ministry was marked by personal austerity, devotion to the care of orphans, the sick, captives, and the poor, and reform of the local clergy. He died on September 8, 1555, and was canonized in 1658. Universities have been named after him in the United States, Australia, and Cuba. His feast is not on the General Roman Calendar.

23 PADRE PIO, FRIAR

Padre Pio (1887–1968) was an Italian Capuchin friar known for his bearing of the wounds of Christ (the stigmata) on his body from 1918 until the day after his death on September 23, 1968. Born Francesco Forgione in a village near Naples (Pio, or Pius, was his religious name), he was a renowned confessor, said to have heard as many as twenty-five thousand confessions a year. In 1956 he established a hospital and an international research center in the field of biomedicine. He was beatified in 1999 in the presence of some 250,000 people and was canonized in June 2002.

24 GERARD SAGREDO, MARTYR

Gerard Sagredo (d. 1046) is venerated as Venice's first martyr. He is also regarded as the "apostle of Hungary," where he is known as Collert. He had been a Benedictine monk and later prior at San Giorgio Maggiore in Venice before setting out on a pilgrimage to Jerusalem. He took a circuitous route, traveling through Hungary. King Stephen [August 16] invited him to become his son's tutor. Not long afterward, the diocese of Csanad was established, and Gerard was named its first bishop in 1035. He devoted himself to combating paganism and reclaiming imperfectly converted Christians. When Stephen died in 1038, a fierce conflict broke out among competing claimants to the throne and there was also a revolt against Christianity. At Buda Gerard was attacked and killed by one of the factions. His feast is not on the General Roman Calendar.

25 SERGIUS OF RADONEZH, ABBOT

Sergius of Radonezh (ca. 1315–92) is regarded as the greatest of the Russian saints and the first Russian mystic, venerated by Orthodox and Catholics alike. Considered the patron saint of Russia, he has been called "the Russian Orthodox Francis of Assisi" [October 4]. He was also the founder of some forty monasteries and a mediator and peacemaker in political disputes, preventing four civil wars between princes. Born of noble parents at Rostov and baptized as Bartholomew, as a teenager he fled with his family to Radonezh, a small village about fifty miles northeast of Moscow. After his parents' death, he took up a life of monastic solitude in the forests of Radonezh. In 1336 he built a chapel in honor of the Trinity and soon attracted disciples. He became their abbot and was ordained a priest. His name was changed to Sergius.

In 1354 he and his disciples adopted a cenobitic (communal) Rule, that of Theodore the Studite, and the great monastery that developed, now known as the Trinity–St. Sergius Lavra, became a center of pilgrimage and the spiritual heart of Russian Orthodoxy. Sergius died on September 25, 1392. His feast is celebrated in the Russian and Greek Orthodox Churches and by the Church of England and the Episcopal Church in the United States. However, it is not on the General Roman Calendar.

26 COSMAS AND DAMIAN, MARTYRS

Cosmas and *Damian* (d. ca. 287) are the patron saints of physicians, along with Luke [October 18] and Pantaleon [July 27]. They are also patron saints of nurses, surgeons, pharmacists, dentists, barbers, the sightless, and even confectioners. Unfortunately, there is little reliable information about them. Their legend says that they were twin brothers born in Arabia and doctors who practiced medicine without taking any fees for service. They made no secret of their Christian faith and were arrested during the Diocletian persecution and beheaded in Cyrrhus, north of Antioch, in Syria. Their feast is on the General Roman Calendar and is celebrated in the Russian and Greek Orthodox Churches on both July 1 and November 1.

27 VINCENT DE PAUL, PRIEST

Vincent de Paul (1581–1660) was the founder of the Vincentians and the Sisters of Charity and is the patron saint of all charitable societies and works. Vincent himself always signed himself "Depaul," not "de Paul." The latter would ordinarily convey noble parentage. Born of a peasant family at Pouy in southwestern France, he studied for the priesthood at a local Franciscan college and then at Toulouse University and was ordained at the early age of nineteen. He became a court chaplain, but then his biography becomes clouded. According to one version, he was falsely accused of theft and underwent some sort of religious conversion, perhaps while in prison. He is also reported to have been captured by pirates during a boat trip from Marseilles to Narbonne in 1605 and to have spent two years as a slave in Tunisia, before finally managing to escape. Some scholars tend to dismiss this account as legendary.

What does seem certain is that Vincent did spend a year in Rome, possibly studying, before returning to France. In Paris he joined a group of priests headed by his friend and mentor Pierre de Bérulle (later a cardinal), who established the Congregation of the Oratory in France. On Bérulle's advice, Vincent became the parish priest of Clichy, on the northern outskirts of Paris, in 1612, and the following year became tutor in the powerful Gondi family.

While he remained with the Gondi family for twelve years, Vincent also spent some time as a parish priest at Châtillon-les-Dombes, where he discovered the needs of sick and poor families. He decided to form a confraternity of caring individuals who would help these families by turns. The first group—all women—came into being in August 1617 and were known as the Servants of the Poor. Vincent wanted to have male groups as well, but these would not develop until after his death. In 1833 Frédéric Ozanam would found the Society of St. Vincent de Paul. Vincent did establish in 1618 a society of priests known variously as the Priests of the Mission, Vincentians, and Lazarists. Vincent and his new band of priests went from village to village conducting missions. As their work and community grew, the archbishop gave them the priory of Saint-Lazare, which became one of the great centers of spiritual and pastoral renewal in France. Vincent died on September 27, 1660, and was canonized in 1737. His feast is on the General Roman Calendar.

28 WENCESLAUS, MARTYR; MARTYRS OF CHINA

Wenceslaus (907–29) is best known as the subject of the Christmas carol "Good King Wenceslaus," although its contents are not based on any known incident in his life. He is the patron saint of the Czech Republic, Slovakia, Bohemia, and Moravia. The son of a duke, Wenceslaus seized the reins of power in 922, becoming duke of Bohemia, in order to bring an end to the struggle between Christian and anti-Christian factions and also to block the invasion of Bohemia by the Bavarians. When a son was born to Wenceslaus, his brother Boleslav saw that he had lost his chance to succeed to the throne. Boleslav invited his brother to his residence and murdered Wenceslaus as he was on his way to chapel for the singing of Matins. His feast is on the General Roman Calendar.

The *martyrs of China,* eighty-seven native converts and thirty-three foreign missionaries, were put to death between 1648 and 1930. Most had been killed during the anti-Western and anti-Christian Boxer Rebellion (1898–1900). Included among them were four young girls who had been raised in a Catholic orphanage: Wang Cheng, Fan Kun, Ji Yu, and Zheng Xu. Canonized by Pope John Paul II on October 1, 2000, they were the first Chinese Catholics to be raised to sainthood.

29 MICHAEL, GABRIEL, AND RAPHAEL, ARCHANGELS

September 29 is known as Michaelmas Day because it is the feast of *Michael the Archangel,* the leader of the ranks of angels and the guardian and protector of the people of Israel (Dan. 10; 12). According to Jude 9 Michael (Heb., "Who is like God?") conducted warfare with the devil over the body of Moses, and in Revelation 12:7–9 he and his angels fight the dragon and hurl him and his followers from heaven. He is venerated as the head of the heavenly armies and as patron saint of soldiers. He is also believed to protect Christians against the devil, especially at the hour of death, and to lead their souls to God. He is patron saint of the sick, radiologists, grocers, mariners, police officers, paratroopers, and cemeteries. In the revision of the General Roman Calendar in 1969, his feast was joined with those of Gabriel and Raphael.

The archangel *Gabriel* (Heb., "man of God") is portrayed in the Old Testament as an instrument of revelation (e.g., Dan. 8:15–26; 9:20–27) and in the noncanonical *1 Enoch* (9:1) as a heavenly intercessor. He is one of those who stand in the presence of God (Rev. 8:2), and he is sent to announce the birth of John the Baptist [June 24; August 29] to Zechariah [November 5] (Luke 1:11–20) and the conception of Jesus to Mary [March 25] (Luke 1:26–38), addressing the Blessed Virgin in the memorable words, "Hail, full of grace. The Lord is with you." He is patron saint of messengers, diplomats, postal employees, and stamp collectors.

Raphael (Heb., "God heals") is God's messenger who hears people's prayers and brings these before God (Tob. 12:12, 15). He is identified as the angel who healed the earth when it was defiled by the sins of the fallen angels (*1 Enoch* 10:7). He is patron saint of travelers, physicians, nurses, lovers, health inspectors, and the sightless. Raphael's cult, unlike those of other two archangels, developed late and then only infrequently. A universal feast was instituted for him in 1921, but it has been merged now with that of Michael and Gabriel.

30 JEROME, PRIEST AND DOCTOR OF THE CHURCH

Jerome (ca. 345–420) is the most famous biblical scholar in the history of the Church, also known for his cantankerous temperament and sarcastic wit. He is patron saint of scholars, librarians, and those who study Sacred Scripture. Born Eusebius Hieronymus Sophronius at Stridon, near Aquileia, in Dalmatia, he was well educated, especially in grammar, rhetoric, and the classics, and was baptized sometime before 366. (It was the custom then to defer baptism until later in life.) After a period of travel, he decided to become a monk, along with a number of friends, ca. 370 in Aquileia, which was a major Christian center at the time. Because of a chance meeting with a priest from Antioch, Jerome and three of his friends left for the East, arriving in Antioch in 374. Two of his friends died there, and Jerome himself became seriously ill. While sick, he had a dream in which he appeared before the judgment seat of God and was condemned for being a Ciceronian rather than a Christian. He became a hermit at Chalcis in the Syrian desert for four or five years, gave up the study of the classics, and learned Hebrew in order to study the Scriptures in the original languages (he already knew Greek). He was ordained a priest in Antioch, even though he had no real desire to be a priest and, in fact, never celebrated Mass.

In 382 Jerome returned to Rome to act as interpreter for Paulinus, one of the claimants to the see of Antioch, at a council called by Pope Damasus I (366–84) [December 11]. Once the council was over, he was enlisted by the aged pope to serve as his secretary. While in Rome, Jerome did some biblical translations and began the enormous task of producing a Latin text of the entire Bible that would be faithful to the original languages. This would later be called the Vulgate version, which became the official Latin translation of the Bible. He also wrote a number of biblical commentaries.

In August 385, he returned to Antioch and eventually settled in Bethlehem, where he would spend the remainder of his life—living in a cell hewn from a rock near the traditional birthplace of Jesus—teaching, studying, and writing. Jerome died in Bethlehem on September 30, 420. He was proclaimed one of the four original Latin Doctors of the Church in 1298, along with Ambrose [December 7], Augustine [August 28], and Gregory the Great [September 3]. His feast is on the General Roman Calendar and is also observed by the Church of England, the Episcopal Church in the United States, and the Evangelical Lutheran Church in America.

OCTOBER

1 THERESA OF THE CHILD JESUS, VIRGIN AND DOCTOR OF THE CHURCH

Theresa of the Child Jesus (1873–97), or Thérèse of Lisieux, is better known as The Little Flower, a name drawn from the subtitle of her famous autobiography. Born Marie Francoise Thérèse Martin at Alençon, France, she became a Carmelite nun with the special permission of her bishop, because she was only fifteen. In the convent at Lisieux, Theresa eschewed the traditional medieval and Baroque path of excessive self-mortification and visionary experiences as well as the rigidity and formalism of much nineteenth-century spirituality and instead followed a simple and straightforward path to holiness.

In 1895, she had a hemorrhage, the first sign of tuberculosis that would eventually bring about her death. In June 1897, Theresa was moved to the convent infirmary and, after a period of spiritual as well as intense physical suffering, she died on September 30, at age twenty-four. It is likely that she would have remained unknown if she had not written a short autobiography, *The Story of a Soul,* which was translated into several languages and became widely popular. Many people attributed cures to her intercession, and her cult spread rapidly. Canonized by Pope Pius XI in 1925, St. Theresa became a highly influential model of sanctity for Catholics in the first half of the twentieth century because of the simplicity of her approach to spiritual life. Pope John Paul II declared her a Doctor of the Church in 1997. Her feast is on the General Roman Calendar.

2 GUARDIAN ANGELS

According to the belief of many Catholics (and of some pagans and Jews before the time of Christ), guardian angels are spiritual beings who protect individual persons from spiritual and physical harm. The belief has some basis in the New Testament (e.g., Matt. 18:10; Acts 12:15), and the *Catechism of the Catholic Church* assumes their existence and traditional function (n. 336). However, the Church has never defined anything about them. The guardian angels were originally commemorated with Michael the Archangel on September 29, but an independent feast, first found in Portugal in 1513, was later extended to the whole Church by Pope Clement X in 1670 and assigned to this day. It remains on the General Roman Calendar.

3 FRANCIS BORGIA, PRIEST

Francis Borgia (1510–72) was the third superior general of the Society of Jesus and is sometimes referred to as the second founder of the Jesuits. Of noble blood, he was born Francisco de Borja y Aragón in Valencia, Spain. He studied philosophy at Saragossa and then in 1529 married the empress Isabella's lady-in-waiting, Eleanor de Castro of Portugal. He and his family (eight children) lived happily at court for the next ten years. When the empress died in 1539, he was profoundly affected by the transitoriness of life and thereafter dedicated himself to a life of prayer and striving for holiness.

In 1545 he founded a Jesuit university and a hospital in Gandía. When his wife died in 1546, Francis vowed to become a Jesuit. On February 1, 1548, while still living in a manner befitting his noble rank, he secretly pronounced his first vows as a Jesuit and in August 1550 earned a doctorate in theology from the university he himself had founded. In late 1550 he went to Rome to meet Ignatius of Loyola [July 31]; while there he assisted Ignatius in the founding and financing of the Roman College (later the Pontifical Gregorian University). In February 1551, back in Spain, he resigned his title and put on the Jesuit habit for the first time. He was ordained a priest on May 26. Francis spent the next three years fulfilling the role of a parish priest, but in 1554 Ignatius appointed him commissary general of the order for Spain. While in this post he founded some twenty colleges and Spain's first Jesuit novitiate.

In 1565, Pope Pius IV named him vicar general of the order in Rome. He would remain in the position for seven years, during which he revised the Society's Constitutions, supervised the order's expansion into Poland, France, and elsewhere, promoted its missions in India and North and South America, and began the famous

Gesù Church in Rome. During the great plague of 1566, he raised large sums of money for the sick and sent his priests out to serve in hospitals and the poorest sections of the city. His spiritual writings during this period stressed self-knowledge and humility, the humanity of Jesus and his sufferings, the Eucharist, prayer, and the importance of sanctifying all of our daily actions. On September 30, 1572, Francis died at age sixty-one. He was canonized in 1671. His feast is celebrated by the Jesuits on this day, but it is not on the General Roman Calendar.

4   FRANCIS OF ASSISI, FRIAR

Francis of Assisi (1181/82–1226) was the founder of the Franciscans and is one of the most popular saints in the history of the Church. Born Francesco Bernardone, he was baptized Giovanni in honor of John the Baptist [June 24; August 29]. His father was a wealthy merchant, and Francis's early life was marked by high living and a concern for social status. After a serious illness in 1203, he experienced a profound change in his values, which caused him to be drawn increasingly to a life of prayer, penance, pilgrimages, and almsgiving. Francis began to spend more time working among social outcasts and the poor. He renounced his patrimony, gave back his fine clothes, and lived for several years as a hermit, caring for lepers and repairing ruined churches in the town.

In the spring of 1208 his life took yet another turn. In response to what he took to be a personal call (reflected in Matt. 10:7–19) during Mass in the Portiuncula, he donned the simple tunic and hood of a shepherd, with a cord tied around the waist. He began to preach publicly and to attract followers. By the next year there were twelve in his company, which became known as Penitentiaries of Assisi, although Francis preferred the name *fratres minores* (Lat., "lesser brothers"), which eventually became their official ecclesiastical name, Friars Minor. Francis wrote a brief statement on their way of life, based on a few Gospel texts, and took this primitive Rule to Rome to secure papal approval in 1210 (the Rule was revised and the order approved in 1223). Francis also became a deacon around this time, but, out of humility and a high regard for the priesthood, did not proceed to the next step of ordination.

When Francis returned to Assisi, his friars took up residence together at the rural chapel of the Portiuncula. This became the base from which they spread out in small groups through central Italy, doing manual labor and preaching. Wherever the Franciscans settled, they lived in simple wood huts without tables or chairs, their churches were modest and small, they slept on the ground, and they had very few books. At the first general chapter of 1217 Francis sent his friars beyond the Alps and even to the Near East, where the Crusaders had established their rule, and himself went to Egypt in 1219, where he was appalled by the behavior of the Crusaders themselves.

By 1223 his health had begun to fail, and he had to withdraw from normal activities for long periods of rest and prayer. He is said to have experienced the first recorded case of stigmata in 1224. Francis died at age forty-five on October 3, 1226, and was canonized two years later. His simple lifestyle and piety, devotion to the poor, and love for the whole of God's created order, including animals, have made him one of the Church's most beloved saints. His feast is on the General Roman Calendar and is also observed on this day by the Church of England, the Episcopal Church in the United States, and the Evangelical Lutheran Church in America.

5 BLESSED RAYMOND OF CAPUA, PRIEST

Raymond of Capua (1330–99) was the spiritual director of Catherine of Siena [April 29] and master general of the Dominican order. Born Raymond delle Vigne of a noble family in Capua, north of Naples, he studied at the University of Bologna and, while there, joined the Dominicans. He held various positions within the order in Rome and Florence before moving to Siena in 1374. It was there that he met Catherine of Siena, who, while attending one of his Masses, heard a voice saying: "This is my beloved servant; this is he to whom I shall entrust you." For the last six years of her life, he offered her spiritual guidance and encouragement. They also collaborated on apostolic works, beginning with the people of Siena who were suffering from an outbreak of plague. Raymond took ill and seemed to be at the point of death, until Catherine prayed for an hour and a half at his bedside. The next day he was completely recovered.

Catherine died in 1380, and Raymond was elected master general of that part of the Dominican order that supported Urban VI's claim to the papacy. His first concern was to revitalize the order in the aftermath of the Black

Death and in the midst of the Great Schism (1378–1417). He placed renewed emphasis on the monastic side of Dominican life and established a number of houses of strict observance in several provinces. Raymond of Capua died on October 5, 1399. His feast is not on the General Roman Calendar.

6   BRUNO, PRIEST

Bruno (ca. 1032–1101) was the founder of the Carthusian order. Born in Cologne, he became a canon at the Cologne cathedral before being ordained a priest in 1055. He was appointed a lecturer in grammar and theology at the prestigious cathedral school in Reims, where he himself had been a student. He held the post for more than eighteen years. After a time, he resigned his various offices, gave away his money, and retired with a few companions to the abbey of Molesmes, where he placed himself under the direction of its abbot, Robert, the founder of the Cistercians. He and his six companions lived in a hermitage away from the monastery, but Bruno felt that their solitude was not severe enough. They applied to Hugh [April 1], the bishop of Grenoble, for permission to settle in his diocese. Hugh gave them a remote, forested, mountainous piece of land called Cartusia or La Chartreuse, and in 1085 they built an oratory with some small cells around it. This was the beginning of the Carthusian order and its motherhouse, La Grande Chartreuse.

Their eremitical way of life, which emphasized poverty, solitude, and austerity, was inspired by the Desert Fathers of Egypt and Palestine rather than the Rule of

St. Benedict [July 11]. Their daily life consisted of prayer, reading, and manual work. Bruno founded a second hermitage at La Torre, in Calabria, where died on October 6, 1101. He was never formally canonized (he was simply declared a saint by Pope Leo X in 1514). His feast is on the General Roman Calendar.

7 OUR LADY OF THE ROSARY

The Rosary, also known as the "Psalter of Mary" because its 150 Hail Marys correspond to the number of psalms in the Bible, is a form of prayer, originating sometime in the twelfth or thirteenth century, in which fifteen decades of Hail Marys are recited, using beads as counters, while meditating on a sequence of Mysteries associated with the life of the Blessed Virgin. The Mysteries of the Rosary are divided into Joyful, Sorrowful, Glorious, and Luminous. The Joyful Mysteries are the Annunciation [March 25], the Visitation (of Mary to her cousin Elizabeth) [May 31], the Nativity [December 25], the Presentation (of Jesus in the Temple) [February 2], and the Finding of Jesus in the Temple. The Sorrowful Mysteries are the Agony in the Garden, the Scourging at the Pillar, the Crowning with Thorns, the Carrying of the Cross, and the Crucifixion. The Glorious Mysteries are the Resurrection, the Ascension, the Descent of the Holy Spirit upon the Apostles (Pentecost), the Assumption [August 15], and the Coronation of Mary (as Queen of Heaven) [August 22]. The Mysteries of Light, added by Pope John Paul II on this feast day in 2002, are the Baptism of Jesus in the Jordan, the Wedding at Cana, the proclamation of the Kingdom of God, the Transfiguration [August 6], and the institution of the Eucharist at the Last Supper.

The Rosary gained popularity through Rosary confraternities in the fifteenth century, experienced an upsurge in the nineteenth, especially because of the Marian apparitions at Lourdes (she carried a rosary), and remained a highly popular Catholic devotion through most of the twentieth century. Many Catholics prayed it daily, either individually or as a family. It was often prayed during the Latin Mass as a substitute for the missal. However, with the Second Vatican Council's reformed Mass in the vernacular with full congregational participation, private devotions receded in importance. Indeed, Pope Paul VI made it clear that the Rosary is not to be recited during Mass (*Marialis cultus*, 1974). The feast of Our Lady of the Rosary is on the General Roman Calendar.

8   PELAGIA, VIRGIN

The genuine *Pelagia* (d. ca. 311) was a young virgin martyr of Antioch, who was venerated there on October 8, at least since the fourth century. As a young girl of fifteen, she was arrested during a persecution. She asked the soldiers to allow her to go upstairs to change her clothes, whereupon she jumped off the roof to her death in the river below in order to escape dishonor. The story of this Pelagia became enmeshed in one told by Chrysostom in his sixty-seventh homily on Matthew's Gospel. It concerned a morally notorious, but nameless, actress from Antioch who had a sudden conversion and pursued thereafter a life of extreme austerity and solitude. She put on men's clothes and went to live as a solitary in a grotto near the Mount of Olives; only upon her death was her true identity revealed. This legendary Pelagia is the one commemorated on this day on the Greek and Russian Orthodox calendars. Her feast, however, is not on the General Roman Calendar.

9   DENIS, BISHOP, AND
COMPANIONS, MARTYRS

Denis (d. ca. 258), also known as Denys and Dionysius, is the principal patron saint of France. Italian by birth, he was one of six (or seven) missionary bishops sent by the pope ca. 250 to evangelize Gaul. He preached in Paris with great success and established a Christian presence on an island in the River Seine, aided by the priest Rusticus and the deacon Eleutherius. They were so effective that they were arrested, imprisoned, and then beheaded during the Valerian persecution. Their bodies were thrown into the river, but later recovered and buried. A chapel, built over their graves, served as the foundation in the seventh century of the great abbey of Saint-Denis, later the burial place of French kings. Denis has been recognized as the first bishop of Paris. His feast is on the General Roman Calendar

10 PAULINUS OF YORK, BISHOP

Paulinus of York (d. 644), one of the second group of monks sent to England by Pope Gregory the Great [September 3] in 601, was the first "apostle of Northumbria"

in England and the first bishop of York. After being consecrated a bishop in 625, Paulinus traveled north as chaplain to Ethelburga, Christian daughter of the king of Kent, in the hope of converting her pagan husband-to-be Edwin and his subjects in Northumbria. Paulinus eventually did so and baptized Edwin and his infant daughter at Easter 627 in a wooden church at York. He began building a cathedral in York, but his northern apostolate was cut short in 633 by the death of Edwin in battle against pagan forces. Queen Ethelburga fled back to Kent, and Paulinus went with her. Paulinus served as bishop of Rochester for the remainder of his life. He died on October 10, 644. His feast is not on the General Roman Calendar.

11   MARY SOLEDAD, VIRGIN

Mary Soledad (1826–87) was for thirty-five years the head of the Handmaids of Mary, a Spanish congregation of sisters whose mission was the service of the sick and the needy. Born Manuela Torres-Acosta in Madrid, she thought at first of becoming a Dominican nun, but was persuaded by the local parish priest, Michael Martinez y Sanz, to become part of his new community founded to minister to the sick. Manuela took the religious name Mary Soledad (Maria Desolata) in honor of Our Lady of Sorrows [September 15], to whom she had a special devotion. Five years later, the priest took half of the community to establish a new foundation in an African colony. Mary Soledad was left in charge of those who remained in Madrid. In 1861 their Rule received diocesan approval, and the community took the name Handmaids of Mary

Serving the Sick. Mary Soledad died on October 11, 1887, and was canonized in 1970. Her feast is not on the General Roman Calendar.

12 WILFRID OF YORK, BISHOP

Wilfrid (634–709) was bishop of York from 664 and a supporter of the Roman position on the dating of Easter. Born in Northumbria of a noble family, he became abbot of Ripon, where he introduced the Rule of St. Benedict [July 11]. He was then chosen bishop of Northumbria (centered in York) by King Alcfrith, but had to cross the English Channel to France to be consecrated. Upon his return to England in 666, he found that Alcfrith had died or was in exile and that his own place as bishop of York had been taken by Chad [March 2], nominated by King Oswiu and dubiously consecrated. Wilfrid retired to Ripon, but was later reinstated by Theodore, the archbishop of Canterbury, in 669.

With the support of King Egfrith and his wife, Etheldreda [June 23], Wilfrid obtained large tracts of land for the building of monasteries and churches. His power and wealth had already become subjects of gossip and criticism when he encouraged Etheldreda to separate from her husband, the king, and become a nun in 672. With the collaboration of King Egfrith and without Wilfrid's consent, Archbishop Theodore divided Northumbria into three, and then five, smaller dioceses. Wilfrid decided to appeal Theodore's action to Rome.

The pope did rule in favor of Wilfrid in the matter of his restoration to his see, but he upheld Theodore's

division of the diocese, with the stipulation that Wilfrid
be allowed to select his own suffragan bishops. The king
accused Wilfrid of having bribed the pope and placed
him in prison for nine months before releasing him on
condition that he leave the kingdom. Wilfrid went to
Sussex, which was the last stronghold of paganism in
Anglo-Saxon England, preaching there and on the Isle of
Wight and founding a monastery at Selsey (which later
developed into Chichester). He was reinstated, then exiled again. His final exile came to an end in 705 when he
agreed to yield his claim to York in return for full episcopal authority over the see of Hexham and the monasteries of Hexham and Ripon. He died in 709. His feast is
celebrated on this day by the Church of England, but it is
not on the General Roman Calendar.

13   EDWARD THE CONFESSOR, KING

Edward the Confessor (1003–66) was the king of England
from 1042 to 1066—the last king of the Anglo-Saxon line—
and virtual founder of Westminster Abbey. The son of
King Ethelred II and his second (Norman) wife, Emma,
Edward was educated at Ely and then in Normandy.
Edward's political record as king is a matter of some
debate within the historical community, but he was accessible to his subjects, generous to the poor, and had a
reputation for visions and healings. He also had a close
working relationship with the papacy. He appointed diocesan priests, sometimes from abroad, to bishoprics,
thereby diminishing the near monopoly of monastic
bishops. His decision to endow Westminster Abbey was

the result of a vow he had once made to visit Rome as a pilgrim if his family fortunes were restored. Later the pope released him from the vow on condition that he should endow a monastery dedicated to St. Peter [June 29]. Edward chose an existing monastic house at Thorney, to the west of London, and that became Westminster Abbey. Edward died on January 5, 1066. His feast is celebrated on this day by the Church of England, but it is not on the General Roman Calendar.

14 CALLISTUS I, POPE AND MARTYR

Callistus I (d. 222, pope 217–22) was the first pope, after Peter [June 29], whose name is commemorated as a martyr in the oldest martyrology of the Roman church, the *Depositio Martyrum* (ca. 354). Callistus was a Roman by birth and in his youth had been a slave of a Christian who set him up in banking. When the business failed, Callistus fled. After his return, he was charged with fighting in a synagogue on the Sabbath and sentenced to hard labor in the mines of Sardinia. Liberated with a number of other Christian slaves, he was later appointed deacon by Pope Zephrynus, with supervisory authority over the clergy of Rome and the church's official cemetery on the Appian Way. Because of Zephrynus's own intellectual and administrative limitations, Callistus exerted enormous influence as the pope's deacon and was elected to succeed him. Hippolytus [August 13], however, refused to accept the election and seems to have sought and received election as bishop by a schismatic group, thereby becoming the first of the Catholic Church's thirty-nine antipopes.

Callistus's five-year pontificate was defined in large part by his constant battles with Hippolytus and his faction, who accused the pope of doctrinal deviations and laxity in discipline (e.g., readmitting heretics and schismatics to the Church without adequate prior penances). Both charges were unfair. Callistus's approach to sinners was actually closer to that of Jesus than to that of the new rigorists in the Church. Although his name appears in the oldest Roman martyrology, it is questionable whether he was, in fact, a martyr. Historians point out that there was no persecution during his pontificate. His feast is on the General Roman Calendar.

15   TERESA OF ÁVILA, VIRGIN AND DOCTOR OF THE CHURCH

Teresa of Ávila (1515–82) was the foundress of the Discalced Carmelites and one of the first two women to be named a Doctor of the Church (with Catherine of Siena [April 29]). She is also the patron saint of Spain. Born Teresa de Ahumada y Cepeda near Ávila, Spain, of a large, aristocratic Castilian family with Jewish ancestry, she entered the Carmelite monastery of the Incarnation at Ávila in 1535 after reading the letters of St. Jerome [September 30] during a period of convalescence from an illness that may have been psychosomatic.

In 1554, while praying before a statue of the wounded Christ, she underwent a profound spiritual conversion. She later wrote: "When I fell to prayer again and looked at Christ hanging poor and naked upon the Cross, I felt I could not bear to be rich. So I besought him with tears to bring it to pass that I might be as poor as he." Between then and 1560, her mystical and visionary experiences became the subject of gossip, and she was exposed to misunderstanding, ridicule, and even persecution.

In 1562, with thirteen other nuns, she established a convent in Ávila where the primitive Carmelite Rule would be strictly observed, and in the same year composed the first draft of her *Life*, a treatise on mystical prayer. Thereafter, she always signed herself Teresa de Jesus. This first reformed convent would become the prototype for sixteen others she would found in her lifetime. Their mode of life would be marked by personal poverty, signified by the coarse brown wool habit, leather sandals, and beds of straw, manual work, abstinence from meat, and solitude. Teresa's many writings, including *The Way of Perfection* and *Meditations on the Song of Songs*, were done under obedience, but also with the encouragement of the Dominican Domingo Báñez, one of the most prominent theologians of the time, who became her spiritual director and confessor and who defended her before civil and ecclesiastical tribunals during a time when her reforms for the Carmelites were being challenged.

In 1577 she began the composition of her masterpiece, *The Interior Castle*, which describes the mystical life through the symbolism of seven mansions. Although Teresa was profoundly contemplative, she led an active life not only as a reformer of Carmelite life, but also as an adviser to and correspondent with countless people of every station in life. She died on October 4, 1582, was canonized in 1622, and was named a Doctor of the Church in 1970. Her feast is on the General Roman Calendar.

16 HEDWIG, RELIGIOUS;
MARGARET MARY ALACOQUE,
VIRGIN

Hedwig (ca. 1174–1243), or Jadwiga, is patron saint of Silesia. Born at Andechs (Bavaria), the daughter of a count, at age twelve she married the eighteen-year-old duke of Silesia. She and her husband helped to found several religious houses, including the first (Cistercian) convent of women in Silesia as well as hospitals and a house for lepers. After the birth of their seventh child, she and her husband took a vow of chastity and lived as brother and sister. Following her husband's death in 1238, she took the habit of a Cistercian nun, but did not take religious vows so that she would still be free to administer her property for the benefit of the poor. Hedwig was said to have foretold her own death at the convent in Trebnitz (Trzebnica), near Breslau in October 1243. She was canonized in 1267. Her feast is on the General Roman Calendar.

Margaret Mary Alacoque (1647–90) was the principal founder of devotion to the Sacred Heart of Jesus. Born in a small town in Burgundy, she was only eight when she was sent away to school with the Poor Clares after the death of her father. She entered the Visitation convent of Paray-le-Monial in 1671 at age twenty. From 1673 to 1675 she is said to have experienced a series of visions of Christ revealing to her the love and mercy of God for all people. The visions urged her to persuade church authorities to have a special feast celebrated on the Friday after the Octave of Corpus Christi and to develop what eventually became the devotion of the First Fridays (attending Mass and receiving Communion on nine consecutive first Fridays of the month, a devotion that was especially popular prior to the Second Vatican Council [1962–65]).

At first Margaret Mary encountered opposition, but then she was supported and encouraged by Claude La Colombière [February 15] and John Eudes [August 19]. The devotion itself consists of veneration of the physical heart of Jesus, united to his divinity, as the symbol of his redemptive love for all. The feast of the Sacred Heart was first celebrated in Visitation convents and then extended to the universal Church in 1856. Margaret May Alacoque died at age forty-three, on October 17, 1690. She was canonized in 1920, and her feast is on the General Roman Calendar.

17 IGNATIUS OF ANTIOCH, BISHOP AND MARTYR

Ignatius of Antioch (ca. 35–ca. 107) is the Apostolic Father whose letters to the various churches in the ancient Christian world serve as a major source of information regarding the life, faith, and structure of the early Church in Asia Minor and Rome. He was also the first writer to use the term "Catholic Church" as a collective designation for Christians. The facts of his early life are largely unknown. He is thought to have been a disciple of John the Evangelist [December 27]. He became bishop of Antioch ca. 69 and was condemned to death during Trajan's persecution of Christians and taken to Rome. During this journey he wrote six letters to six churches and one separate letter to Polycarp [February 23], the bishop of Smyrna, whom he met en route. The letters stress the divinity and the humanity of Jesus Christ, his bodily death and resurrection, the central importance of the Eucharist and the bishop for church unity, and the special reverence owed to the church of Rome as the one founded by Peter and Paul [June 29]. Upon reaching Rome, he was taken to the Colosseum and thrown to the lions, dying almost immediately. From the beginning, Antioch kept his feast on October 17. The Western Church had observed it on February 1 until 1969, when it transferred it to October 17.

18   LUKE, EVANGELIST

Luke (first century) is the traditional author of the Third Gospel and was a companion of Paul [June 29]. According to a reliable tradition, Luke was a Syrian physician from Antioch who wrote his Gospel in Achaea (Greece) and lived as a celibate to the age of eighty-four, when he died in Boeotia. The *Muratorian Canon*, a list of New Testament books probably from the late second century, identifies Luke as the author of the Third Gospel. Irenaeus [June 28] attributes both the Gospel and Acts of the Apostles to Luke, arguing that Luke is the person intended by the first-person references in Acts. The opening of Acts refers to the Gospel and is dedicated to the same person, Theophilus. He is thought to have accompanied Paul on his second (Acts 16:10–17) and third (Acts 20:5–24) missionary journeys.

The basic point of Luke's New Testament writings is to underscore the love and compassion of Christ and his concern for the poor. Some of the most moving and memorable parables emphasizing these themes are in Luke's Gospel, for example, the prodigal son (15:11–32) and the rich man and Lazarus (16:19–31). Women also figure more prominently in his Gospel than in any other. Luke's feast is on the General Roman Calendar and is celebrated on this day by all the major Christian Churches, Eastern and Western alike.

19 ISAAC JOGUES, JOHN DE BRÉBEUF, AND COMPANIONS, MARTYRS

Isaac Jogues (1607–46), *John de Brébeuf* (1593–1649), and their companions are known collectively as the North American Martyrs and are patron saints of North America. Isaac Jogues was born in Orléans, France, became a Jesuit in 1624, and was ordained a priest in early 1636. He was sent to Canada, or the New France, to preach the gospel to the Hurons. After some limited success at Sainte-Marie, he returned to Quebec to ask for more missionaries. Since there were no Jesuits available, he was given the services of *René Goupil,* a lay assistant. During their return trip to Sainte-Marie, they were attacked by Mohawks, taken captive, and brought to the Mohawk village. On the way, Jogues accepted Goupil's vows as a Jesuit. When they reached the village on the bank of the Mohawk River, they were tortured for three days, then handed over to the chief to act as his personal slaves. A few weeks later, on September 29, 1642, Goupil was tomahawked to death for making the sign of the cross on a child. Jogues, however, endured months of slavery, before eventually escaping and finding his way back to France.

The following June he returned to New France. He attended a lengthy peace conference between the French and the Iroquois federation. The Mohawks would also have to give their approval, and Jogues was chosen to go to the Mohawks to secure it. When he and his party arrived at the Mohawk village, the Indians were amazed to see their former slave acting as the envoy of the powerful French nation. He returned to Quebec, but asked permission to return to the Mohawks as a missionary once again, now that they had agreed to the treaty. He was accompanied by *John de la Lande,* a layman, and several Hurons.

In the meantime, however, the Mohawks had suffered both a crop failure and an epidemic and blamed their misfortune on Jogues. They stripped and beat Jogues and his two companions and dragged them to the village. The next day, October 18, 1646, Jogues was tomahawked to death. His killer hacked off Jogues's head and dragged his body through the village. De la Lande was killed the next day.

Three years later *John de Brébeuf* and *Gabriel Lalement,* who had worked successfully among the Hurons, were brutally tortured, mutilated, burned, and then eaten when the Hurons' village was attacked by their deadly enemies, the Iroquois. They, along with Isaac Jogues, René Goupil, *Charles Garnier, Anthony Daniel,* and *Noel Chabanel,* were beatified in 1925 and canonized in 1930. Their feast is on the General Roman Calendar.

20 MARIA BERTILLA BOSCARDIN, NUN; JERZY POPIELUSZKO, PRIEST

Maria Bertilla Boscardin (1888–1922) was a nun and nurse whose life bore a striking spiritual resemblance to that of Thérèse of Lisieux [October 1], whose own sanctity was rooted in the faithful performance of the daily, simple duties of her state in life. Born Anna Francesca, in northern Italy, of a poor family, with an alcoholic and abusive father, she lacked the advantage of a normal education and was disparaged by many for her seeming lack of intelligence. When, in 1904, she joined the Sisters of St. Dorothy, she was given the name Maria Bertilla and assigned to work in the kitchen and laundry; however, she was also allowed to train as a nurse. Three years later, she was transferred to the children's diphtheria ward, where she demonstrated a special gift for relating to ill and disturbed children. With the outbreak of World War I the hospital was taken over by the military for the care of the wounded, and by 1917 it was in the front line of the fighting. Maria Bertilla cared for those patients who could not be moved, even in the face of constant air raids and bombings. Maria Bertilla died on October 20, 1922, and was canonized in 1961. Her feast is not on the General Roman Calendar.

This is also the day of death of *Jerzy Popieluszko* (1947–84), a Polish diocesan priest who was murdered by agents of the Communist government in retaliation for his activities in support of the Solidarity movement.

21   HILARION, HERMIT

Hilarion (ca. 291–371), also known as Hilarion the Great, was the founder of monasticism in Palestine. Born of pagan parents in a village in the south of Gaza in Palestine, Hilarion became a Christian while still in his mid-teens. For a short time he stayed with Anthony in the Egyptian desert, but left because of the many visitors who came to see the famous master. He retired to Majuma, between the sea and a swamp, where he lived a life of extreme austerity in imitation of Anthony. His fame spread after several years, and people began flocking to see him in order to obtain spiritual guidance. Eventually, he decided to leave his native country in search of a place where he could enjoy complete solitude. His travels took him to Egypt, Sicily, Dalmatia, and finally Cyprus. He found some solitude in that last place, but he was still disturbed by visitors. He died at the age eighty. His fame derives from a popular biography of him written by Jerome. Hilarion's feast is not on the General Roman Calendar, but it is celebrated on this day by the Greek and Russian Orthodox Churches.

22   PETER OF ALCÁNTARA, FOUNDER

Peter of Alcántara (1499–1562) was the founder of the Franciscans of the Observance of St. Peter of Alcántara, or Alcantarines, and spiritual adviser to Teresa of Ávila [October 15]. Born Pedro Garavita at Alcántara, Spain, he studied at the University of Salamanca and joined the strict Franciscan Friars of the Observance in 1515. He followed an extremely austere regime of mortification, similar to that of the Desert Fathers, eating sparingly and sleeping as little as possible and then usually in a sitting position. Because of this practice, he was later designated as the patron saint of night watchmen. Ordained a priest in 1524, he became superior of a number of Franciscan houses and was a provincial from 1538 to 1541.

In 1554 he went to Rome to seek permission to found a stricter congregation of friars. This was the beginning of the Franciscans of the Observance of St. Peter of Alcántara, or Alcantarines. The Alcantarine Rule required that cells be only seven feet in length and that the friars go about barefoot, abstain from meat and wine, practice three hours of mental prayer daily, and subsist on almsgiving. Peter died in 1562 and was canonized in 1669. Although his feast day is in the *Roman Martyrology* on October 19 (but is not on the General Roman Calendar), Franciscans celebrate it on this day.

23 JOHN OF CAPISTRANO, PRIEST

John of Capistrano (1386–1456) was a renowned Franciscan preacher who is the patron saint of military chaplains and jurists. Born at Capistrano in the Abruzzi region of Italy, he studied law at Perugia, married, and became governor of Perugia in 1412. He was imprisoned for a time during a civil war and claimed to have had a vision of St. Francis [October 4] that generated a spiritual conversion. He joined the Franciscans in 1415 and was ordained a priest four years later. John studied with Bernardino of Siena [May 20] and became a successful preacher, attracting large crowds. In 1443 John became vicar general of the Cismontaine family of the Observants. John always insisted that efforts at reform should begin with oneself. He went about barefoot, wore a hair shirt, and ate and slept little.

After Constantinople fell to the Turks in 1453, Pope Pius II called upon John to preach a new crusade against the Turks. John's moral support and help in raising an army was credited in part with the victory of the Hungarian forces in defense of Belgrade. John died at Ilok (or Villach), Austria, on October 23, 1456. He was canonized in 1690 (two sources say 1724.) His feast was extended to the calendar of the universal Church in 1890 (one source says 1880) and is on the General Roman Calendar today.

24 ANTHONY CLARET, BISHOP

Anthony Claret (1807–70) was the founder of the congregation of the Missionary Sons of the Immaculate Heart of Mary, better known as the Claretians. Born Antonio Juan Claret i Clará at Sallent in northern Spain, he was ordained a diocesan priest in 1835, went to Rome to offer his services as a missionary, and became a Jesuit novice. Because of health problems, however, he had to return to Spain, where for ten years he gave retreats and missions and engaged in other forms of pastoral work in Catalonia. During this period he founded in 1849 the congregation of the Missionary Sons of the Immaculate Heart of Mary (the Claretians). In 1850 he was appointed archbishop of Santiago, Cuba, a diocese that had been vacant for fourteen years, where he encountered much opposition from powerful anti-Christian groups, including even an assassination attempt. After seven years of dedicated pastoral ministry of every kind, he resigned in 1857 and returned to Spain to become confessor to Queen Isabella II. He died on October 24, 1870, and was canonized in 1950. His feast is on the General Roman Calendar.

25 FORTY MARTYRS OF ENGLAND AND WALES

This feast celebrates the martyrdoms of forty English and Welsh Catholics executed for their faith between 1535 and 1679. Their names were selected by Pope Paul VI in 1970 from a list of some two hundred martyrs already beatified by previous popes. There were four laywomen, three laymen, thirteen diocesan priests, ten Jesuits, three Benedictines, three Carthusian monks, one Brigittine nun, two Franciscans, and one Augustinian friar. The forty include those who were executed for refusing to take the Oath of Supremacy, simply being priests, or harboring priests.

The first of these martyrs were executed in 1535 for refusing to recognize Henry VIII as supreme head of the Church in England. There were no executions of Catholics during the reign of Edward VI (1547–53) or Mary I (1553–58), but in the latter's reign some 280 Protestants were put to death. The succession of Elizabeth I in 1558 brought a return to Protestantism, but there was little active persecution of Catholics for the first twelve years of her reign. The change came after the Northern Rebellion of 1569, the excommunication of the queen by Pope Pius V in 1570, and the Ridolfi Plot of 1571 to depose the queen.

Twenty of the Forty Martyrs suffered under the legislation that followed the papal action. Altogether about 190 were martyred between 1570 and Elizabeth's death in 1603. The feast of the Forty Martyrs is not on the General Roman Calendar.

26 CEDD, BISHOP;
ALFRED THE GREAT, KING

Cedd (d. 664) was the bishop of the East Saxons and the brother of Chad of Lichfield [March 2]. Educated at Lindisfarne by Aidan, he became a monk there and was ordained a priest. Cedd was consecrated bishop of the East Saxons at Lindisfarne. As bishop he founded two monasteries in the region, and then another in North Yorkshire at Lastingham in 658. Soon after the Synod of Whitby (664), where he acted as a mediator between those favoring the Roman system for the dating of Easter and those favoring the Celtic, Cedd died of the plague at Lastingham, where he was buried, on October 26. His feast is not on the General Roman Calendar, but it is commemorated on this day by the Church of England.

Also on this day the Church of England and the Episcopal Church in the United States celebrate the feast of *Alfred the Great* (849–99), king of Wessex from 871 and one of the most successful Christian leaders in English history. He promoted church reform and learning and founded monastic communities. He has no feast day in the Catholic Church.

27 BLESSED BARTHOLOMEW OF VICENZA, FRIAR

Bartholomew of Vicenza (ca. 1200–1271) was a Dominican friar. Born Bartholomew Breganza in Venice, he was educated at Padua, entered the Dominicans ca. 1220, and served as prior of several Dominican houses. In 1233, with John of Vicenza, he founded the *Fratres Gaudentes* (Lat., "Joyful Brothers"), a military order, for the purpose of keeping the civil peace in Bologna. The order spread to towns all over Italy. He left a legacy of sermons, biblical commentaries, and a treatise on one of the writings of Dionysius the Areopagite. He died on July 1, 1271, and was beatified in 1793. His feast is not on the General Roman Calendar, but it is celebrated on this day by the Dominicans.

28 SIMON AND JUDE, APOSTLES

Simon (first century) was one of the twelve apostles. His nickname was the "Cananaean" (Matt. 10:4; Mark 3:18), Aramaic for "Zealot" (Luke 6:15; Acts 1:13). He is often called Simon the Less to distinguish him from Simon Peter [June 29]. According to tradition, he engaged in missions to Egypt and Persia, where he and Jude were martyred together on the same day. *Jude* (first century) was also one of the twelve apostles, best known as the patron saint of hopeless causes as well as of hospitals. There are only three brief mentions of him in the New Testament: Luke 6:16, John 14:22 (where the author is careful to distinguish him from Judas Iscariot), and Acts 1:13. These few texts imply that, like Simon, Jude was an obscure figure who is often confused with others with the same name. Ancient legends mention his missionary work in Mesopotamia and Persia. Only in the twentieth century did he become known as the patron saint of hopeless causes. It may be that no one wanted to pray to him because his name was so close to that of Judas, the one who betrayed Jesus, and that people turned to Jude only after all other intercessors had apparently failed. The feast day of Simon and Jude is on the General Roman Calendar. In the Greek and Russian Orthodox Churches they have separate feast days: Simon's on May 10, and Jude's on June 19.

29 NARCISSUS OF JERUSALEM, BISHOP

Narcissus of Jerusalem (d. 215) was a venerable figure in second- and third-century Jerusalem, thought to have been 160 years old at the time of his death. A Greek by birth, he became bishop of Jerusalem ca. 190 and is reported to have performed many miracles, including the changing of water into oil for the church lamps on the Easter Vigil. Despite his reputation for holiness, he was often attacked by people who resented the rigor with which he imposed church discipline. In a letter written soon after in 212, Alexander, coadjutor bishop in Jerusalem, refers to Narcissus as still alive at the age of 116. There are no details of his death, and his feast is not on the General Roman Calendar.

30 BLESSED BENVENUTA OF CIVIDALE, VIRGIN

Benvenuta of Cividale (1254–92) was a Dominican tertiary. Born Benvenuta Boiani at Cividale in Fruili, Italy, of well-to-do parents, she derived her Christian name from her father's remark upon learning that he had a daughter rather than a hoped-for son, "She is welcome (It. *benvenuta*) all the same!" Drawn to a contemplative rather than an active spiritual life, she took a vow of lifelong chastity at a young age and joined the third order of St. Dominic [August 8]. She went to excess, however, in some of her ascetical practices, sometimes using the discipline (self-flagellation) on herself three times a night or tying a rope around her waist so tightly that it dug into her flesh and gave her great pain. She died on October 30, 1292. Her feast is not on the General Roman Calendar.

31 ALPHONSUS RODRÍGUEZ, RELIGIOUS

Alphonsus Rodríguez (1533–1617) was a Spanish Jesuit lay brother. Born in Segovia, Spain, of a well-to-do wool merchant, Alphonsus inherited his father's business when he was twenty-three. Within the space of three years, his wife, daughter, and mother died. He began to think of what God expected of him in this life. When his son died some years later, he decided to join the Jesuits, but was rejected for lack of education. He applied a second time and was accepted as a lay brother in 1571. For forty-five years he served as the doorkeeper at the Jesuit College of Montesión in Majorca, integrating a life of prayer and self-mortification with his daily responsibilities. He was allowed to take his final vows in 1585. His reputation for holiness grew, and soon people came to him for spiritual guidance. Alphonsus died October 31, 1617. In 1633 he was declared patron saint of Majorca and was canonized in 1888. Alphonsus's feast is not on the General Roman Calendar, but it is celebrated by the Jesuits on this day.

NOVEMBER

1 ALL SAINTS

The feast of *All Saints* celebrates the triumph of Christ's grace in every person who now enjoys the eternal vision of God in heaven. The scope of this feast includes those who have officially been recognized by the Church as saints; those whose lives of sanctity were known only to their families, friends, and associates or to members of their parish, diocese, or other religious community; and those, like Pope John XXIII (1881–1963) [June 3] or Dorothy Day (1897–1980) [November 29], who enjoyed an international reputation for holiness but whose causes for canonization have not yet been completed.

The first explicit mention of November 1 as the day for observing such a feast seems to come from England, where the feast was introduced during the first quarter of the eighth century, probably by Egbert of York. By the twelfth century, November 1 was securely established as the date of the celebration. In England and Ireland this feast was formerly known as All Hallows. This explains the name for the secular celebration of Halloween, on the "eve" of the feast itself (thus, Hallowe'en, or Hallow evening). The theology underlying this feast is well expressed in the Second Vatican Council's Dogmatic Constitution on the Church: "In the lives of those . . . who are more perfectly transformed into the image of Christ God shows, vividly, to humanity his presence and his face. He speaks to us in them" (n. 50). This feast is on the General Roman Calendar with the rank of a Solemnity.

2   ALL SOULS

The feast of *All Souls,* also known as the Commemoration of All the Faithful Departed, is a celebration of the lives of loved ones who have gone before us in death, but who may still be in need of the Church's prayers of petition for their deliverance from purgatory into heaven. Unlike the ecumenical feast of All Saints [November 1], this feast is theologically rooted in the distinctively Catholic doctrine of purgatory, an after-death state of purification from the temporal punishment still due to sins that have already been forgiven, sacramentally (i.e., in the Sacrament of Reconciliation, or Penance) or through a personal act of contrition. Eastern Christians rejected the West's juridical approach and stressed instead the more mystical nature of the purgative state as a process of maturation and spiritual growth. However, the Council of Trent defined the existence of purgatory and insisted that the souls detained there are helped by acts of intercession of the faithful and especially by the sacrifice of the Mass (*Decree on Purgatory,* 1563).

The first evidence of this feast is in seventh-century Spain. Two centuries later, in 988, Odilo, abbot of Cluny, directed his community to observe November 2 as a day of prayer for the dead. From Cluny the practice spread rapidly and widely, but it was not until after another two or three centuries that the feast was commonly found on November 2 in liturgical calendars and martyrologies. The Commemoration of All the Faithful Departed is on the General Roman Calendar and is also celebrated on this day by the Church of England and the Episcopal Church in the United States. The month of November, and especially this day, is a traditional time for visiting the graves of loved ones.

3   MARTIN DE PORRES, RELIGIOUS

Martin de Porres (1579–1639) is the patron saint of race relations and of social justice. He was born out of wedlock in Lima, Peru, to a Spanish knight and a freed slave from Panama. To his father's disappointment, Martin inherited his mother's features and complexion. In his early years, Martin served as an apprentice to a barber-surgeon. Already a Dominican tertiary, in 1595 he entered a Dominican convent in Lima as a lay helper and in 1603 was invited to become a lay brother, devoting himself to the care of the sick and the poor, regardless of race, and to menial tasks of barbering, gardening, and the like. He gained a reputation for spiritual insight and for the power of healing. His Dominican confreres called him "father of charity," but Martin referred to himself as "mulatto dog." Because his desire to become a foreign missionary and suffer martyrdom was thwarted, he committed himself instead to a life of prayer and rigorous penances. He died on November 3, 1639, at age sixty. He was beatified in

1837 and canonized by Pope John XXIII in 1962. His feast is on the General Roman Calendar.

4   CHARLES BORROMEO, BISHOP

Charles Borromeo (1538–84) was one of the most important bishops in the history of the Church and one of the outstanding figures in the Catholic Reformation. He is the patron saint of bishops, catechists, and seminarians. Born of an aristocratic and wealthy family in a castle on Lake Maggiore, Carlo Borromeo was educated in Milan and then in Pavia, where he earned a doctorate in civil and canon law. He had received tonsure (entrance into the clerical state) at age twelve. His uncle became Pope Pius IV in 1559. Under his uncle, Charles became administrator of the diocese of Milan, a cardinal, secretary of state, an active participant in the third session of the Council of Trent (1562–63), and papal legate for all of Italy.

After Pius IV died in 1565, Charles returned to his diocese of Milan (he had been ordained a priest and then bishop in 1563). He adopted a simple standard of living for himself and gave away to the poor much of his substantial revenue. He held councils and synods, made regular visits to his parishes, reorganized the diocesan administration, established seminaries for the education of future priests, enforced standards of morality for his clergy, and founded a confraternity to teach Christian doctrine to children. His reforms were so energetic and far-reaching that some disgruntled members of a rival lay movement attempted to assassinate him in 1569. Charles was only slightly wounded, and the group was later suppressed.

When in 1578 his cathedral canons refused to cooperate with some of his reform programs, Charles founded a society of diocesan priests, the Oblates of St. Ambrose [December 7], to carry out his wishes. The society still exists as the Society of St. Ambrose and St. Charles (Ambrosians). He died in Milan on November 3, 1584, at age forty-six and was canonized in 1610. His feast is on the General Roman Calendar.

5   ZECHARIAH AND ELIZABETH

Zechariah and *Elizabeth* (first century) were the parents of John the Baptist [June 24, August 29]. According to Luke 1:5–25, 57–80, while performing his priestly duties in the Temple, Zechariah learned of John's forthcoming birth from the angel Gabriel [September 29]. When he expressed doubt about the news and requested a sign, he was struck speechless. After John was born, Zechariah was still unable to speak until the eighth day, when an argument arose about his name. Relatives wanted him to be named after his father, but Elizabeth insisted that his name would be John. Zechariah asked for a writing tablet and wrote: "His name is John." At that moment he recovered his power of speech, whereupon he pronounced the prophetic oracle known as the Benedictus (Luke 1:68–79). Some of the Fathers of the Church believed that Zechariah died a martyr, but there is no historical evidence of that. Nevertheless, he has been venerated throughout the East.

   Elizabeth, the wife of Zechariah and mother of John the Baptist, was aged and barren when she conceived her son. At her cousin Mary's visit, Elizabeth pronounced the second verse of the Hail Mary prayer: "Blessed are you among women and blessed is the fruit of your womb" (Luke 1:42). Unlike her husband Zechariah's feast, Elizabeth's has never been celebrated on its own. Their joint feast is not on the General Roman Calendar.

6   PAUL OF CONSTANTINOPLE, BISHOP

Paul of Constantinople (ca. 300–ca. 350) was a strong defender of the teaching of the Council of Nicaea (325) against the Arians (who denied that Jesus Christ was equal in divinity to God the Father). Born in Thessalonica, Paul succeeded Alexander in the see of Constantinople ca. 336. But he himself was soon displaced by an Arian, Eusebius of Nicomedia, who had the support of the emperor Constantius. After Eusebius's death, Paul was reelected, but encountered resistance from the Arians. This, in turn, provoked a popular rebellion in support of Paul in 342, during which the emperor's representative was killed in a skirmish. As a result, Paul was exiled to Pontus. Under pressure from the West, Paul was reinstated in Constantinople, but Paul was later exiled, first to Mesopotamia, then to Emesa, and finally to Cucusus in Armenia, where he was strangled to death—according to legend—by the Arians. His feast is not on the General Roman Calendar, but it is celebrated on this day by the Greek and Russian Orthodox Churches.

7   WILLIBRORD, BISHOP

Willibrord (658–739) was the "apostle of Frisia" and archbishop of Utrecht, and is patron saint of the Netherlands (Holland) and Luxembourg. Born in Northumbria,
England, he was educated by Wilfrid [October 12] at
Ripon Abbey and went to Ireland at age twenty for further study. Willibrord stayed in Ireland for twelve years
and at some point was ordained a priest. He returned
to England in 690 and, under the inspiration of the monastic leader Egbert, he went with twelve companions
as a missionary to Frisia, along the coast of what is now
the Netherlands. With the support of the Frankish ruler
Pepin II and then of Pope Sergius I, Willibrord's mission prospered. In 695 he was consecrated archbishop of
the Frisians by the pope, given the additional name of
Clement, and sent back to his mission territory with a
papal mandate to establish a metropolitan diocese with
its center at Utrecht. Willibrord built churches and monasteries and consecrated bishops for the new dioceses. He
died on November 7, 739, at age eighty-one. His feast is
not on the General Roman Calendar.

8   BLESSED JOHN DUNS SCOTUS, FRIAR

John Duns Scotus (ca. 1265–1308) was a Franciscan philosopher and theologian known as the "Subtle Doctor" and
the "Marian Doctor." Born John of Duns, in Duns, Scotland (thus, the name "Scotus"), he became a Franciscan at
age fifteen and went to study at Oxford. He was ordained

a priest in 1291. After ordination he studied in Paris, then lectured at Cambridge, then completed his master's degree at the University of Paris in 1305 and spent the next two years lecturing there. At the end of 1307 he publicly defended the view, controversial at the time, that Mary was conceived free from original sin, a forerunner of the dogma of the Immaculate Conception [December 8]. Because of the vehemently negative reaction to his defense of the Immaculate Conception, Scotus was moved to the University of Cologne, where he lectured and defended the Catholic faith against various dissident groups. He died in Cologne on November 8, 1308, at age forty-three. His feast is not on the General Roman Calendar.

9   DEDICATION OF ST. JOHN LATERAN

The oldest of the four major basilicas of Rome, *St. John Lateran* (whose official title is the Patriarchal Basilica of the Most Holy Savior and St. John the Baptist at the Lateran) stands on the site of an ancient palace on the Celian Hill, which formerly belonged to the Laterani family. The Lateran Basilica (not St. Peter's), originally known as the Church of the Savior, is the pope's cathedral church in his primary role as Bishop of Rome. It is considered "the mother and head of all churches of Rome and the world." Five ecumenical councils were held there (in 1123, 1139, 1179, 1215, and 1512–17). This feast, which commemorates the original dedication of the basilica by Pope Sylvester I on November 9, 324, is on the General Roman Calendar.

10 LEO THE GREAT, POPE AND
    DOCTOR OF THE CHURCH

Leo the Great (d. 461, pope 440–61) is one of only two popes given the title "the Great" (the other being Gregory the Great [September 3]). Born in Rome of Tuscan parents at the end of the fourth century, he served as an adviser to Celestine I (422–32) and Sixtus III (432–40). As pope, he proved to be a strong advocate of papal authority and of the teachings of the Council of Chalcedon (451) on the humanity and divinity of Jesus Christ. So forcefully articulated were Leo's claims for the pope's universal and supreme authority over the Church, in fact, that his own pontificate constituted a major turning point in the history of the papacy. He was the first pope to claim to be Peter's heir, which, according to Roman law, meant that all the rights and duties associated with Peter [June 29] lived on in Leo. Thereafter, the popes increasingly regarded themselves as standing in the place of Peter, exercising authority not only over all of the faithful, but over all of the other bishops as well.

Indeed, Leo himself exercised firm control over the bishops of Italy, enforcing uniformity of pastoral practice, correcting abuses, and resolving disputes. Other areas, e.g., Spain and North Africa, eagerly sought his instructions on combating heresy and on irregularities in elections and other conflicts. The East, however, was much less disposed than the West to accept Leo's papal claims. In June 449 he sent an important letter (*Letter 28*), or *Tome*, to Bishop Flavian of Constantinople, condemning the Monophysite teaching that in Christ there is only a divine nature and not a human nature as well. After much dispute, however, an ecumenical council endorsed the Christological teaching of Leo and others; namely, that in Jesus Christ there are two natures, one divine and one human, which are hypostatically united in one divine Person. Leo's *Tome* was respectfully received and approved as a standard of orthodoxy and as an expression of "the voice of Peter."

Leo is also celebrated for his courageous personal confrontation with Attila the Hun near Mantua in 452, persuading him to withdraw northward. Leo died on November 10, 461, and was declared a Doctor of the Church in 1754. His feast is on the General Roman Calendar and is celebrated by the Russian Orthodox Church on February 18.

11   MARTIN OF TOURS, BISHOP

Martin of Tours (ca. 316–97) is a patron saint of France and was the founder of monasticism in Gaul (present-day France). His father was a pagan officer in the Roman army, and Martin was pressured to serve in the military as well. While still a catechumen, he refused military service as a matter of conscience and was imprisoned and then discharged in 357. It is in this period of his life that the legendary episode so often depicted by artists was said to have occurred at Amiens. After he cut his cloak in half to clothe a naked beggar, he is said to have seen Christ in a dream wearing the same cloak. In 360 Hilary of Poitiers [January 13] gave Martin land at Ligugé on which to live as a hermit. Disciples soon joined him there, forming the first monastery in all of Gaul and the first known monastic foundation north of the Alps. Martin was popularly acclaimed bishop of Tours in 372, but continued to live as a monk and founded other monasteries to assist in his evangelization of rural areas. His twenty-five-year reign was marked by healings as well as the ordinary pastoral activities of a bishop. He died on November 8, 397, at Candes. His feast is on the General Roman Calendar.

12 JOSEPHAT, BISHOP AND MARTYR

Josephat (1580–1623) was the first Eastern saint to be formally canonized by the Catholic Church. Born Ioann Kuncevyč in Ukraine, he entered the Holy Trinity monastery in Vilna in 1604 and soon thereafter was ordained to the diaconate and the priesthood, taking the name Josephat. He became a popular preacher, especially in support of extending the union with Rome to the province of Kiev, and gained a reputation for asceticism. He and a monastic colleague initiated a movement in Ruthenian monasticism that eventually developed into the Order of St. Basil [January 2]. In 1617, he became archbishop of Polock and was tireless in preaching and other pastoral activities. He also promoted adherence to the Union of Brest (1596), an agreement that brought the Orthodox metropolitan province of Kiev into full communion with the Catholic Church (at least until the expansion of Orthodox Russia into the area). In 1623, Josephat was murdered by supporters of a rival bishop in Vitebsk, and his body was thrown into the Dnieper River. His feast is on the General Roman Calendar.

13 FRANCES XAVIER CABRINI, VIRGIN

Frances Xavier Cabrini (1850–1917), better known as Mother Cabrini, was the first U.S. citizen canonized by the Catholic Church and is the patron saint of immigrants and hospital administrators. Born Maria Francesca Cabrini near Pavia, Italy, she tried twice to enter a convent, but was refused both times for health reasons. She became a schoolteacher and took a private vow of virginity. When the local bishop encouraged her to become a missionary, she founded a small community of sisters in 1880, establishing convents in Grumello, Milan, and Rome. After receiving papal approval for her Missionary Sisters of the Sacred Heart in 1887, she sought an audience with the pope to explain her plans to embark on a mission to China. Leo XIII listened in silence and then said that her mission was to be "not to the East, but to the West." He urged her instead to minister to Italian immigrants in the United States. She arrived in New York in 1889, where there were some fifty thousand Italian immigrants living for the most part in poverty and apart from the Church.

She began work among the Italian immigrants, teaching their children, visiting the sick, and feeding the hungry. As the sisters' reputation grew, local shopkeepers donated whatever they could for their work. Mother Cabrini eventually established an orphanage, then a novitiate and a house for her congregation. Additional foundations were made in Chicago, New Orleans, and other U.S. cities. She eventually extended her missionary outreach to Central and South America. By 1907, there were foundations in France and Spain as well as Italy and the

Americas. While wrapping Christmas presents for Italian parochial-school children in Chicago on December 21, 1917, Mother Cabrini collapsed, and she died the next day. She was canonized in 1946. Her feast is on the Proper Calendar for the Dioceses of the United States. It is not on the General Roman Calendar.

14 LAWRENCE O'TOOLE, BISHOP; JOSEPH PIGNATELLI, RELIGIOUS

Lawrence O'Toole (1128–80) was one of the most important archbishops of Dublin. Born Lorcán Ua Tuathail in County Kildare, the product of a marriage between the O'Toole and O'Byrne royal clans, he was taken hostage, at age ten, for two years by a local king, but was eventually released to the custody of the bishop of Glendalough. When Lawrence's father came to take him home, Lawrence told him of his wish to become a monk. He was left in the care of the bishop, became a monk at Glendalough abbey, and was elected its abbot in 1153 at age twenty-five. In 1162, he was elected archbishop of Dublin.

One of his first acts as archbishop was to import some Augustinian canons of Arrouaise into the principal churches of the diocese, and he himself donned their religious habit, observed their Rule of life, and imposed it on his own cathedral canons as well. He also gained a reputation for his commitment to the poor, his tireless preaching, and the quality of his liturgical celebrations. When England invaded Ireland in 1170, he served as peacemaker, and later as mediator between the king of England and Irish leaders at the synod of Cashel. In

1179 he and five other Irish bishops attended the Third
Lateran Council in Rome and was appointed papal legate for the Ireland. Lawrence died on November 14, 1180,
and was canonized in 1225. His feast is not on the General
Roman Calendar.

On this same day the Jesuits celebrate the feast of
Joseph Pignatelli (1737–1811), who played a vital part in
sustaining the Society of Jesus between the time of its
suppression in 1773 and that of its restoration in 1814. With
the suppression of the Jesuits on July 21, 1773, twenty-
three thousand Jesuits, including Joseph Pignatelli, were
no longer under vows. When he learned that Catherine
the Great refused to enforce the suppression in Russia, he
wrote to the superior of the Jesuits there and asked for
readmission. He renewed his vows on July 6, 1797, and
in 1799 became master of novices at Colorno, the only
Jesuit novitiate in Western Europe at that time. Joseph
Pignatelli died on November 15, 1811. Three years later,
Pius VII restored the Society of Jesus throughout the
world. Joseph Pignatelli was canonized in 1954. His feast
is not on the General Roman Calendar.

15   ALBERT THE GREAT, BISHOP AND
DOCTOR OF THE CHURCH

Albert the Great (1200–1280), also known by his Latin
name, Albertus Magnus, was Thomas Aquinas's [Janu-
ary 28] teacher and is the patron saint of scientists and
medical technicians. Born in Swabia, near Ulm, he joined
the Dominicans while studying at the University of
Padua in 1223 and taught at Hildesheim, Regensburg, and

other cities as well as Cologne, where Aquinas was his student. Albert became Master at Paris in 1248 and in the same year organized the Dominican house of studies at Cologne. He served as prior provincial of Germany for three years (1254–57), during which time he also served as the pope's personal theologian. He participated in the Second Council of Lyons in 1274, despite the shock of Thomas Aquinas's death on his own way to the council, and publicly defended his former student against attacks on his orthodoxy. Albert's own work, filling thirty-eight volumes, covers subjects ranging from astronomy and chemistry to geography and physiology. His teaching also influenced another, more mystical theological school represented by Meister Eckhart and Johannes Tauler. His contemporaries gave him the title "the Great" and also referred to him as the "Universal Doctor." He died on November 15, 1280, and was canonized and declared a Doctor of the Church in 1931. Albert the Great's feast is on the General Roman Calendar.

16 MARGARET OF SCOTLAND, QUEEN

Margaret of Scotland (1046–93) is the patron saint of Scotland. Born probably in Hungary, where her father had taken refuge from the Danish rule in England and married the sister of the Hungarian king, Margaret was educated in Hungary and then returned to England with her parents just before the Norman Conquest in 1066. As one of the few surviving members of the Anglo-Saxon royal family, she was unsafe in England and went with her mother, brother, and sister to Scotland, where she married King Malcolm III ca. 1070. They had six sons and two daughters. Margaret used her influence at court to promote the reform of the Church in Scotland, bringing various liturgical practices into conformity with those observed in Rome. She founded monasteries and was devoted to her children and to the poor, but also found time for a rich prayer life. She died on November 16, 1093, and was canonized until 1250. Her feast is on the General Roman Calendar, one of the few saints of Scotland so honored.

17 ELIZABETH OF HUNGARY, RELIGIOUS

Elizabeth of Hungary (1207–31) was the queen of Hungary and is the patron saint of Franciscan tertiaries and Catholic charities. Born in Bratislava, the daughter of the king of Hungary, at fourteen she married Ludwig, the eldest son of the duke of Thuringia. Their brief marriage was a happy one and yielded three children. Elizabeth devoted herself to a life of prayer and almsgiving. She built a hospital in the basement of their castle and daily provided food, money, and work to the poor lined up at her door. When in September 1227 her husband died of plague on the way to join the Crusade in the Holy Land, Elizabeth was devastated.

Instead of remarrying, Elizabeth became a Franciscan tertiary in 1228 and settled just outside Marburg, where, out of the resources of her inheritance, she established a hospice for the sick, aged, and poor. At this time, care of the sick was something that only men performed.

Elizabeth is said to have retained her good humor and to have continued in her work on behalf of the needy, carving out new paths for the future of this ministry, but her health was broken within two years, and she was just twenty-four when she died on November 17, 1231. She was canonized only four years later. Her feast is on the General Roman Calendar.

18 DEDICATION OF THE CHURCHES OF PETER AND PAUL

This feast celebrates the anniversaries of the *dedications of St. Peter's Basilica and St. Paul's Outside the Walls,* two of the four major basilicas in Rome. St. Peter's is built on Vatican Hill, over the site where the Apostle Peter [June 29] is thought to have been buried. The original building, in basilica style with a large courtyard (atrium) at its entrance, was constructed ca. 330, during the reign of the emperor Constantine (d. 337). The present church was begun in 1506 under the direction of a succession of architects (Bramante, Raphael, Peuzzi, and Sangallo), but its final shape derives from Michelangelo (d. 1564), who did not live to see the erection of the great dome. Excavations in the twentieth century showed that the church is built over a large Roman cemetery. Peter's grave is thought to be under the main altar. The crypts and altars of the basilica contain the burial places of over 130 popes.

St. Paul's Outside the Walls derives its name from its location on the Via Ostia, outside the walls of the city. It was first built over the relics of the Apostle Paul [June 29]

by Constantine in the fourth century and was later en-
larged. The basilica burned to the ground in 1823 and was
rededicated, after a complete rebuilding, on December
10, 1854. The feast of the dedication of these two basilicas
is on the General Roman Calendar.

19 MECHTHILDE OF MAGDEBURG, ABBESS

Mechthilde of Magdeburg (ca. 1207–82), descended from a
noble family in Saxony, was a mystic who left home to
become a Beguine (a member of a nonmonastic community of women) at Magdeburg under the spiritual
guidance of Dominicans. She recorded her mystical experiences in a book of revelations entitled *Flowing Light
of the Divinity,* which contains dialogues with the Lord,
bridal mysticism, and some trinitarian theology and es-
chatology. She suffered from illnesses, personal threats,
and much disapproval from official sources. Ca. 1270, she
became a nun at the convent at Helfta. Her revelations
are considered among the most forceful and poetic examples of women's writings to have survived from the
Middle Ages. Her feast is not on the General Roman Calendar, nor was she ever formally canonized.

20 EDMUND, KING AND MARTYR

Edmund (841–69) was the king of East Anglia. Born of
Saxon stock, he was raised a Christian and became king
of the East Angles sometime before 865. During the
great war with the Vikings in 869–70, he was defeated

and captured. He refused to renounce his Christian faith or to rule as the Viking king's vassal. He was then killed at Hellesden (Suffolk), whether by being scourged, shot with arrows, and beheaded, as the traditional account has it, or by being spread-eagled as an offering to the Viking gods. His feast is not on the General Roman Calendar.

21 PRESENTATION OF MARY

The feast of the *Presentation of Mary* commemorates an event not described in the New Testament. According to the apocryphal *Protevangelium of James,* when the Blessed Virgin Mary was three years old, her parents took her to the Temple in Jerusalem and left her there to be educated. The priest received her with a kiss, saying: "The Lord has magnified thy name in all generations. In thee, on the last of days, the Lord will manifest his redemption to the sons of Israel." Then the priest set Mary on the third step of the altar, and the Lord sent grace upon her; she danced and "all the house of Israel loved her." Nowhere in the Roman liturgy, however, is there any indication that this is the event commemorated in this feast. Because the feast is also celebrated on this day in the East, it is thought that it originated there, probably in the eighth century. The feast of the Presentation of Mary was celebrated in the West sporadically from 1372. It is on the General Roman Calendar and is celebrated on this day by the Greek and Russian Orthodox Churches.

22 CECILIA, VIRGIN AND MARTYR

Cecilia (third century) was a Roman martyr of whom almost nothing is known for certain. She is the patron saint of musicians, singers, and poets. Her popularity is rooted in a fifth-century legend, according to which she refused to consummate a marriage because of her vow of virginity, and when she also refused to sacrifice to the gods, an attempt was made unsuccessfully to suffocate her. Then a solider was sent to behead her, but three blows to the head failed to kill her. She survived half dead for three days. However, there is no mention of Cecilia in any of the near contemporary martyrologies. Her feast is on the General Roman Calendar.

23 CLEMENT I, POPE AND MARTYR;
COLUMBAN, ABBOT

Clement I (d. ca. 101, pope ca. 91–ca. 101), also known as Clement of Rome, is best known for his likely authorship of the letter referred to as *1 Clement,* the most important first-century Christian document outside the New Testament and treated by some in the ancient Church as if it were, in fact, part of the New Testament canon. The Roman community at this time was probably divided into a number of small house churches scattered throughout the city, each presided over by a presbyter. There would have been no united and coordinated leadership within the city's Christian community as a whole, but Clement and others in his position would have functioned as a kind of foreign minister of the Roman church rather than as its pope in the modern sense of the word.

This first letter of Clement was sent ca. 96 from the church in Rome to the church in Corinth, instructing the Corinthians to reinstate elders (presbyters, or senior priests) who had been improperly deposed and to exile the younger persons who had instigated the rebellion. The form of Clement's intervention seems to have been modeled on the relations of the imperial capital of Rome (its senate and emperor) with its outlying provinces. Recommending exile and sending three witnesses along with the letter, which Clement also did, were mirrored secular Roman practice. Indeed, the letter is marked throughout by a laudatory attitude toward the Roman state. Underlying the text is the conviction that the empire and its rulers have been established by God as the earthly counterpart of the heavenly kingdom. The influence of the existing Roman political system on the evolving Roman ecclesiastical system, therefore, cannot be discounted. There is no historical evidence to support the claim that Clement died a martyr. His feast is on the General Roman Calendar.

Columban (ca. 543–615) was one of the greatest Irish missionary monks of the sixth and seventh centuries. Born in Leinster, he became a monk first on an island in Lough Erne and then at Bangor, where he remained many years. Not until 590 or thereabouts did he set sail with twelve companions for Gaul. Columban and his monks began their work with energy and enthusiasm. Their reputation soon reached the king of Burgundy, who gave Columban a plot of land on which to found a monastery. The success of the first led quickly to the founding of a second and a third. The essence of his Rule was love of God and love of neighbor. It also prescribed harsh penances for every conceivable fault, however slight.

After twelve years of ministry, however, Columban and his monks began to sense hostility from the local Frankish bishops, who resented their independence and their Celtic (as opposed to Roman) ways. In 610, after Columban publicly chastised him for personal faults, the king ordered Columban and his Irish monks to leave the country. After spending time at the court of the Austrasian king at Metz, Columban, by now about seventy, moved yet again, walking across the Alps to Milan. With a donated piece of land, Columban made his final monastic foundation, at Bobbio, between Genoa and Piacenza. He died on November 23, 615. His feast is on the General Roman Calendar.

24 ANDREW DUNG-LAC AND COMPANIONS, MARTYRS

Andrew Dung-Lac (d. 1839), a Vietnamese diocesan priest, was one of 117 martyrs, also known as the Martyrs of Tonkin, who were canonized in 1988. Catholicism was first introduced into Vietnam in 1533, but did not take hold until early in the next century when Jesuits established roots there. Severe persecution broke out in 1698, then three more times in the eighteenth century, and again in the nineteenth. Between one hundred thousand and three hundred thousand Catholics suffered in some way during the fifty years before 1833, when the French moved in and secured religious freedom for Catholics. Most of the 117 martyrs were put to death (mostly by beheading) during this fifty-year period. Their feast is on the General Roman Calendar.

25 MOSES OF ROME, MARTYR

Moses of Rome (d. 251) was a member of the Roman clergy who was a leading candidate for the papacy at one time and would very likely have been elected if he were not in prison and eventually martyred under the emperor Decius. Possibly of Jewish origin, Moses and his fellow priest-prisoners exchanged regular letters of encouragement with Cyprian [September 16], bishop of Carthage. The previous pope, Fabian [January 20], had died more than a year earlier, but the election of a successor was delayed because of the persecution. By the time the persecution subsided in the spring of 251, however, Moses had died in prison and was immediately proclaimed a martyr. His feast is not on the General Roman Calendar.

26 LEONARD OF PORT MAURICE, FRIAR

Leonard of Port Maurice (1676–1751) was a Franciscan priest who was an indefatigable preacher and a vigorous promoter of devotion to the Stations of the Cross. Born Paulo Girolamo Casanova in Liguria, Italy, he joined the Franciscans, was ordained a priest in 1702, and became guardian (superior) of a Florentine friary, then of St. Bonaventure's [July 15] in Rome in 1730. He established some five hundred Stations of the Cross in Italy, including a set in the Colosseum in Rome during the Jubilee year of 1750. He died in Rome on November 26, 1751, and was canonized in 1867. He is patron saint of parish missions. His feast is not on the General Roman Calendar.

27 JAMES THE PERSIAN, MARTYR

James the Persian (d. ca. 421), or James Intercisus (Lat., "cut to pieces"), was the best-known victim of the second great persecution in Persia, beginning ca. 420. According to the largely legendary account of his martyrdom, James was a friend of the pagan king. Because he did not want to lose the king's friendship, he abandoned his faith after the king declared war on Christians. His apostasy greatly distressed James's wife and mother. When the king died, they wrote to James to reproach him. He was greatly moved by their letter, repented, renounced his position at court, and publicly declared himself a Christian. His body was stretched, limb by limb, and then cut to pieces. A Greek Orthodox source says that he died on November 27, 389. His feast is celebrated by the Greek and Russian Orthodox Churches on this day, but is not on the General Roman Calendar.

28 CATHERINE LABOURÉ, VIRGIN

Catherine Labouré (1806–76) was a French Sister of Charity whose reported visions of the Blessed Virgin Mary gave rise to devotion to the Miraculous Medal. Born Zoë Labouré in the Côte d'Or of France, she joined the Sisters of Charity of St. Vincent de Paul [September 27] in 1830, taking the religious name Catherine. She was sent to Paris, where she had the first of her claimed visions in the convent chapel on the Rue de Bac. The Blessed Virgin was said to have appeared to her standing on a globe with shafts of light streaming from her hands and the words "O Mary, conceived without sin, pray for us who have recourse to thee" surrounding the image. Catherine also claimed to have heard a voice urging her to reproduce on a medal what she had seen in the vision. The archbishop of Paris gave permission to have the medal struck, and the first fifteen hundred, issued in June 1832, came to be known as the "Miraculous Medal" because of its origin. From 1831 until her death on December 31, 1876, Catherine lived a quiet life out of the public eye. Her feast is not on the General Roman Calendar.

29 SATURNINUS OF TOULOUSE, BISHOP AND MARTYR; DOROTHY DAY, FOUNDRESS

Saturninus of Toulouse (third century), also known as Sernin, was the first bishop of Toulouse. Little is known of him before he became a bishop, but his name suggests that he was an African. In Toulouse, he opposed idol worship, for which he was dragged by the pagan temple priests into the temple and warned that he must sacrifice to the offended gods. Saturninus insisted that he worshiped only the one true God and that their gods were evil. Enraged, the priests tied his feet to a bull that then dragged him to his death. His feast is observed in the

Mozarabic Rite and also in parts of France, but it is not on the General Roman Calendar.

This is also the day of death of *Dorothy Day* (1897–1980), cofoundress of the Catholic Worker movement, a community of laypeople. Her whole life was dedicated to the service of the poor, the hungry, and the homeless and to peace.

30 ANDREW, APOSTLE

Andrew (d. ca. 70) was one of Jesus' first disciples and one of the twelve apostles. Indeed, his name is prominent on all lists of the apostles (Matt. 10:2; Mark 3:18; Luke 6:14; Acts 1:13). He is the patron saint of Scotland, Russia, and Greece. Born in Bethsaida, on the northeast shore of the Sea of Galilee (John 1:44), he was the brother of Simon Peter [June 29]. Both were residents of Capernaum (Mark 1:29), where they worked as fishermen (Mark 1:16). Andrew learned of Jesus through John the Baptist [June 24; August 29], whose disciple he was. Andrew then introduced Jesus to Peter (John 1:40).

Second-century apocryphal literature recounts Andrew's missionary ventures. The *Acts of Andrew and Matthias* tells us of Andrew's rescue of Matthias [May 14] from cannibals. The *Acts of Andrew* reports miracles performed in Greece and Asia Minor. The account of Andrew's crucifixion at Patras, Greece, on an X-shaped cross (called St. Andrew's Cross) also circulated independently of these documents. (The cross is incorporated into the Union Jack to represent Scotland.) Andrew's feast is on the General Roman Calendar and is also celebrated on this day by the Greek and Russian Orthodox Churches, by the Church of England and the Episcopal Church in the United States, and by the Evangelical Lutheran Church in America.

DECEMBER

1   EDMUND CAMPION, RALPH SHERWIN, ALEXANDER BRIANT, AND ROBERT SOUTHWELL, MARTYRS

Edmund Campion (1540–81) was the first Jesuit martyr in Elizabethan England. Born in London, the son of a bookseller, he was a brilliant student at Oxford. He was ordained a deacon in the Church of England in 1569 and in the same year took the Oath of Supremacy. But he was having personal doubts about the newly reopened breach between England and the pope, so he left for Ireland, where he helped to revive the university in Dublin (later Trinity College) and wrote a history of the country. He returned to England in 1571, a year after Pope Pius V [April 30] excommunicated and deposed Queen Elizabeth. Soon thereafter Edmund crossed the Channel to the (Catholic) English College at Douai, where he joined the Roman Catholic Church in 1573 and left for Rome to join the Society of Jesus. He was ordained a priest in 1578.

The following year he and Robert Persons were chosen to inaugurate a Jesuit mission in England. Campion's eloquence, learning, and personality, as well as his effective use of the printing press, made him a formidable presence the government could not ignore. As he continued to evade the government's scrutiny by his mobility and effective disguises, he published his most famous work, *Decem Rationes* (Lat., "Ten Reasons"), a defense of Catholicism and a challenge to Protestants to debate him. A few weeks later he was arrested and imprisoned in the Tower of London. No amount of bribes (from the queen herself), torture (on the rack), or theological argument could induce him to conform. On December 1, 1581, he and Alexander Briant and Ralph Sherwin were hanged, drawn, and quartered at Tyburn. He was beatified in 1588 and then canonized in 1970 as one of the Forty Martyrs of England and Wales [October 25]. Edmund Campion's feast is not on the General Roman Calendar, but it is observed on this day by the Jesuits.

On this day the Jesuits also observe the feast of Ralph Sherwin, Alexander Briant, and Robert Southwell. *Ralph Sherwin* (1549–81) was the first to volunteer for the mission to England, accompanying Campion and Robert Persons as far as Reims in 1580. Sherwin set out from there by himself and was arrested soon after his arrival while preaching in a private home. Like Campion, he was severely tortured on the rack and bribed with a bishopric if he would conform. After more than a year's imprisonment, he was brought to trial and met the same fate as Campion. He was beatified and canonized with Campion as one of the Forty Martyrs of England and Wales.

Alexander Briant (1556–81) was a young diocesan priest who had been ordained at the English College at Douai and who returned to England to carry out a mission in the West Country. He was arrested and tortured in the Tower. In a letter from the Tower to Jesuits in England, he reflected on his plight and asked to be admitted to the order. Consequently, he is numbered among the martyrs of the Society of Jesus. He was beatified and canonized as one of the Forty Martyrs of England and Wales.

Robert Southwell (ca. 1561–95), an accomplished poet, was ordained a Jesuit priest in 1584 and returned to England from the English College at Douai, where he was prefect of studies. As in the case of the other Jesuit missionaries, Southwell's goal was not the conversion of Protestants, but the reconciliation of lapsed Catholics to the Church, especially those in the aristocracy and intellectual community. Southwell was eventually betrayed, imprisoned, brutally tortured, and then, three years later, condemned, hanged, drawn, and quartered at Tyburn. He was canonized, with the others, in 1970.

2 CHROMATIUS, BISHOP; MAURA CLARKE, ITA FORD, DOROTHY KAZEL, AND JEAN DONOVAN, MARTYRS

Chromatius (d. 407) was one of the most distinguished bishops of his time. Born in Aquileia, near Trieste, he participated in the anti-Arian council of Aquileia in 381 while still a presbyter. He was elected bishop of his hometown in 388. He was a friend and correspondent of Jerome [September 30], whom he had met while Jerome was residing in Milan and who dedicated several of his works to him, and of Ambrose [December 7], archbishop of Milan. He was himself an able commentator on Sacred Scripture, especially Matthew's Gospel. His feast is not on the General Roman Calendar.

December 2 is also the day on which four missionaries, followers of Oscar Romero [March 24], were raped and murdered in El Salvador in 1980: *Maura Clarke* and *Ita Ford*, both Maryknoll sisters; and *Dorothy Kazel,* an Ursuline sister, and *Jean Donovan,* a lay missioner, both from Cleveland, Ohio.

3   FRANCIS XAVIER, PRIEST

Francis Xavier (1506–52) was one of the greatest missionaries in the history of the Church and is patron saint of foreign missions. He is also known as the "apostle of the Indies and of Japan." He is the patron saint of India, Japan, Pakistan, the East Indies, Outer Mongolia, and Borneo. Born at the castle of Xavier (Javier) in Navarre, Spain, he was educated at the University of Paris, where he met Ignatius of Loyola [July 31] and became one of the original group of seven Jesuits who took their vows at Montmartre in 1534 and were ordained priests in Venice three years later. In 1540 he joined Simon Rodriguez at Lisbon and, after several months, went to Goa, India, to evangelize the East Indies. Francis was named papal nuncio in the East.

He enjoyed extraordinary success over the remaining ten years of his life. In Goa he spent the mornings visiting prisons and hospitals, and in the afternoons teaching catechism to children and slaves. He also worked in southern India among the low-caste Paravas and in Ceylon, Malacca, the Molucca islands, and the Malay Peninsula. In 1549 Francis Xavier went to Japan, where he made a hundred converts in a year at Kagoshima. By the time he left Japan, there were some two thousand Japanese Christians. In 1552 Francis fell ill on his way to China and died almost alone on the island of Shang-chwan (Sancian), six miles off the coast of mainland China, on December 3. He was forty-six years old. His feast is on the General Roman Calendar and is also commemorated by the Evangelical Lutheran Church in America.

4   JOHN DAMASCENE, PRIEST AND DOCTOR OF THE CHURCH

John Damascene (ca. 657–ca. 749), also John of Damascus and John Chrysorrhoas (Gk., "Golden Speaker"), was one of the most influential Greek theologians in the medieval West; his thought impacted the work of Thomas Aquinas [January 28], Peter Lombard, and others. Born in Damascus, Syria, of a wealthy Christian family, John divided his wealth among his relatives, the Church, and the poor and became a monk and later a priest at the monastery of St. Sabas [December 5], near Jerusalem. John invested his time, energy, and considerable intellectual gifts in the composition of hymns and theological works, the most important of which was his *Fount of Wisdom*, which was divided into three parts: philosophy, heresies, and the Orthodox faith. John had a quintessentially Catholic sacramental vision. "The one who seeks God continually will find him," he wrote, "for God is in everything." He also wrote three tracts against the iconoclasts. He died at Mar Saba ca. 749. He was declared a Doctor of the Church in 1890. His feast is on the General Roman Calendar.

5   SABAS, ABBOT

Sabas (439–532) was the founder of the large monastery of
Mar Saba, near Jerusalem, and was the superior of all the
hermits in contemporary Palestine. Born in Cappadocia,
the son of an army officer, he entered a monastery near
his hometown of Mutalaska when only eight years of age.
He later became a hermit, at one stage of his life spending four years alone in the wilderness, subsisting on wild
herbs and water from a brook. Eventually consenting to
the entreaties of disciples, he founded a *laura* (a monastic
community consisting of hermit's cells, or huts, clustered
around a church). His disciples grew to 150. Since none of
the hermits was a priest, some of the monks appealed to
the patriarch of Jerusalem, who insisted in 491 that Sabas
should be ordained. In 493 the patriarch appointed Sabas
archimandrite over all the monks of Palestine who lived
a semi-eremitical life. Sabas also preached in opposition
to the heresy of Monophysitism, which posited only a
divine nature in Christ, while denying that he also had a
human nature. Sabas died on December 5, 532. His feast
is not on the General Roman Calendar.

6   NICHOLAS OF MYRA, BISHOP

Nicholas (fourth century) was the bishop of Myra who is
the basis of the legend of Santa Claus (St. Nicholas). Said
to have been born at Patara in Lycia (southwestern Turkey), he became bishop of Myra, the province's capital,
where he enjoyed a reputation for piety and pastoral zeal.
He was imprisoned during the Diocletian persecution

(303–5) and was later present at the Council of Nicaea (325), where he joined in the condemnation of Arianism, the heresy that denied the full divinity of Christ. The accounts are unanimous that, by whatever means, Nicholas died at Myra, and there was a basilica built in his honor in Constantinople by the emperor Justinian. Nicholas's cult became almost universal in the West. He also has had an important place in the Byzantine liturgical tradition. He is thought to have been the most frequently represented saintly bishop for several centuries.

The practice of giving gifts to children on his feast began in the Low Countries and became popular in North America through the Dutch settlers of New Amsterdam. Nicholas's patronage of pawnbrokers is linked with yet another legend about his throwing three bags of gold through a window to be used as dowries for three young women who would otherwise have been given over to a life of prostitution. The legend is said to be the origin of the pawnbroker's three golden balls. Nicholas's feast is on the General Roman Calendar and is also observed by the Greek and Russian Orthodox Churches, the Church of England and the Episcopal Church in the United States, and the Evangelical Lutheran Church in America.

7   AMBROSE OF MILAN, BISHOP AND DOCTOR OF THE CHURCH

Ambrose (339–97) was the bishop of Milan whose sermons influenced Augustine's [August 28] decision to become a Christian. Born in Trier, he was appointed governor of Aemilia and Liguria, with his residence in Milan, the administrative capital of the Western Empire. Upon the death of Auxentius, the Arian bishop of Milan, in 374 there was street fighting between Arians (who held that Christ was the greatest of creatures, but not equal to God the Father) and orthodox Catholics. Ambrose appealed for peace between the two sides and was himself chosen as bishop even though he had not yet been baptized! Within a week, however, he was baptized and consecrated the bishop of Milan. Ambrose gave his wealth to the poor and the Church and steeped himself in Sacred Scripture and the writings of the Church Fathers. He became an advocate of their thought in the West and encouraged monasticism (himself following a quasi-monastic style of life within his episcopal household) and the cult of martyrs. He also proved to be a committed pastor who was always accessible to his people. He also emerged as an important political figure, advising the emperor Gratian about Arianism, reminding Valerian, Gratian's successor, that the emperor is in the Church, not above it, and persuading the usurper Maximus to confine his ambitions to Gaul, Spain, and Britain. When Theodosius defeated Maximus, Ambrose excommunicated him for the massacre of 390 people.

Ambrose was a prolific, if not original, writer on a wide range of theological and pastoral topics, including the sacraments, the priesthood (clerical ethics), and the Gospel of Luke. He was the first of the Fathers and Doctors of the Church to address the question of Church-state relations, stressing the supremacy of the Church in its own domain and as the guardian of morality. He died on Good Friday, April 4, 397. He was named one of the four Latin Doctors of the Church, alongside

Augustine, Jerome [September 30], and Gregory the Great [September 3] in 1298. His feast day, which is on the General Roman Calendar, commemorates not the day of his death, but of his consecration as a bishop.

8   IMMACULATE CONCEPTION

The feast of the *Immaculate Conception* of the Blessed Virgin Mary celebrates the conception of Mary in her mother's womb without the stain of original sin. In Pope Pius IX's bull *Ineffabilis Deus,* issued on December 8, 1854, Mary's preservation from original sin was a "singular grace and privilege" given her by God "in view of the merits of Jesus Christ" as the Savior of the human race.

This feast was known as early as the seventh century in Palestine as the Conception by St. Anne [July 26] of the Theotokos (Gk., "Mother of God"), celebrated on December 9, but the doctrine itself has never been accepted in the East because of Eastern Christianity's different theological understanding of original sin. (For the East, humans share in the guilt of Adam's and Eve's sin only insofar as they willingly imitate the first parents by sinning. Adam's and Eve's sin is a model or prototype only.)

In 1476 Pope Sixtus IV approved the feast with its own Mass and Office, and in 1708 Pope Clement XI extended it to the universal Church and made it a holy day of obligation. The Council of Trent (1545–63) explicitly declared that its teaching on the universality of original sin did not include the Blessed Virgin Mary. In 1858, Mary is thought to have appeared to Bernadette Soubirous [April 16] in Lourdes, France, saying, "I am the Immaculate Conception." Five years after that, in 1863, a new Mass and Office were prescribed. This feast (now called the Immaculate Conception of the Blessed Virgin Mary) is on the General Roman Calendar.

9 BLESSED JUAN DIEGO (CUATITLATOATZIN), HERMIT

In 1531 the Blessed Virgin Mary is believed to have appeared four times to *Juan Diego Cuatitlatoatzin* ("the talking eagle") at Tepeyac, a hill near Mexico City, and to have instructed him, in the Nahuatl language, to tell the local bishop of her wish that a church be built on that site. She also left a life-size figure of herself on the peasant's mantle. The first appearance is said to have occurred on December 9. An Amerindian of the Chichimeca tribe, Juan Diego subsequently devoted himself to the pilgrims who came to see this miraculous image of Mary imprinted on his cloak. It is now preserved in the Basilica of Our Lady of Guadalupe [December 12] in Tepeyac. Juan Diego was beatified in 1990 and canonized in 2002. His feast is not on the General Roman Calendar.

10 MENNAS, HERMOGENES, AND EUGRAPHUS, MARTYRS; EDWARD GENNINGS, POLYDORE PLASDEN, JOHN ROBERTS, SWITHIN WELLS, AND EUSTACE WHITE, MARTYRS; THOMAS MERTON, MONK

Mennas (third century), also known as Kallikelados (Gk., "sweet and beautiful voice"), was a civil servant in Rome who kept his Christian faith secret and rose eventually to high office under the emperor Maximian. Mennas's friend and secretary was *Eugraphus,* also a Christian. It was not until he was assigned to Alexandria that Mennas revealed himself to be a Christian. The emperor sent one of his magistrates, *Hermogenes,* to investigate. When his trial began, Mennas spoke at length in his own defense. Although the spectators were moved by his eloquence, Hermogenes ordered Mennas's tongue cut out. After a time both Mennas and Eugraphus were summoned before Hermogenes. When the tongueless Mennas spoke in a "sweet and beautiful voice," Hermogenes fell to his knees in acceptance of Christ. All three were beheaded at the command of the Roman governor. Their feast is not on the General Roman Calendar.

Edward Gennings (1567–91), *Polydore Plasden* (1563–91), *John Roberts* (ca. 1576–1610), *Swithin Wells* (1536–91), and *Eustace White* (d. 1591) are among the Forty Martyrs of England and Wales [October 25], canonized in 1970. Four of the five were executed on December 10, 1591, and one, John Roberts, was put to death on December 10, 1610.

And this is the day of death of *Thomas Merton* (1915–68), a Trappist monk and activist in the cause of world peace, social justice, and interfaith harmony, who influenced millions of people of all faiths and of no faith with his spiritual writings, especially his autobiographical classic, *The Seven Storey Mountain* (1949).

11   DAMASUS I, POPE

Damasus I (ca. 304–384, pope 366–84) was one of the most aggressive advocates of the primacy of Rome in the early

Church. Born in Rome, the son of a priest, Damasus was ordained a deacon and accompanied Pope Liberius into exile in 355. He soon returned to Rome, however, and was in the service for a time of the antipope Felix II. This was a remarkably significant lapse in one who, later as pope, would argue vigorously on behalf of the supremacy of the papacy.

When Liberius died, a faction consistently loyal to Liberius met immediately in the Julian basilica of Santa Maria, elected the deacon Ursinus, and had him consecrated Bishop of Rome. Another, larger faction loyal to Felix met in the church of San Lorenzo and elected the deacon Damasus, who hired a gang of thugs to storm the Julian basilica, routing the Ursinians in a three-day massacre. Damasus was consecrated in the Lateran basilica on October 1 after his supporters had seized the church. As the violence continued, Damasus dispatched his own forces to attack Ursinus's supporters, who had taken refuge in the Liberian basilica (now St. Mary Major). A contemporary historian reported that 137 died in the battle.

Significantly, Damasus himself took no part in the ecumenical council of Constantinople in 381, which defined the divinity of the Holy Spirit and placed the bishop of Constantinople, "the new Rome," second only to the Bishop of Rome. Although the claims of Constantinople were based on synodal decisions and political considerations, Damasus's claims for the Roman primacy were based exclusively on his being the direct successor of Peter and the rightful heir of Christ's promises given in Matthew 16:18. Damasus organized the papal archives, established Latin as the principal liturgical language, and commissioned Jerome [September 30] to revise existing translations of the New Testament. He died in 384. His feast is on the General Roman Calendar.

12   OUR LADY OF GUADALUPE; JANE FRANCES DE CHANTAL, RELIGIOUS

The *Blessed Virgin Mary* is believed to have appeared four times (between December 9 and 12) in 1531 to an Amerindian, Juan Diego [December 9], on Tepeyac hill outside Mexico City, ten years after the bloody defeat of the Aztec Empire at the hands of the Spanish conquerors. A painted, life-size figure of the Virgin as a young, dark-skinned American Indian woman with the face of a mestizo was imprinted on Juan Diego's cloak. The image gave Indians the assurance that Christianity was not only the faith of their European conquerors, but a faith for them also. In 1754 Pope Benedict XIV authorized a Mass and Office to be celebrated on December 12 under the title of Our Lady of Guadalupe, and he named Mary as patron saint of New Spain. She was designated patron saint of all of Latin America in 1910 and as "Queen of Mexico and Empress of the Americas" in 1945. The feast is observed throughout Latin America. It is not on the General Roman Calendar.

Jane Frances de Chantal (1572–1641) was a close friend and spiritual associate of Francis de Sales [January 24] and cofoundress with him of the Visitation Sisters. Born Jeanne Frémyot in Dijon, the daughter of the president of the parliament of Burgundy, she took the additional name Françoise at her Confirmation. After the accidental death of her husband, Baron de Chantal, Jane took a vow of chastity. In 1604 she heard Francis de Sales preach and persuaded him to become her spiritual director.

In 1607, when she informed Francis of her desire to enter the cloister, he advised against it and proposed instead that they establish a religious community for women who were prevented from entering the enclosed religious orders. This community would not be enclosed and would devote itself to the needs of society. It would be called the Congregation of the Visitation of the Virgin Mary, and its members would imitate the virtues exemplified in Mary's visit to Elizabeth [November 5] as well as engage in works of mercy toward the poor and the sick. Because of opposition to the idea of nonenclosure, however, Francis de Sales had to modify the Rule in 1613, but without completely sacrificing flexibility. Jane Frances was able to attend to her children, settled the affairs of her deceased father, and founded new convents in various cities in France. In 1618 the institute was raised to a religious order. Jane Frances died in 1641 and was canonized in 1767. Her feast is on the General Roman Calendar.

13 LUCY, VIRGIN AND MARTYR

Lucy (d. ca. 304) is the patron saint of those suffering from diseases of the eye and is traditionally portrayed carrying a tray containing two eyes. She is thought to have been born in Syracuse, Sicily, of noble and wealthy parents. Intending to give her fortune to the poor, she was the victim of an attempted rape during the Diocletian persecution. When she resisted, she was denounced as a Christian, arrested, tortured, and killed. Many legends were associated with her name (which is derived from the Latin word *lux,* "light"). One story is that she tore out her own eyes rather than yield to the rapist and is sometimes depicted offering her eyes to him. Her feast is celebrated in Sweden as a festival of light. The popular song "Santa Lucia" commemorates her. Her feast is on the General Roman Calendar and is also celebrated on this day by the Church of England.

14 JOHN OF THE CROSS, PRIEST AND DOCTOR OF THE CHURCH

John of the Cross (1542–91) was a mystic who founded the Discalced Carmelite friars. Born Juan de Yepes y Alvárez in Fontiveros, between Ávila and Salamanca, in conditions of poverty, he was sent to an orphanage, but displayed no skill in almost any trade. Eventually he found work as a nurse's assistant in a hospital for those with venereal diseases. John developed a love for the sick and the poor and a capacity to handle the most menial and unpleasant tasks. John felt drawn to the monastic life and was admitted to the Carmelites. He was accepted in 1563 and took the name John of Matthias. He studied theology at the University of Salamanca and was ordained a priest in 1567.

While at home to celebrate his first Mass, he met Teresa of Ávila [October 15], who was involved in the reform of Carmelite nuns and was trying to effect a similar reform of Carmelite friars. She urged him to join in her efforts. John adopted the Discalced habit and changed his

name to John of the Cross. In 1571, Teresa became prioress
of an unreformed convent in Ávila and sent for John to be
its spiritual director and confessor. However, because of
continued opposition from other Carmelites against the
Discalced movement, John was arrested and imprisoned
in the Carmelite priory in Toledo. He spent most of his
nine months in prison in total darkness. He was able to
pray the Divine Office only when a ray of sunlight pene-
trated through the tiny slit window high on the wall. The
cell was bitterly cold in winter and stifling in summer.
John was half starved, covered with vermin, and flogged
to induce him to leave the Discalced. However, he wrote
some of his greatest poetry there. In August 1578 he managed to escape and was smuggled out of Toledo.

When John was safely out of Toledo and had recovered from his ordeal, he was sent as prior of the house
of El Calvario, near Baeza, as confessor to the Discalced
nuns. During this period he composed his famous works,
which are usually commentaries on his poems: *The Ascent
of Mount Carmel*, *The Dark Night of the Soul*, *The Spiritual
Canticle*, and *The Living Flame of Love*. John of the Cross
died on December 14, 1591. He was canonized in 1726 and
declared a Doctor of the Church in 1926. His feast is on
the General Roman Calendar.

15 MARY DI ROSA, FOUNDRESS

Mary di Rosa (1813–55) was the foundress of the Handmaids of Charity. Born Paula di Rosa in Brescia, Italy, she
devoted her early years to social work, particularly the
welfare of the young girls who worked in her father's

factory. She attended to the sick during a cholera epidemic in 1836 and, after the disease had run its course, directed a house for poor and abandoned girls. She cofounded the congregation of the Handmaids of Charity, devoted to the care of the sick. During the political upheavals in Italy, she set up a military hospital to care for the military and civilian wounded. In 1850 the constitutions of her congregation were given papal approval and in the summer of 1852 Paula and twenty-five sisters pronounced their vows. Paula took the name Maria Crocifissa (It., "Mary of the Crucified"). She collapsed from physical exhaustion in Mantua and died three weeks later in her native Brescia at age forty-two. She was canonized in 1954. Her feast is not on the General Roman Calendar.

16 ADELAIDE OF BURGUNDY, NUN

Adelaide (931–99) was the foundress of many monasteries of monks and nuns. The daughter of Rudolph II of Upper Burgundy, at age sixteen she married Lothair, who was by that time at least nominally the king of Italy. Lothair was poisoned three years later by the father of one of Adelaide's disappointed suitors. She was imprisoned in a castle and either was freed by the German king, Otto the Great, or escaped on her own. On Christmas Day, 951, she married Otto at Pavia. The marriage consolidated his authority in northern Italy, and in 962 he was crowned emperor in Rome. Their marriage ended after twenty-two years with the death of Otto. For many years thereafter, Adelaide devoted herself to peacemaking and generosity to the poor. She founded and restored many monasteries and worked for the conversion of the Slavs. She died on December 16, 999, and was canonized ca. 1097. Her feast is not on the General Roman Calendar.

17 JOHN OF MATHA, FOUNDER; LAZARUS

John of Matha (d. 1213) was the founder of the Order of the Most Holy Trinity, popularly known as the Trinitarians. Born at Faucon in Provence of a well-to-do family, he retired to a hermitage after his schooling was completed. When he found that his privacy was often disturbed, he went to study theology in Paris, received a doctorate, and was ordained a priest. After the Second Crusade of 1147–49, he felt an inspiration to devote his life to the ransoming of Christian slaves from the Muslims. He traveled to Rome to secure papal approval for his venture. Innocent III was so impressed that he approved the foundation of the Order of the Most Holy Trinity in 1198. They were given a white habit with a red and blue cross on the breast. Members of the order went to Morocco, Tunis, and Spain, and several hundred captives were said to have been released. John spent his last two years in Rome and died there on December 17, 1213. His feast is not on the General Roman Calendar.

Lazarus (first century) was the brother of Martha [July 29] and Mary and a close friend of Jesus, who raised him from the dead (John 11:1–44). According to an Eastern tradition, Lazarus, with his two sisters, was put into a leaking boat by the Jews, but they were miraculously saved and landed on Cyprus, where he was made bishop of Kition. An eleventh-century Western legend maintained that Lazarus had been the bishop of Marseilles. Devotion to Lazarus was widespread in the early Church. His feast is not on the General Roman Calendar.

18 FLANNAN OF KILLALOE, BISHOP

Flannan (seventh century) was the bishop of Killaloe in Ireland. He is thought to have been the son of a chieftain named Turlough in the west of Ireland. According to an Irish legend, he was the disciple of Molua, the founder of the monastery at Killaloe, and made a pilgrimage to Rome floating on a millstone. Actually, the millstones that accompanied the Celtic saints on their journeys were small in size and were used as altars for Mass. Flannan was an itinerant preacher. The cathedral at Killaloe housed his relics, and the remote Flannan Islands off the coast of Scotland are named after him. They have long been a center of religious devotion. On one island, where there is a lighthouse, there are the remains of a tiny chapel called the chapel of Flannan. There are cults of this saint in both Ireland and Scotland. His feast is not on the General Roman Calendar.

19 ANASTASIUS I, POPE;
BLESSED URBAN V, POPE

Anastasius I (d. 401, pope 399–401) is best known for his condemnation of the great third-century theologian Origen (d. ca. 254), with whose writings he was not even familiar. He did little else that was memorable in his very brief pontificate, except perhaps fathering his own successor, Innocent I. His feast is not on the General Roman Calendar.

Urban V (1310–70, pope 1362–70) was the sixth—and probably the best—of the Avignon popes. He restored the papacy to Rome for three years. Born Guillaume de Grimoard, he was a Benedictine monk, a canon lawyer, abbot of Saint-Victor in Marseilles, and papal legate in Italy—but not a cardinal—when elected pope in Avignon on September 28, 1362. During the conclave when the cardinals could not agree on one of their own number, they turned to the deeply spiritual Abbot Grimoard and elected him unanimously. Retaining his black Benedictine habit and Rule, Urban V continued his predecessor's reformist agenda.

He failed to achieve one of the main goals of his pontificate, the reunion with the East and the liberation of the holy places in Palestine from Turkish control. At the same time, he sincerely hoped to return the papacy once and for all to Rome. The city was in chaos and the Vatican was uninhabitable. On April 30, 1367, against the strong objections of the French cardinals and the Curia, Urban V left Avignon and entered Rome with an impressive military escort on October 16. He is said to have wept at the condition of the city. By the end of his pontificate, with the situation in Italy still unsettled, Urban V returned to Avignon. Less than two months afterward, he fell gravely ill and died. Urban V was beatified by Pope Pius IX in 1870. His feast is not on the General Roman Calendar.

20 DOMINIC OF SILOS, ABBOT

Dominic of Silos (ca. 1000–73) is especially venerated by the Dominicans because, nearly a century after his death, Joan of Aza made a pilgrimage to his tomb, where she had a vision in which Dominic of Silos promised that she would bear another son. She named the child Dominic [August 8], and he became the founder of the Order of Preachers. Born in Navarre, Spain, of a peasant family, Dominic of Silos became a monk at San Millán de la Cogolla. He was ordained a priest and became novice master and then prior of the monastery. After a dispute with the king of Navarre over property rights, Dominic and two companions were sent into exile. The ruler of Old Castile welcomed them and in 1041 gave them the run-down monastery of St. Sebastian at Silos, near Burgos. Dominic, chosen its abbot, rebuilt the church, planned the cloisters, and established a renowned scriptorium. Dominic's reputation for holiness, learning, generosity to the poor, and healings grew. Three years after his death in 1073, his remains were moved into the church, which was the equivalent of local canonization. His feast is not on the General Roman Calendar.

21 PETER CANISIUS, PRIEST AND DOCTOR OF THE CHURCH

Peter Canisius (1521–97) was called by Leo XIII (1878–1903) the "second apostle of Germany," after Boniface [June 5], and is generally regarded as one of the principal theologians of the Counter-Reformation. Born of an aristocratic family in Nijmegen, the Netherlands, he was educated at the universities in Cologne and Louvain. He set aside a legal career and marriage and returned to Cologne to study theology. He joined the Jesuits in 1543. After ordination to the priesthood, he became a prominent preacher, attended two sessions of the Council of Trent as a theological consultant, and was recalled to Rome to work with Ignatius of Loyola [July 31] for five months.

In 1552 Ignatius sent him to Vienna to help reenergize a moribund church. Many Catholics no longer practiced their faith. Peter displayed extraordinary pastoral energy and won the admiration of the Viennese people by his ministry to the poor, the sick, and prisoners. He worked tirelessly during a plague in the fall of 1551. He was invited to become archbishop of Vienna, but he agreed only to administer the diocese for a year.

In 1555, he published his famous Catechism, entitled *Summa Doctrinae Christianae* (Lat., "Synthesis of Christian Doctrine"), which was translated from Latin into fifteen languages during Peter's lifetime. Later he produced a *Smaller Catechism*, translated into German for children and the general public, and then the *Shortest Catechism* on an even simpler level. In 1556 he was appointed provincial of a new Jesuit province for Austria, Bavaria, and Bohemia, with his residence in Prague. He established a college there (and others in Augsburg, Munich, and Innsbruck), to which even Protestants were happy to send their sons.

In his formal discussions with Lutherans, he was always courteous and tried to stress common elements of faith rather than differences. He insisted on the importance of schools and publications and took a leading role in the founding of several Jesuit colleges in northern Germany. During his eight years in Switzerland, he preached throughout the canton and is said to have played a large part in keeping it Catholic during a critical period of its history. In 1591 he suffered a stroke that left him partially paralyzed for the remainder of his life. He died in Fribourg on December 21, 1597. He was canonized and declared a Doctor of the Church in the same ceremony in 1925, the first such instance in history. His feast is on the General Roman Calendar.

22 ANASTASIA, MARTYR

Anastasia (d. ca. 304) was a martyr venerated in Rome since the fifth century and is mentioned in the Canon of the Roman Mass. In the Roman Catholic liturgical calendar her feast shares December 25 with Christmas and by tradition the second Mass (of three) on Christmas commemorates her. Popes in the past sang their second Christmas Mass in the Roman church under her title. The legend of Anastasia indicates that she was the daughter of a noble Roman and had Chrysogonus as her spiritual director. She is said to have married a pagan and also to have cared for Christians who were in prison during the persecution of Diocletian. After her husband's death, she went to Aquileia to minister to suffering Christians there. For this reason, she is known by the Greeks as Anastasia the healer. She herself was eventually arrested and executed. A more credible account is that she was not born in Rome and never lived there. Her cult originated in Sirmium, where it is more likely she was martyred during the Diocletian persecution (303–5). The feast of Anastasia is not on the General Roman Calendar, but it is celebrated on this day in the East.

23   JOHN OF KANTY, PRIEST; MARY
MARGARET D'YOUVILLE, FOUNDRESS

John of Kanty (1390–1473), also Kanti or Cantius, is a patron saint of Lithuania. Born of a well-to-do family at Kanti, near Oswiecim (Auschwitz) in Poland, he was educated at the University of Kraków and was ordained a priest soon after completing his courses. He was appointed a lecturer there and was said to have been effective as both a teacher and a preacher. He later occupied a chair of theology at the university. He was renowned not only for his teaching, but also for the austerity of his life (he slept on the floor and never ate meat) as well as his generosity to the poor. He died on December 24, 1473, and was canonized in 1767. His feast is on the General Roman Calendar.

Mary Margaret d'Youville (1701–71) was foundress of the Grey Nuns, or the Sisters of Charity of the General Hospital, and the first native-born Canadian saint. Born at Varennes, Quebec, Mary was married for eight years and had six children, only two of whom survived. After her husband's death, she and some companions devoted themselves to the care of poor, sick, and aged women in Montreal in 1737. Because of the types of people they nursed, their work aroused opposition in the neighborhood, even inspiring a mob scene with stone throwing and angry shouts of "Down with the *soeurs grises* (Fr., "tipsy nuns")!" Although *gris* also means "grey" in French, the allegation here was that the four women were drunk and that the widow d'Youville was carrying on her husband's liquor trade with the Indians. Eventually, however, the people were won over by the nature and quality of their work, for which the sisters adopted a simple Rule. They embraced the title given them by the crowd and transformed it by adopting a grey habit and calling themselves Grey Nuns. They nursed the wounded during the war between the English and French and later built schools and orphanages. Mary Margaret d'Youville died in 1771 and was canonized in 1990. Her feast is not on the General Roman Calendar, but is celebrated in Canada.

24 SHARBEL MAKHLOUF, HERMIT; ABRAHAM JOSHUA HESCHEL, RABBI

Sharbel Makhlouf (1828–98) was a Lebanese hermit. Born Joseph Makhlouf of a poor family in a remote village in Lebanon, near the great cedars, he was a shepherd in his early years and spent time in a cave praying and meditating. In 1851, he entered the Maronite monastery of Our Lady of Maifouk, taking the name Sharbel, after a second-century Syrian martyr. He was ordained a priest in 1859 and, following the example of the Desert Fathers, eventually moved to a small hermitage owned by the monastery consisting of four tiny cells and a chapel. Food was brought to him once a day from the monastery. Sharbel lived in the hermitage for more than twenty-three years, with the Eucharist at the center of his daily spiritual life. His reputation for wisdom and sanctity brought many visitors seeking spiritual guidance and healing. He died on Christmas Eve, 1898, and was canonized in 1977. His feast is not on the General Roman Calendar.

This is also the day of death of *Abraham Joshua Heschel* (1907–72), a Polish-born Hasidic rabbi who was a strong supporter of the civil rights and peace movements in the United States. A scholar, he had an appreciation for the Catholic principle of sacramentality and wrote works that recalled Christians to their Jewish roots.

25 THE NATIVITY OF OUR LORD

The feast of the *Nativity of Our Lord,* or Christmas, is second in importance only to Easter. It celebrates the incarnation of the Son of God in Jesus of Nazareth, who was virginally conceived by Mary, his mother. The Christmas season begins on December 24 with Evening Prayer I, or First Vespers, and the evening vigil Mass and concludes on the Sunday after Epiphany, the feast of the Baptism of the Lord. It is preceded by a four-week period of vigil and preparation known as Advent, which begins on the fourth Sunday before December 25.

Although the actual date of Christ's birth is unknown, this date was selected for the celebration of the event by the early fourth century in Rome. There is no evidence of a celebration of the Nativity of Our Lord before this time. It has been commonly believed that the date was chosen to counteract the pagan feast of the sun god, the Sun of Righteousness, which the emperor Aurelian established in 274. Christ was portrayed as the true "sun of justice." Another theory holds that the cult of the sun was particularly strong in Rome and that the symbolism of Christ-as-sun was deeply rooted in Christian consciousness.

In the East January 6 was celebrated as the feast of the Epiphany, which focused on both the Nativity and the Baptism of the Lord. (The focus of the Epiphany in the West was on the visit of the Magi.) Christmas is traditionally celebrated in the West by three Masses: one at midnight, one at dawn, and the third during the day, which have been thought to symbolize the threefold birth of Christ: in the bosom of the Father, from the womb of the Blessed Virgin Mary, and mystically in the souls of the faithful. The religious as well as secular customs (for example, the Christmas tree and the singing of carols) associated with this day were a much later development in Germany. This solemn feast is on the General Roman Calendar.

26 STEPHEN, FIRST MARTYR

Stephen (d. ca. 35) was the first Christian martyr and one of the seven chosen by the twelve apostles to serve tables, to look after the distribution of alms, especially to widows, and to assist in the ministry of preaching (Acts 6–7). He is the patron saint of deacons and in the Middle Ages was invoked against headaches. A Greek-speaking Jew living in Jerusalem, he was converted to Christ and became a leader of the Hellenistic Christians. The Hellenists argued that the new faith could not develop except by separating itself from Judaism and in particular by placing distance between itself and the Temple and the Mosaic law.

The Hellenists also urged the expansion of the Church's mission to the Gentiles. The elders of certain synagogues opposed Stephen and the other Hellenists on every count and charged him with blasphemy for saying that the Temple would be destroyed and that Jesus had set aside the Mosaic law. When given permission to speak before the Sanhedrin, Stephen made an eloquent defense (Acts 7:2–53) in which he accused his accusers of resisting the Holy Spirit, of persecuting the prophets, and of betraying and murdering Jesus, "the righteous one." The members of the council shouted out, covered their ears, and ordered him to be dragged outside the city and stoned to death, apparently without any formal trial. Stephen's feast is on the General Roman Calendar and is celebrated on this day by the Church of England, the Episcopal Church in the United States, and the Evangelical Lutheran Church in America.

27 JOHN, APOSTLE AND EVANGELIST

John the Evangelist (d. ca. 101), the son of Zebedee, was one of the twelve apostles and considered to be the author of the Fourth Gospel. Like his brother James [July 25], he was a fisherman and among Jesus' first disciples (Matt. 4:21; Mark 1:19; Luke 5:10). According to Mark 3:17, Jesus gave John and James the nickname "sons of thunder." They may have been cousins of Jesus through their mother, who may have been, in turn, the sister of the Blessed Virgin Mary (cf. Matt 27:56; Mark 15:40; John 19:25). John played a leading role in the first Christian community in Jerusalem (Gal. 2:9) and is listed in the Acts of the Apostles as second to Peter in the upper room (Acts 1:13). He accompanied Peter to preach in the Temple, where they were both arrested (Acts 3–4), and he traveled with Peter to Samaria to examine the new converts there (Acts 8:14–25).

John is traditionally regarded as the author of five New Testament books: the Fourth Gospel, the book of Revelation, and three Letters. John is thought to have died a natural death in Ephesus in about the third year of the reign of Trajan (98–117), when he was around ninety-four. His feast is on the General Roman Calendar.

28 HOLY INNOCENTS, MARTYRS

The *Holy Innocents* (first century) were put to death by King Herod in an effort to destroy the One who was to be born king of the Jews out of fear for his own throne (Matt. 2:16–18). They are venerated as martyrs who died not *because* of Christ, but *instead* of Christ. When Herod learned that wise men, or Magi, were coming from the East to pay homage to the new king, he asked the chief priests and scribes where the Messiah would be born. They told him Bethlehem in Judea (Mic. 5:1). Then he questioned the Magi and ordered them to return and tell him where the child could be found, so that he too could go and worship him. According to the Scriptures, the Magi were warned in a dream to return home by a different route. Then Joseph [March 19], fearing for the child, took Mary and the infant Jesus into Egypt, where they remained until Herod was dead (Matt. 2:12–15). When Herod realized that the wise men had ignored his command, he ordered all male children under the age of two in the Bethlehem district to be killed. Their number has been estimated at between six and twenty-five. This feast is on the General Roman Calendar and is celebrated also by the Church of England, the Episcopal Church in the United States, and the Evangelical Lutheran Church in America.

29 THOMAS BECKET, BISHOP AND MARTYR

Thomas Becket (1118–70), or Thomas of Canterbury, was archbishop of Canterbury when slain in the Canterbury cathedral upon orders from King Henry II. He was the most popular saint in medieval England. Born in London of a wealthy Norman family, he studied at Merton Abbey in Surrey and in Paris. After the death of both of his parents, he had to work as a clerk and then, at age twenty-four, obtained a post in the household of Theobald, archbishop of Canterbury, who conferred minor orders on him and provided him with several benefices. Thomas was later ordained a deacon and sent to study law in Bologna and Auxerre. In 1154 he was named archdeacon of Canterbury. At only twenty-one, Henry II was crowned king of England in the same year and appointed Thomas as chancellor of England the following year. Thomas and the king became close friends as well as allies. When Theobald died in 1161, the king wanted to make Thomas the new archbishop, but Thomas strongly resisted, predicting grave political tensions and the eventual end of their friendship. The king paid no heed to Thomas's warnings and pressed forward with the appointment. Thomas continued to resist until urged to accept by the papal legate in 1162.

As archbishop, Thomas wore simple clerical dress and a hair shirt close to his skin. He rose early to read the Bible and celebrated or attended Mass at nine o'clock. He distributed alms to the poor every day and established a certain monastic regularity in his own household. Conflicts with the king became increasingly serious. Thomas refused to pay tax on church lands and hand over a canon for trial in the royal court. The king was insisting on the end of clerical immunity from civil prosecution, receipt of revenues from vacant church benefices, and other issues. Thomas left secretly for France for an audience with the pope. Thomas remained abroad for six years, returning to England after the archbishop of York defied his orders and crowned the heir to the throne, Prince Henry. Although the practice of crowning a successor while the incumbent still lived was common on the Continent, it had not been done before in England.

Thomas excommunicated, from the pulpit of Canterbury cathedral, the archbishop of York and the bishops who had assisted at the young prince's coronation. When the king heard the news, he asked who would rid him of this turbulent priest, or words to that effect. On the afternoon of December 29, four knights rushed into the cathedral at Canterbury and hacked Thomas to death between the altars of Our Lady and St. Benedict [July 11]. The pope excommunicated the king. Thomas Becket's feast is on the General Roman Calendar and is also celebrated by the Church of England.

30 EGWIN OF WORCESTER, BISHOP

Egwin of Worcester (d. 717) was the founder of Evesham,
one of the great Benedictine abbeys in medieval England.
Born of royal blood, he became bishop of Worcester ca.
693 and later founded Evesham Abbey, which became one
of the greatest in medieval England. He was so committed to the reform of the clergy that he evoked the enmity
of a faction, which denounced him to the king and the
archbishop of Canterbury. As a consequence, Egwin was
forced to withdraw from his see for a time. He made a
penitential pilgrimage to Rome, where he received papal
vindication. Egwin died at Evesham and was buried in
the monastery. His feast is not on the General Roman
Calendar.

31 SYLVESTER I, POPE

The pontificate of *Sylvester I* (d. 335, pope 314–335) lasted
for nearly twenty-one years, the tenth-longest in history,
and overlapped with most of the imperial reign of Constantine (306–37). In spite of the length of his pontificate
and the importance of the Constantinian period in which
the pope served, Sylvester seems to have made little or
no lasting impact on the Church or on the papacy itself.
Indeed, it is what he did not do as pope that is more significant than what he did do.

   During Sylvester's pontificate, the first ecumenical
council was held at Nicaea, the emperor's summer residence (in modern northwest Turkey), in July 325. This
was the council that first defined the divinity of Jesus

Christ, teaching that he is of the same being, or substance (Gk. *homoousios*), with God the Father (against the Arians, who held that Jesus Christ was the greatest of creatures, but not equal to God). Significantly, the pope played no part in the proceedings of this ecumenical council. The emperor himself convened and presided over it. Sylvester declined to attend, pleading old age. In spite of Sylvester's lackluster pontificate, the Roman church benefited immensely from Constantine's generosity, which included the building of great churches such as the original St. Peter's Basilica on the Via Ostiensis and the Basilica Constantiniana and its baptistery (later known as St. John Lateran, which still serves as the pope's cathedral church even today). Sylvester died in 335. His feast is on the General Roman Calendar.

INDEX OF NAMES